# Through Bosnian Eyes

# Central European Studies

Editors
*Charles W. Ingrao*
*Gary B. Cohen*

This series aims at enriching our understanding of the great stretch of "middle Europe" between the present European Community and the former Soviet Union. Building on Purdue University Press's extensive list of attractively produced titles in Balkan and Danubian history, the series focuses on the lands and people of the former Habsburg Empire and those areas on its periphery.

# Through Bosnian Eyes

## The Political Memoir of a Bosnian Serb

Mirko Pejanović

Introduction by Robert J. Donia
Translated by Marina Bowder

Purdue University Press
West Lafayette, Indiana

First U.S. edition published 2004. Published in 2002 by TKD Šahinpašič, Sarajevo. All rights reserved.

ISBN 1-55753-359-8

Printed in the United States of America

**Library of Congress Cataloging-in-Publication Data**
Pejanovic, Mirko, 1946–
  [Bosansko pitanje. English]
  Through Bosnian eyes : the political memoir of a Bosnian Serb / by Mirko Pejanovic ; introduction by Robert J. Donia.
    p. cm. — (Central European studies)
  Includes bibliographical references and index.
  Originally published: Sarajevo : TKD Sahinpasic, 2002.
  ISBN 1-55753-359-8 (pbk.)
    1. Pejanović, Mirko, 1946– 2. Politicians—Bosnia and Hercegovina—Biography. 3. Serbs—Bosnia and Hercegovina—Biography. 4. Bosnia and Hercegovina—Politics and government—20th century. 5. Bosnia and Hercegovina—Ethnic relations. 6. Yugoslav War, 1991–1995—Bosnia and Hercegovina. I. Title. II. Series.

DR1755.P45A3 2004
949.703—dc22                                                2004044407
[B]

# CONTENTS

| | | |
|---|---|---|
| Foreword by Charles W. Ingrao | | vii |
| Preface | | xi |
| Introduction | | 1 |
| I. | On the Eve of Political Pluralism | 13 |
| II. | Ante Marković's Failure | 27 |
| III. | The Election Coalitions | 33 |
| IV. | The Triumph of the National Parties | 43 |
| V. | The Civic Parliament — Protest against the War | 53 |
| VI. | Secret Mission to Krajišnik | 59 |
| VII. | The Presidential Platform and Its Destiny | 73 |
| VIII. | The Bosnian Army and Its First Commander, Sefer Halilović | 85 |
| IX. | Kecmanović Goes to Belgrade | 101 |
| X. | Herceg-Bosna — A New Political Fact | 115 |
| XI. | The Fate of Serbs in the Cities | 129 |
| XII. | Haris Silajdžić Resigns | 153 |
| XIII. | The Geneva Peace Talks | 159 |
| XIV. | The Vance Owen Peace Plan | 169 |
| XV. | The Owen-Stoltenberg Plan for a Union of Three Republics | 177 |

| | | |
|---|---|---|
| XVI. | The SGV: Its Foundation, Principles, and Activities | 187 |
| XVII. | Wartime Visits to Moscow and Belgrade | 197 |
| XVIII. | Joint Action for Dayton by the SGV and the HNV | 209 |
| IXX. | The Dayton Peace Agreement | 219 |
| XX. | The Serb National Question in Bosnia | 225 |
| XXI. | Constitutional Change | 233 |
| Index | | 239 |

# FOREWORD

The war in Bosnia (1992–95) has produced a prodigious number of publications. Journalists were among the first to chronicle the outbreak of Europe's first war—and commission of genocide—since World War II. Most of their accounts were compiled during the fighting in Croatia and Bosnia as they followed in the path of the ethnic cleansers or dodged artillery barrages and snipers during the three-year siege of Sarajevo. They were soon followed by a small number of scholars whose narratives also relied heavily on media accounts, but who nonetheless provided a broader —and substantially better informed—historical context and analysis to the epiphenomena of war and destruction. With the approach of peace, several key western military and diplomatic figures published wartime memoirs that offered much more detailed accounts of the byzantine negotiations, secret understandings and, oftentimes, outright duplicity of the increasingly desperate belligerents. The conclusion of the Bosnian conflict has somewhat reduced, but hardly ended, the flow of new books. By 1999, Noel Malcolm and Quintin Hoare had catalogued no fewer than 350 volumes in their *Books on Bosnia,* yet still felt compelled to admit that theirs did not even represent a comprehensive listing of the western-language studies they examined.

Meanwhile the passage of nearly a decade since the conclusion of the Dayton Peace Accords (1995) has given a second and more numerous group of scholars the time to conduct research more thoroughly. It has also afforded several of Bosnia's leaders the opportunity to reflect and compile their wartime memoirs. With official government documents still under seal, their accounts represent the most valuable source for classified "inside" information about wartime policy making. Yet, for many of the most senior actors, only a narrow window remains in which to make a contribution while they are still alive and their memories relatively fresh.

Although virtually all of these accounts published so far have appeared in the trinity of languages that westerners discreetly term Bosnian-Croatian-Serbian (or BCS), some of the most prominent figures have also published their memoirs in English. Central European Studies is pleased to play a role in this process by publishing Mirko Pejanović's memoir in collaboration with the Sarajevo publishing house TKD Šahinpašič. Indeed, we anticipate that it will be only the first of several series volumes devoted to the recent history of what was once Yugoslavia, but which the U.S. State Department now groups with other Balkan countries as "South

Central Europe." The significance of this relatively new characterization is not lost on those of us who appreciate the demographic similarities between *Mitteleuropa's* Habsburg and Ottoman spheres.

This dualism is readily evident in the work of Robert Donia, who first brought Dr. Pejanović's memoir to our attention and has contextualized it here with a preface and introduction. His *Islam under the Double Eagle: Muslims of Bosnia and Herzegovina, 1878–1914* (1981) is well known to Habsburg and Ottoman scholars alike, much as the wartime survey that he co-authored with John A. L. Fine, *Bosnia-Hercegovina: A Tradition Betrayed* (1994) filled an enormous conceptual gap for journalists, policy makers, and NGO staffers who were grappling with the challenges of ethnic conflict in the post-Communist era. As one of the few western academics who actually spent time in Sarajevo during the siege and has remained active there as a faculty member at the University of Sarajevo, Professor Donia readily appreciates the vital contribution that Mirko Pejanović has played in the struggle to preserve a part of multiethnic central Europe.

—Charles W. Ingrao
Senior Series Editor

# PREFACE

Mirko Pejanović is not the kind of Bosnian that most of us have come to know through media reports. Those narratives left us with the sense that every Bosnian is either a victim to be pitied or a war criminal hardened to indifference by unfathomable brutality. Pejanović was neither of these. He formed no paramilitary group, organized no concentration camps, and ravaged no civilian populations. He neither gave riveting interviews to international journalists nor struck photogenic poses while toting menacing weaponry or sporting a flamboyant hairstyle.

Pejanović spent the war in a quiet but unrelenting quest to find a peaceful exit from war and to end the violence against his people. As a member of the highest governing body of Bosnia and Herzegovina for all but a few months of the war, he both witnessed and participated in that regime's struggle to acquire international respectability and protect its citizens from their enemies. He tells of that struggle in the following pages: it is a story of some successes and at least as many failures. Pejanović was buoyed by the triumphs but largely undaunted by losses. Such indomitable optimism, coupled with a well-defined vision of a future for Bosnia, led him to spend the war coping with the complex challenges that confronted the members of Bosnia's collective presidency in the difficult conditions of wartime Sarajevo.

Pejanović is a Serb. In fact, he was the most prominent Bosnian Serb politician of his time to remain loyal to the internationally recognized government of Bosnia. Such loyalist Serbs constituted a perpetual bone in the throat to Radovan Karadžić and other nationalists of the Serbian Democratic Party (SDS — *Srpska demokratska stranka*) who urgently wanted the world to believe that they, and only they, spoke on behalf of all Bosnian Serbs. As a participant in his government's delegation to the Geneva peace negotiations in 1993, Pejanović sat across from fellow Bosnian Serbs (now indicted war criminals) who sought in vain to entice him to defect and join their separatist project. But this was not an isolated incident. The SDS Serbs campaigned relentlessly, using arguments, enticements and threats to despoil the Bosnian government's claim that it encompassed Bosnians of all nationalities. Unable to explain why thousands of Serbs and Croats had elected to endure shelling and deprivation to remain with their neighbors in Bosnia's cities, the nationalists portrayed such stay-behinds as hostages being held against their will or, more effectively, marginalized them as inconsequential people of no political conviction. It was critical to their nationally exclusive territorial units to dismiss the significance of those Serbs and Croats who favored the "civic option" and supported tolerance of other nationalities.

Pejanović and his ilk were likewise a standing inconvenience to the international negotiators who hoped that the war could be ended by simple territorial division. In Chapter XIX Pejanović relates the apparent complicity of Lord David Owen, the principal international convener of peace talks, in an effort to entice his defection from the government delegation. (In Chapter III, it should be noted, the author portrays a somewhat different Owen, one quite sympathetic to the plight of besieged Sarajevans and their practices of mutual coexistence.) International representatives viewed their task as pacifying the "guys with the guns," as one of them put it. It suited the diplomats well to have the advocates of the civic option languish in shadowy obscurity. Neither the pragmatic demands of international diplomacy nor the marketing needs of the international media found room for highlighting the peace-seeking idealists who led the the non-national opposition.

Mirko Pejanović is very much a "son of the Sarajevo asphalt," to borrow a phrase from the local vernacular. Born in 1946 in Matijevići in north-central Bosnia, he completed his studies at the University of Sarajevo, obtained a doctorate in political science there, and subsequently became both a Professor of Political Science and a Vice Rector of the University. He was active for many years in the Sarajevo branch of the Socialist Alliance. Not until 1990 did he become President of the Socialist Alliance of Bosnia and Herzegovina, just at a time when waves of democratization and the collapse of communism were sweeping across Eastern Europe. His accession to higher office thus corresponded with the epochal changes that were sweeping the land.

In the former Yugoslavia, the road from communism proved also to be the road to war. Pejanović and others favoring the "civic option" lost decisively in the 1990 elections, but his relatively strong showing aided his ascent to the Presidency after its two nationalist Serb members resigned in 1992. Pejanović became a Presidency member just in time to witness from the inside Bosnia's nightmare of protracted war and Sarajevo's seemingly endless siege. So his is a tale of persistence in the face of daunting obstacles. In the early months of the war, Pejanović and other Serbs in Sarajevo faced a double threat. They were being terrorized by the shells launched by Serbian extremists in the surrounding hills and simultaneously by uncontrolled Bosniak gangs and military units conducting retaliatory violence against the Serbs who had stayed. After he joined the

Presidency in June 1992, he was able to oppose both forms of violence with equal vigor, and he describes each with equal candor.

Many will find this narrative most remarkable for what it does not include. Hatred, resentment, and personal animus are wholly absent from the following pages. Perhaps more than any political leader of the past decade, Pejanović practiced tolerance at a personal level. From his office in the Presidency Building he became an unofficial ombudsman for Serbs living in Sarajevo and was able to translate his personal compassion into efforts to extricate many prospective victims from threats of violence. Equally notable is the lack of personal animus. Pejanović is critical at one point or another of almost every political and military leader with whom he dealt, but never does such criticism mutate into personal animosity. He manages to find sympathetic words for even the crudest rogues of the Bosnian war (with the exception of Karadžić), and his disagreements with each of them were habitually framed as principled disagreements.

There can be no mistaking Pejanović's commitment to the "common life" of Bosnia's peoples, as he so often expresses it. His attachment to that term speaks to his belief in historical values. Not until the 1990s and the arrival of UN forces did the terms "multiethnic" and "multicultural" enter the Bosnian vocabulary; before that, "common life" was valued, along with the shared values and joint historical experiences implied by that term. In March 1994 Pejanović and other Serbs formed the Serbian Civil Council (SGV — *Srpsko građansko vijeće*) to promote the rights of Serbs by peaceful means. A vital founding principal of the SGV was the notion that rights for Serbs could be fully achieved without diminishing those of their Croat and Bosniak neighbors. In that fundamental premise Pejanović is the polar opposite of the nationalist exclusivity and hate-mongering practiced by the Serbs of the SDS.

The SGV became the primary vehicle for Pejanović's transition from a member of the Presidency to being a lobbyist for Serb equality and restoration of common life. The SGV was founded just as the Bosnian Parliament was considering the draft Constitution of the Federation as proposed in the Washington Agreements. That Constitution gave equal rights to the Bosniaks and Croats as "constituent" nations in the Federation, but it left out the Serbs. The SGV asked that they be included, but its proposal was ignored. After the Dayton Peace Agreement was signed in 1995, the quest for equal national rights became a campaign to implement the Dayton Agreement's constitutional provisions in both the Republika Srpska (RS) and the Federation. Annex 4 of the Dayton Agreements specified that the Serbs, Croats, and Bosniaks were all "constituent" nations of Bosnia and

Herzegovina, but neither entity constitution contained that provision. In 1998, the SGV and several other non-governmental organizations won the support of President Alija Izetbegović in urging the Constitutional Court to rule on the equality of all three nations.

This initiative finally bore fruit in July 2000, as described in the book's last chapter. The Constitutional Court, after deliberations over many months, ruled that all three nations must be regarded as "constituent" nations on all territory of Bosnia and Herzegovina. While this ruling in itself changes little, it has the potential to serve the same role as the "interstate commerce" clause of the US Constitution, which has been employed to justify all manner of expanded central government authority and Congressional legislation. Pejanović spells out his assessment of this decision in the last chapter. Even if only some of those changes are forthcoming, the "constituent nations" ruling will probably be noted as a key development in the rebuilding of post-war Bosnia. It already stands out as a major milestone in the already rich legacy of Pejanović's political career.

This work originally appeared as *Bosansko pitanje i Srbi u Bosni i Hercegovini* (Sarajevo: Bosanska knjiga, 1999) as an extended interview with Mirko Šagolj, the managing editor of the Sarajevo daily newspaper *Oslobođenje*. Šagolj's questions have been removed, editorial notes have been added, and certain passages have been rearranged in the interest of topical cohesion. The editor has added some dates to the English-language version to place events in a chronological context and provided certain clarifying comments based on the author's responses to specific inquiries. The last chapter is excerpted from other sections of the original book and from an extensive interview given by the author to *Oslobođenie* after the Constitutional Court decision on constituent nations.

—Robert J. Donia

# INTRODUCTION
## ROBERT J. DONIA

In early 1990, when this memoir begins, communism was collapsing throughout Eastern Europe. Responding to massive dissatisfaction with single-party rule, communist party leaders agreed to hold multiparty elections. In the Federal Socialist Republic of Yugoslavia (SFRY), elections were held on different dates in each of the country's six republics, but country-wide elections were never called. In February 1990, the communist-dominated Assembly of the Republic of Bosnia-Herzegovina approved constitutional changes that paved the way for elections later in the year, and leaders of the other three republics were making similar plans. The first voting took place in the republics of Croatia and Slovenia in April and May 1990. Elections in other republics followed in November and December 1990.

Concurrent with the dawn of multiparty politics in 1990, Mirko Pejanović emerged in Bosnia-Herzegovina as a leader of the Socialist Alliance, the mass-participation organization tasked with implementing the policies of the League of Communists. Pejanović was born in 1946 in the northern Bosnian town of Matijevići. He received his doctorate from the University of Sarajevo and then became professor of political science at that institution. He also worked in the Sarajevo branch of the Socialist Alliance during the 1970s and 1980s, and in March 1990 he was elected President of the Socialist Alliance of Bosnia-Herzegovina with a mandate to transform the organization into a competitive western-style political party.

## INTERGROUP RELATIONS IN BOSNIA-HERZEGOVINA

Transition to democracy held particular perils for the Socialist Republic of Bosnia-Herzegovina. Unlike the other five republics of federal Yugoslavia, Bosnia-Herzegovina had no single nationality with an absolute majority. The republic's population consisted of 44% Bosniaks (known prior to September 1993 as "Bosnian Muslims"), 35% Serbs, 17% Croats, and lesser numbers of Yugoslavs, Jews, Romany, and others. Members of all three major groups spoke the same South Slavic language (known as "Serbo-Croatian" during the socialist era) and traced their origins to Slavic migrations from north-central Europe in the 5th to 8th centuries A.D. Each of the three major nationalities had roots in religious identity (Bosniaks with Islam; Serbs with Serbian Orthodoxy; and Croats with

Catholicism), but in the 19th and 20th centuries each group asserted an identity as a secular nation that superseded its religious origins.

In the communist era, leaders of the three major groups in Bosnia-Herzegovina normally worked together to promote the republic's interests while remaining loyal to the SFRY. Members of the republic's assembly showed deep concern for nationalism's potentially corrosive effects by enacting constitutional changes and laws in anticipation of multiparty elections in 1990. In February 1990 the assembly reaffirmed the special rights of Bosnia's three major groups by adopting Amendment #60 to the republic's constitution:

> The Socialist Republic of Bosnia and Herzegovina is a democratic, sovereign state of equal citizens, peoples of Bosnia and Herzegovina—Muslims, Serbs, and Croats, and members of others nations and nationalities living therein.[1]

Although the amendment recognized the three major peoples as "constituent nations," it neither specified the nature of group rights nor spelled out the means by which they could be asserted. Implementing legislation and legal interpretation were required to give substance to the amendment's provisions.

Despite efforts to avoid friction among the three national groups, disharmony among them was increasing by the late 1980s. More ominously, annexationist aspirations loomed large among nationalists in the neighboring republics of Croatia and Serbia. Serbian President Slobodan Milošević and Croatian President Franjo Tudjman each sponsored a nationalist political party in Bosnia-Herzegovina, and in March 1991 the two presidents held extensive talks on partitioning most of Bosnia-Herzegovina between their two countries.

## THE YUGOSLAV CONTEXT: TRANSITION TO MULTIPARTY RULE

After decades of centralized rule, political power in the SFRY during the 1970s and 1980s gradually devolved to the communist party organizations of the country's six republics and two autonomous provinces. De-

---

[1] Amendment 60 restated the provisions of Article One of the 1974 Constitution but omitted the clumsy and outdated socialist nomenclature. The original 1974 Article One stated, "The Socialist Republic of Bosnia and Herzegovina is a socialist democratic state and socialist self-administered democratic community of working peoples and citizens, nations of Bosnia-Herzegovina—Muslims, Serbs, and Croats, and members of other nations and nationalities living therein."

centralization was enshrined in the 1974 Yugoslav constitution, the last to be promulgated during the life of Josip Broz Tito (1895–1980). Republican particularism, albeit in the hands of the governing League of Communists, accelerated in the late 1980s with the growing prospect of democratic pluralism. Since a single nationality dominated in all republics but Bosnia-Herzegovina, nationalism often reinforced the autonomist ambitions of leaders in those republics.

Prospects for peaceful transition from communism to democracy were dimmed by the rise of Slobodan Milošević in the Republic of Serbia in 1987. Milošević, a banker and long-time party member, regularly invoked loyalty to Yugoslavia and to socialist principles. But in 1988 and 1989 he roused Serbian nationalists to conduct mass demonstrations to overthrow communist leaders in the Republic of Montenegro and the Autonomous Provinces of Vojvodina and Kosovo. Milošević replaced the ousted officials with appointees loyal to him. These appointments helped him control the SFRY's two key central institutions, the collective state Presidency and the Yugoslav National Army (JNA—*Jugoslovenska narodna armija*). Milošević's ascension fueled separatist impulses among non-Serbs who feared that Serbs and Serbian interests would come to dominate Yugoslavia.

## NATIONALIST TRIUMPH IN THE NOVEMBER 1990 ELECTIONS

Many Yugoslavs thought Bosnia-Herzegovina might become a bastion of non-nationalist political strength that would buffer the rising national tensions. Yugoslav Federal Prime Minister Ante Marković harbored hopes for non-nationalist political party that would prevail in all republics of the Yugoslav federation. At a rally in July 1990 in northwestern Bosnia, Marković announced the formation of the Alliance of Reformist Forces of Yugoslavia (SRSJ - *Savez reformskih snaga Jugoslavija*, commonly called the "Reformists."). Marković hoped to foster identification with the Partisan legacy and to mobilize support for market-oriented economic reforms he had advocated as federal Prime Minister. The rally was held on Mount Kozara, site of a near-miraculous Partisan escape from German forces in 1942 and of a monument to that achievement erected in the 1970s. The location evoked Partisan traditions of national equality and wartime revolutionary resistance and avoided association with communism's signal economic failures.

Along with the Reformists, transformed versions of the League of

Communists and the Socialist Alliance competed in the 1990 elections. The League of Communists altered its name to the "League of Communists—Social Democratic Party" (SK-SDP—*Savez komunista—socijalistička demokratska partija*), evoked the Partisan legacy, and warned against national intolerance. The Socialist Alliance changed its name to the Democratic Socialist Alliance (DSS—*Demokratski socijalistički savez*). Led by Pejanović, the DSS claimed a hundred thousand members and endorsed a program indistinguishable from that of the SK-SDP. As campaigning began, the two transformed communist political bodies agreed to campaign jointly for the November elections.

At the Reformists' inaugural rally on Mount Kozara, Pejanović and leaders of the SK-SDP offered to support the Reformist campaign. Such an alliance would have pitted the major non-nationalist parties against the three nationalist contenders. But Marković, fearing his party would be tainted by association with communist incumbents, rejected the offer. Marković's decision proved fateful. Reformists and the former communists split the non-nationalist vote in the elections, and both went down in defeat.

Three nationalist parties rose to prominence in the fall campaign. Bosniaks (at that time called "Bosnian Muslims"), led by former dissident Alija Izetbegović, organized the SDA (*Stranka demokratska akcija*—Party of Democratic Action). Bosnian Croats formed the HDZ (*Hrvatska demokratska zajednica*—Croatian Democratic Community) under the tutelage of Croatian President Franjo Tudjman. Bosnian Serbs, under the guidance of Serbian President Milošević, formed the SDS (*Srpska demokratska stranka*—Serbian Democratic Party) and elected Radovan Karadžić as party president.

Faced with polls showing former communists in the lead and Reformists in second place, the nationalist parties warily agreed to limited cooperation in order to defeat their rivals. Despite sharp differences among them, the three nationalist parties thus achieved a modicum of cooperation that evaded the anti-nationalist contenders. To prevent mutual recriminations, the nationalist leaders agreed not to attack one another, to share power should they collectively emerge victorious, and to urge their followers to vote only for candidates of their own nationality. They urged voters to reject Reformists and transformed communists and sought, with considerable success, to discredit those parties as guardians of the failed socialist order.

The November 1990 elections catapulted nationalist parties into power by large majorities. In accord with the terms of their pre-election interparty agreement, the nationalists apportioned among themselves the leading positions of state. Alija Izetbegović, the SDA nominee, became President of the seven-member Presidency. Momčilo Krajišnik, the SDS nominee, became President of the Assembly. Jure Pelivan, the choice of the HDZ, became Prime Minister. Leaders of the defeated non-nationalist parties formed an opposition coalition, the Left Bloc. With the victory of the three nationalist parties, Pejanović and his hopes for the "civic option" in Bosnian society were sidelined.

## THE ROAD TO WAR

The period of good will among the nationalists was short-lived. The interparty agreement proved more a charter to divide institutions than a formula for sharing power. The parties disagreed about matters great and small, and the Assembly of Bosnia-Herzegovina became deadlocked in spring 1991 over symbolic matters such as the wording of the oath of office and the official name of the republic. Meanwhile, war clouds gathered in neighboring Croatia. Croatian police loyal to President Tudjman found their authority challenged by rebellious local Serbs with the increasingly overt support of the JNA. Milošević, posing as a Serbian nationalist to the many JNA senior officers of Serbian nationality, gradually asserted influence over the army and goaded its commanders into siding with Croatia's Serbs to oppose Croatia's secession from Yugoslavia. By August 1991, Croatian police and a nascent Croatian army were at war with the JNA.

Milošević urged the Bosnian Serbs to send volunteers to fight alongside Croatia's Serbs. By September 1991, the JNA increasingly drew Serbs into its ranks but repelled non-Serbs. After a few months of such "mobilizations," the JNA had effectively been converted into an all-Serb army. Milošević's efforts to militarize the Bosnian Serbs widened the existing rift among the ruling nationalist parties of Bosnia-Herzegovina. Karadžić, Krajišnik, and their SDS colleagues openly sided with the JNA against the Croatian army and police. Counting on the JNA's backing, they became bolder in demanding that Bosnia-Herzegovina remain a part of federal Yugoslavia. The SDS rhetoric alarmed non-Serbs, who feared that Milošević and the JNA would support the Bosnian Serbs as they had the Serbs of Croatia. The HDZ and SDA strengthened their alliance in summer and fall 1991, and all three nationalist parties organized armed forces among their constituents and allies.

In summer and fall 1991, leaders of the nationalist parties negotiated in vain for a compromise in Bosnia-Herzegovina's constitutional relationship with the SFRY. Adil Zulfikarpašić, a leading Bosniak politician, held several meetings with Karadžić in Sarajevo and with Milošević in Belgrade to forge a power-sharing arrangement between Serbs and Bosniaks. Called the "Belgrade Initiative," these negotiations collapsed when Izetbegović withdrew his support in fall 1991. Thereafter the SDA-HDZ coalition and the SDS moved inexorably toward confrontation over the future of Bosnia-Herzegovina.

Events led to heated debates in the Assembly of Bosnia-Herzegovina on the night of 14–15 October 1991. As delegates debated rival platforms for the future of Bosnia-Herzegovina, Karadžić ominously warned that Bosnia's Muslims might disappear if they insisted on independence for Bosnia-Herzegovina. Izetbegović responded that such threats that were driving the republic to separate from Yugoslavia. Krajišnik subsequently adjourned the session. HDZ and SDA delegates, lingering in the hall until the early hours of 15 October, reconvened in the absence of SDS delegates and passed their platform asserting the "sovereignty" of Bosnia-Herzegovina. Bosnian Serb leaders, enraged by declaration's passage, stepped up their campaign for separatism. They convened the "Assembly of the Serbian People of Bosnia-Herzegovina" on 24 October 1991 and invited many politically active Serbs, including Pejanović, to attend. He declined. The assembly organized a "Referendum of the Serbian People" for early November to put a stamp of legitimacy on the Serbian separatist project.

In asserting their competing claims, Bosniak and Serbian nationalists cited irreconcilable constitutional interpretations. HDZ and SDA leaders cited constitutional provisions, including Amendment 60, that attributed sovereignty to the *Republic* of Bosnia-Herzegovina. Serbian polemicists, on the other hand, emphasized the special rights allocated to the *peoples* in the republic, also as found in Amendment 60 and other constitutional documents, and argued that "constituent peoples" retained the right of secession. Under the rationale of this interpretation, Bosnian Serb leaders accelerated plans to form separate institutions and assume political control over territory they claimed as Serbian, even though hundreds of thousands of non-Serbs also lived in those areas. HDZ and SDA leaders, on the other hand, moved toward declaring the republic's independence. Most members of the Left Bloc supported the Bosniak-Croat position, but hoped to avert a catastrophic breach that many feared would end in war.

International diplomacy accelerated the pace of events. From the first days of the Yugoslav crisis in June 1991, the European Community

("EC") sought to mediate the conflict. As the war in Croatia intensified, the EC in September 1991 established a semi-permanent body, the European Community Conference on Yugoslavia (ECCY), based first in The Hague and then in Brussels. Furthermore, the EC called upon an Arbitration Commission (usually called the "Badinter Commission" after its chairman, Robert Badinter) to recommend a consistent approach to recognizing republics seeking independence from Yugoslavia.

In mid-December, the Badinter Commission invited each Yugoslav republic desiring independence to apply for EC recognition. The commission's final rulings were closer to the interpretations of constitutional law advanced by the HDZ and SDA. Twice quoting Amendment 60 of the Bosnian Constitution, the commission interpreted the group rights guaranteed to constituent peoples as human and civil rights guaranteed by the existing government rather than as unconditional rights of secession. Noting that Bosnian Serbs had already convened an assembly and declared their intention to form a separate state, the commission concluded that the will of the people of Bosnia-Herzegovina regarding independence had not yet been clearly expressed. The commission suggested a referendum. Against opposition and eventual abstention by Serbian nationalists, the Assembly of Bosnia-Herzegovina scheduled such a referendum for 29 February and 1 March 1992.

The HDZ urged Croats to vote "Yes" in the independence referendum, but Croatian support for a united Bosnia-Herzegovina was becoming increasingly tenuous. Croatian President Tudjman, in writings dating to the 1970s, held that part or all of Bosnia-Herzegovina should belong to Croatia. In November 1991, Bosnian HDZ member and Tudjman loyalist Mate Boban took a first step toward partition by proclaiming the "Croatian Community of Herzeg-Bosna" in territories with significant Croatian populations. "Herzeg-Bosna" was obviously modelled on the Serbian Autonomous Regions proclaimed two months before, and bore similar ominous implications for the integrity of Bosnia-Herzegovina. Then in February 1992, on orders from Tudjman, pro-Bosnian party president Stjepan Kljuić was ousted and subsequently replaced by Boban. Limited Croatian cooperation with the Bosnian government continued for another year after Kljuić's ouster, but Croats maintained separate military units and coordinated their activities with the army of the Republic of Croatia.

The SDS urged all Serbs to boycott the independence referendum, arguing that the "Serbian people" had already expressed its will at an SDS-sponsored plebiscite in November 1991. Most Serbs observed the boycott, although the exact number of Serbs who voted will never be known because voters were not required to identify themselves by nationality. But just under two-thirds of registered voters participated. Over 99% of them voted for independence.

The EC Council of Ministers accepted the referendum results as proof that most citizens of Bosnia-Herzegovina wanted independence. It established 6 April 1992 as the effective date for EC recognition. Meanwhile, an ECCY working group headed by Portuguese diplomat Jose Cutileiro sought to avert armed conflict through negotiations. Those efforts proved futile, despite promising concurrence on many issues reached on 22 February and again on 18 March 1992. In the first days of April 1992, Serbian paramilitary forces crossed into Eastern Bosnia and began the Serbian nationalist military seizure of power.

The date of EC recognition, 6 April 1992, was a watershed in the history of Bosnia-Herzegovina. The SDA and HDZ achieved international recognition of an independent Bosnia-Herzegovina, but reports of Serbian military attacks on several cities in the republic muted the jubilation. So did the resignations of Biljana Plavšić and Nikola Koljević, the two Serbian members of the collective Bosnian Presidency. In Sarajevo, paramilitary forces loyal to Radovan Karadžić fired on demonstrators demanding that nationalist leaders renounce the use of force. Urged by SDS leaders, thousands of Serbs left Sarajevo for Serbian enclaves elsewhere in Bosnia or for the Republic of Serbia. JNA tank and artillery shells bombarded the city. Bosnia-Herzegovina's independence and recognition thus coincided with the outbreak of war.

## WAR

Owing to advance preparations and superior firepower, the triumph of Serbian arms was swift and widespread. By mid-May, Serbian nationalist forces controlled 70% of the Republic of Bosnia-Herzegovina, and many non-Serb inhabitants had fled, been driven out, killed, or interned in camps. Serb forces conquered most areas with only token resistance, but hastily-organized Bosnian government forces and Croatian military units held off JNA and Serbian irregulars in some regions. In May 1992 the heavily-armed JNA, renamed the "Bosnian Serb Army," sealed off Sarajevo and prevented all but a trickle of supplies escorted by the United Nations Protection Force (UNPROFOR) from entering the city.

For the approximately 300,000 inhabitants remaining in Sarajevo, life was grim and treacherous. Over the almost four years of the city's siege, thousands of innocent civilians were killed, thousands more were injured, and the infrastructure and buildings throughout the city were damaged or destroyed. Much of Pejanović's memoir recounts his struggle to cope with the hardships of war in the besieged capital of Sarajevo.

Following the Koljević and Plavšić resignations from the Presidency of Bosnia-Herzegovina, the remaining five Presidency members sought to replace them with the runners-up among Serbian candidates for the Presidency in the 1990 elections. The two runners-up in that category were Reformist candidate Nenad Kecmanović, with 500,783 votes, and Pejanović, with 335,392. (Plavšić had received 573,812 votes, and Koljević 556,218). Like the Serbs they were invited to replace, Pejanović and Kecmanović were respected intellectuals and professors at the University of Sarajevo. Kecmanović, a former Rector of the University of Sarajevo, had been an unsuccessful candidate in 1988 to represent Bosnia-Herzegovina on the Federal Presidency. In a difficult decision, both men agreed to accepted their nominations to the Presidency. SDS leaders, having fled Sarajevo for the nearby resort village of Pale, denounced the two men as traitors to the Serbian people for agreeing to serve.

There could hardly have been a darker hour for Kecmanović and Pejanović to join the highest governing body of Bosnia-Herzegovina. Together they resolved to pursue a peaceful solution, if at all possible. With Izetbegović's authorization, they undertook a clandestine mission to the makeshift suburban headquarters of Bosnian Serb leaders Radovan Karadžić and Momcilo Krajišnik. As Pejanović relates, their initiative was rejected by the Bosnian Serb leaders, who were then busily consolidating military control over much of Bosnia-Herzegovina.

Pejanović also became the informal ombudsman for Serbs who remained to share the fate of Sarajevo's Croatian and Bosniak citizens. For those who stayed, the Serbian military triumph was accompanied by daily bombardments from JNA artillery and tanks in the hills around the city. Many of Sarajevo's Serbs fled or were victimized by pogroms of Croat and Bosniak paramilitaries that were tolerated, although probably not directed, by the Bosnian government. In one of his memoir's most illuminating sections, Pejanović relates the suffering of Sarajevo's Serbs as they faced dangers from uncontrolled paramilitaries from within the city and shelling by fellow Serbs from the surrounding hills.

Membership on the Presidency did not suit Kecmanović. In June 1992, under the guise of pursuing further negotiations with Serbian nationalists in Pale, he defected to Belgrade. With Kecmanović's departure, Pejanović became the most prominent Serbian politician serving in the wartime government of Bosnia-Herzegovina.

## THE SEARCH FOR PEACE

Under the chairmanship of British Prime Minister John Major, the EC convened an international conference in August 1992 to formulate principles of peacemaking for Bosnia-Herzegovina and to broaden the framework of peace negotiations. The EC formed the International Conference on the Former Yugoslavia (ICFY) under the joint sponsorship of the EC and the UN. The Co-chairmen of the ICFY Steering Committee, Cyrus Vance and former British Foreign Secretary Lord David Owen, were charged with conducting the day-to-day negotiations. The ICFY was based in Geneva, and most negotiating sessions over the next two years took place there.

As a member of the Presidency of Bosnia-Herzegovina, Pejanović participated in many of the Geneva negotiating sessions. In 1993 fellow Bosnian Serbs encouraged him to defect from the Bosnian government. Serbs loyal to the government were a constant aggravation to Karadžić, Krajišnik, and other SDS leaders who urgently wanted the world to believe that they, and only they, spoke on behalf of all Bosnian Serbs. Some international negotiators saw loyalist Serbs and Croats as an inconvenience in their efforts to solve the war through ethnic partition of Bosnia-Herzegovina. In Chapter XIX Pejanović relates the apparent complicity of Lord Owen in an effort to entice his defection. (In Chaper III, it should be noted, the author portrays a somewhat different Owen, one quite sympathetic to the plight of besieged Sarajevans and their practices of mutual coexistence.)

Peace talks continued throughout 1993. International negotiators successively formulated two different peace plans which were accepted by one or more sides but rejected by a third. The Vance Owen Peace Plan, providing for ten ethnic cantons in Bosnia-Herzegovina, was rejected by Bosnian Serb nationalists in May 1993. The successor plan, designed to appease Bosnian Serbs, was rejected by Bosniak representatives in fall 1993. In the meantime, the rift between the HDZ and SDA led to a nasty war between Croat forces and the largely Bosniak Army of Bosnia-Herzegovina from April 1993 to March 1994. By the end of 1993, peace seemed farther away than ever.

American diplomatic intervention broke the deadlock. The US promoted a plan to end the Bosniak-Croat war and issued an ultimatum to Serbian forces to withdraw heavy weapons from around Sarajevo. In February and March 1994, US diplomats hammered out an agreement to end Bosniak-Croat hostilities. Meeting in Washington, Presidents Izetbegović and Tudjman agreed to establish a "Federation of Bosnia-

Herzegovina" consisting of ten cantons. The federation remained a dead letter for the first few years of its existence, but the Washington Agreement functioned as a cease-fire to end the Bosniak-Croat war. Most importantly, the agreement paved the way for Bosniak-Croat cooperation against the previously dominant Bosnian Serb Army.

The agreement also included a constitution drafted by US experts. Article One of the Federation Constitution mentioned "Bosniacs and Croats, as constituent peoples (along with Others)," but failed to mention Serbs. The omission deeply concerned Pejanović. At the time the federation's constitution was submitted for ratification, he and other Serbs were forming the Serbian Civic Council (*Srpska gradjanske vijeće*— SGV) to advance the interests of Serbs in government-controlled territory. Their last-minute appeal to recognize Serbs as a constituent people in the Federation Constitution fell on deaf ears.

Over the next eighteen months, Bosniak and Croat forces turned the tide of battle against the Bosnian Serbs. NATO bombing of Serb military targets, triggered by repeated atrocities against civilians in Sarajevo and eastern Bosnia, coincided with a major Croat-Bosniak offensive in 1995. Faced with determined international opposition, the Bosnian Serbs in late August 1995 begrudgingly authorized Serbian President Milošević to negotiate on their behalf in US-led talks. Negotiations to end the war began shortly thereafter at Wright-Patterson Air Force Base near Dayton, Ohio.

## PEACE AND THE SEARCH FOR EQUALITY OF THREE CONSTITUENT NATIONS

The "General Framework Agreement for Peace in Bosnia-Herzegovina," better known as the "Dayton Agreement," was formally signed in Paris on 14 December 1995. It represented a compromise between the nationalism that had incited the conflict and the democratic principles to which the nationalists paid lip service. To enforce the agreement's military provisions, a NATO-led Implementation Force (IFOR), later renamed "Stabilization Force" (SFOR), was deployed. Civilian compliance was assigned to a High Representative who, by agreement, was to be European.

Like the Washington Accords, the Dayton Agreement included a full-blown constitution, but it was promulgated without providing for ratification by any representative body. The constitution recognized two "entities" in Bosnia-Herzegovina, the Federation and the "Republika

Srpska" (RS), each with its own constitution. The Dayton Agreement thus created a constitutional conundrum. Whereas the constitution of Bosnia-Herzegovina recognized all three peoples as "constituent," the constitutions of its component parts did not. The RS constitution bestowed that status only on Serbs, and the federation constitution recognized only Croats and Bosniaks.

These omissions defined the purpose and program of the SGV under Pejanović's leadership over the next four years. The organization encountered resistance from Bosnian Serbs who opposed the return of Bosniaks and Croats to their former homes in the RS. Many federation politicians likewise opposed granting equal status to Serbs until the RS accommodated the Bosniaks and Croats. Finally, in 1998, Pejanović and other SGV leaders persuaded President Izetbegović to appeal to the Constitutional Court of Bosnia-Herzegovina to recognize all three groups as constituent nations throughout the country.

In an historic ruling in July 2000, the BH constitutional court ruled that the constitutions of both entities should recognize all three nations as constituent peoples. Pejanović and his colleagues celebrated the triumph of the concept they had been championing since the adoption of the federation constitution in 1994.

Both entities were slow to comply, and not until 2002 did the High Representative mandate the appropriate constitutional changes. As of this writing, the impact of the constitutional changes must be judged modest. Still, establishment of the equality of Bosnia's three constituent nations throughout the country has been the most notable legal development in Bosnia-Herzegovina since the signing of the Dayton Agreement.

For the decade covered in this memoir (1990–2000), Mirko Pejanović's role in public life was characterized by an unwavering commitment to national equality and strong convictions regarding the nature of a multiethnic Bosnia-Herzegovina. As a participant in the most important political events of the time, and as a colleague of every major political leader, his personal history is memorable for its insights into the oft-neglected world of Serbs who remained loyal to Bosnia-Herzegovina in its most trying times.

# I. ON THE EVE OF POLITICAL PLURALISM

Elections for the new President of Bosnia's Socialist Alliance were held in March 1990, just when the organization's electoral process was undergoing alignment with contemporary democratic practice. This meant that several candidates - five including myself - presented their programs at the Conference of the Alliance, while the elections themselves were held by secret ballot. Thus I became President of the Socialist Alliance of Bosnia and Herzegovina.

At the time of my election, signs of the shattering changes to come were multiplying fast. But while Yugoslav society was obviously in its final crisis, the election of Ante Marković as Prime Minister of the Yugoslav federal government, had brought hope to many.[1] It was a time of widespread speculation on what route the reform of Yugoslav society would follow - and whether this route would lead to the break-up of the Socialist Federated Republic of Yugoslavia.

My election to the leadership of Bosnia's Socialist Alliance rapidly became the League's moment to face its own future. It had to decide whether to undergo radical reforms and become a party, or to cease functioning altogether. The Socialist Alliance involved by definition the free initiatives of civic organizations, based in the communities where their members lived, combined with the

---

[1] Ante Marković was selected as Prime Minister of Yugoslavia in March 1989. By implementing a comprehensive economic program, he was successful for a time in reducing inflation and introducing some reforms. After facing widespread popular opposition and being undermined by Milošević and other political leaders, he resigned from that position in December 1991. John P. Lampe, *Yugoslavia as History* (Cambridge University Press, 1996), pp. 347-9.

characteristics of a front, a broad association of political movements and parties within the socio-political system. We, the Alliance's leaders, decided our policy would be to offer to its highest body, the Conference of the Socialist Alliance, a concept for transforming the Alliance into a party.

This concept had three components. The first was to change the name from Socialist Alliance to Democratic Socialist Alliance (DSS – *Demokratski socijalistički savez*); the second was a proposal for party goals and programs; and the third was a proposal for party statutes and member recruitment procedures. All three components were discussed extensively in all municipal committees of the Socialist Alliance, and were finally adopted in May and June 1990. Our idea was to simultaneously preserve and develop the popular-based social-democratic traditions already in place: we hoped to build a plural society and multi-party system from the structure of the Alliance. This was a transitional phase, as we worked to turn the Socialist Alliance into a democratic party that would foster a strong feeling of popular involvement in local issues. This built upon the developments of the previous three decades, during which the Alliance had stressed mobilizing civic initiatives to build communal infrastructures.

We also found ourselves compelled to ask what kind of social model would the party born from the Socialist Alliance endorse. This party, it must be said, consisted chiefly of a tight inner circle composed of the Alliance's current activists. Its members were, by and large, mostly of the older generation, and the party relied heavily on the likelihood that rural areas would lend their support, as they had always done in the past. This likelihood was as much as we could guess from the popular mood. I vividly remember a public rally in Milica-Gaj, near Bosanska Dubica: the size of the crowds, and their enthusiastic response to every word from the Alliance's speakers. As President I gave the opening speech at this meeting, which was held on the 27$^{th}$ of July 1990 to celebrate the Day of Uprising. A Partisan woman from Potkozarje told me afterwards, "We must not let national hatred spread among the people."

Of course, this re-examination of the Alliance's role began in the context of widespread turmoil in Bosnia and throughout Yugoslavia, particularly within the League of Communists as it sought a road to reform. There was upheaval in most social organizations, and a universal obsession with creating new formulas for new political parties. At this time the League of Communists, like the Socialist Alliance, underwent an accelerated transformation and was reborn as the League of Communists — Social Democratic Party (SK-SDP – *Savez komunista – Socijalistička demokratska stranka*).[2]

As a public official of Bosnia and as an academic, I wrote and spoke much on the need to pluralize Yugoslav and Bosnian society. I argued for the introduction of a multi-party system, for a parliamentary system of government, and for a plural society based on parliamentary rule. I envisaged this as leading in turn to further economic reforms, all with the aim of building a modern market economy founded on private enterprise. I hoped that our industries would integrate readily into the contemporary European economic scene. Here, however, I found myself faced with the possible consequences of political pluralization. In the historic period surrounding the elections, would the existence of multiple parties, including nationalist parties, prove to be a factor for preserving social stability and growth - or a factor for tension and conflict, finally leading to war?

Given the creation of a multi-party system and the birth of multiple parties, the question arose of what constitutional changes and laws should regulate the consequences: how would the legal basis for a plural system be defined? Certain intellectuals, including Zdravko Grebo, Desimir Međović, Tarik Haverić, and others who were particularly pre-eminent and active in what was then the League of Communists, were the most vocal when it came to ideas for speeding up the introduction of a multi-party system. They cited the Declaration of the ZAVNOBiH, which at the time of its

---

[2] The League of Communists of Bosnia and Herzegovina changed its name in two stages. The first change was to the dual name "League of Communists – Social Democratic Party" (SK-SDP – *Savez komunista – Socijalističa demokratska stranka*). After the party's electoral defeat in the 1990 elections, it dropped its previous name altogether and adopted the shorter of the Social Democratic Party (SDP – *Socijalistička demokratska stranka*) at the Eleventh Party Congress of the League of Communists on February 23, 1991. *Oslobođenje*, 24 February 1991, p. 2.

foundation, in 1943 and 1944, proclaimed a democratic policy upholding the rights of all citizens to freedom of political thought and freedom of association.[3]

Debates were held in Parliament on giving the new system a legal basis, whether by passing appropriate acts, or holding a referendum. There was also widespread discussion of this topic in the media. The situation was resolved when the Bosnian Parliament passed legislation that provided for the introduction of a multi-party system. The Parliament decided that there would be no referendum. Instead, the new law provided that political parties could form freely, on the basis of any interest.[4] The Sarajevo daily *Oslobođenje* contributed its editorial views to the debate. Some of its editorials – especially those of Zlatko Dizdarević and Kemal Kurspahić, offered new insights and ideas to counter the prospects of a social conflict, which held all the potential to become a prolonged social crisis.

With the emergence of a suitable climate for the introduction of a multi-party system, founding committees were formed to prepare for the formal creation of new political parties. Three major new

---

[3] In July 1944 the Partisans held a meeting at Sanski Most in northern Bosnia to formulate its political goals. The declaration of the Regional Anti-fascist Council for the National Liberation of Bosnia and Herzegovina (ZAVNOBiH – Zemaljsko antifašističko vijeće narodnog oslobođenja Bosne i Hercegovine) affirmed the "brotherhood of Serbs, Muslims, and Croats" and advocated a "free and brotherly Bosnia and Herzegovina as an equal federal unit in a democratic federal Yugoslavia." It also affirmed basic human rights and freedoms. Although many of these freedom were subsequently abused, particularly in the immediate post-war years in socialist Bosnia and Herzegovina, the ZAVNOBiH principles proved attractive to many Bosnians seeking a path to democratic transition in the 1990's.

[4] These changes occurred in two phases. On February 21, 1990, the Parliament of Bosnia and Herzegovina passed legislation that provided for the formation of political parties but expressly banned parties based solely on religious or national membership. On June 11, 1990, the Constitutional Court declared that prohibition to be an unconstitutional infringement of the right to free association. *Službeni List socijalistička republika Bosne i Hercegovine*, 21 February 1990 and 17 June 1990. The Court's decision gave a legal green light to the formation and registration of the nationalist parties that were already being contemplated or actually organized.

Bosnian political parties were formed on the basis of nationality. Bosniaks formed the Party for Democratic Action (SDA – *Stranka demokratske akcije*); Bosnian Croats created the Croat Democratic Union (HDZ – *Hrvatska demokratska zajednica*), and Bosnian Serbs formed the Serb Democratic Party (SDS – *Srpska demokratska stranka*). During these events the question arose of the timing of the founding assemblies for the national parties. That of the SDS was already scheduled to take place in June 1990, and Radovan Karadžić was the president of the founding committee. No one thought to seek from him any clarification as to what kind of statement he would make at the founding assembly. He simply said the preparations for the founding session were in their final phase, but that he personally found it all a great burden. He declared publicly that he was exhausted and would not stand, did not want to stand, as a candidate for the party presidency. He claimed that the SDS was still busy consulting with various Serbs who were eminent political professionals, with insight and political experience, and from this group the party president would be chosen. He himself, he said, was out of the question. Later, of course, events went in a very different direction.[5]

Although they never expressly admitted it, the media were heavily engaged with the activities of these three founding committees, and in promoting the campaign events surrounding the inaugural sessions of the SDA, SDS and HDZ. Every commentary that appeared in the press during this period revealed that the ethno-national parties were the most popular with the media. The focus of media attention, and public interest along with it, was drawn towards the national parties and away from any other party or leader. Such was the climate in which these three parties had their birth.

In May 1990 Radio TV Sarajevo broadcast a special program on the hot debates surrounding the newly formed parties´ attitudes to democracy, human rights and freedoms, the national values of

---

[5] The SDS Founding Assembly was held on July 12, 1990, not in June as originally planned. At that assembly, Karadžić was elected President of the SDS despite his public renunciation of interest in the position. He remained SDS President until 1996 when he was forced to withdraw formally from public life under pressure from the International Community.

Bosnian society, and the preservation of peace in Bosnia. I was a guest on behalf of the DSS. Other participants included Ivo Komšić, of the Social Democratic Party; Alija Izetbegović and Adil Zulfikarpašić, of the SDA;[6] Radovan Karadžić, representing the SDS; and Davor Perinović, representing the HDZ. Kosta Jovanović was the host. The televised debate aroused widespread public attention. As might have been expected, everyone used the broadcast as a forum to publicize his own manifesto. Only Komšić and I clung to the theme that what was at stake was not the issue of founding political parties, but rather the degree of commitment that these emerging parties would show when it came to preserving the basic values of society and safeguarding the processes of reform and economic development. Above all, with the country's future itself at stake, what measure of responsibility would they take for ensuring the equality of all peoples in Bosnia, and maintaining stable inter-ethnic relations?

For a considerable period following this broadcast, comments on our statements flooded in. I would say the debate was really launched immediately after the broadcast, at the coffee-session hosted late into the night by the then editor-in-chief of TV Sarajevo, Nenad Pejić. Zulfikarpašić, who was always noted for his courteous behavior to others, spoke at one point to Komšić and myself. He said that he was aware of, and regretted as unjustified, the fact that blame for everything under the sun was laid at the door of the League of Communists. While the League was under constant attack for its exhaustion and mistakes, the younger generation, of which he saw Komšić and myself as representatives, had become the new target. Zulfikarpašić, himself a Partisan during the Second World War and a member of the Communist Party after the war, considered it an injustice that criticism of the old order, which was facing crisis and collapse, should fall upon the new generation, which wanted reform and showed itself serious in pursuit of it.

---

[6] Adil Zulfikarpašić was at this time the Vice President of the SDA, a position he assumed after returning from more than forty years as a successful businessman in Zurich, Switzerland. Later in 1990 he would come into conflict with SDA President Alija Izetbegović and leave to form another party, the Muslim Bosniak Organization (MBO – *Muslimanska bošnjačka organizacija*). See Adil Zulfikarpašić, *The Bosniak* (London: Hurst and Co, 1998), especially pp. 138-45.

Not surprisingly, Komšić and I felt a good deal of personal interest in his comments.

During this period of open controversy, following the introduction of a multi-party system, other issues of legislation were also being debated, including the specific provisions of laws for the elections of parliamentary delegates and members of the Bosnian Presidency.[7] When it came to the Presidency, talks were held on whether this body should keep its current structure, with two representatives from each of the three constituent Bosnian nations, or whether alternatives might be explored.[8] The idea arose of having one member elected from the category of "Others," to represent those who declared themselves to be Yugoslavs or as belonging to nationalities other than Serb, Croat, or Bosniak.[9] One way or another, this debate would always lead to the issue of whether national identity should be focused on or avoided.

---

[7] Discussion about the issues described here consumed the Parliament of Bosnia and Herzegovina throughout June and July 1990. The final package of acts and Constitutional amendments was enacted on July 31, 1990.

[8] The 1974 Constitution of the Republic of Bosnia and Herzegovina incorporated the socialist-era notion of "constituent nations," each of which enjoyed specific rights of cultural development, political representation, and other forms of participation in political life. Article I stated, "The Socialist Republic of Bosnia and Herzegovina is a sicalist democratic state and socialist self-managed democratic community of working people and citizens and nations of Bosnia and Herzegovina – Muslims, Serbs, and Croats, members of other nations and minorities that live within it." *Ustav SFRJ. Ustavi socijalistickih republika i pokrajina.* (Beograd: 1974). Although that language pertaining to working peoples and socialism was erased in the early 1990's, leaders of all three nations held dear their groups' status as "constituent nations" in various constitutional documents.

[9] The Bosniaks were generally known as the Bosnian Muslims until September 1993. Then, a group of their leaders convened in Sarajevo as the Second Bosniak Assembly and voted to change the group's name to "Bosniak." They hoped thereby to be recognized as a national group with status equal to the Serbs and Croats of Bosnia. Various bodies of the international community now accept this designation, and the change was ratified in amendments to the Constitution of the Republic of Bosnia and Herzegovina enacted in September 1995. The terms "Bosniak" and "Bosnian Muslim" are used interchangeably in this work.

Tensions grew, during the drafting of the Law, over the proposal that the Presidency membership should be 3+2+1: three Bosniaks, as the largest nation of Bosnia, two Serbs, and one Croat. This was initially passed by the Parliament as a constitutional solution, but aroused open discontent. Bosnian Croat bodies in particular decried this as an unconstitutional, illegal solution which failed to respect the equality of all three constituent nations of Bosnia. They complained that this inequality would be manifest in the Presidency, the chief of state and highest state body. The protests were loudest in the Croatia-based media: articles in Croatian daily newspapers, such as *Slobodna Dalmacija*, *Vjesnik*, and Zagreb's *Večernji List*, further aggravated the tensions, and worsened inter-ethnic relations. The Bosnian Croat Miro Lasić, a member of the HDZ leadership and later a member of the wartime presidency of Bosnia, was a particularly prolific writer on this topic.

But it has to be said that the arguments of the various eminent Croat intellectuals were sound, and their goal was a just solution that would promote the stability of inter-ethnic relations in Bosnia. As the president of the DSS, I felt deeply responsible, and I finally decided to try and formulate a strategy for resolving this issue. My initiative, which sought changes to the structure of the Presidency, and to the law on the election of its members, was ultimately presented to the Parliament. I requested that the presidency of the DSS should be allowed to speak on this initiative, while I, as party president, signed a letter to the Parliament Speaker, Zlatan Karavdić, giving our position. Karavdić informed all the parliamentary delegates about the letter, and negotiations resumed. This led to the creation of a new political climate, allowing changes to the Law and development of the final formula for Presidency membership: two Bosniaks, two Croats, two Serbs, and one member drawn from the category of "Others".

The tensions relaxed, and the Croats regained confidence that they were, *de jure* and *de facto*, constitutionally an equal nation and would share equal responsibility with the other two constituent nations for the political future of Bosnia. Public reception of this decision was enthusiastic, particularly that of the Bosnian public. I remember one surprise encounter in Banja Luka, during the election campaign of October 1990. Over breakfast at the Hotel Bosna, I found myself face to face with Stjepan Kljuić, already the president of the HDZ.[10] Stjepan introduced me to all the active members of the HDZ in the Banja Luka region, telling them that the initiative of the Socialist Alliance as a front, and my own personal initiative, had led to the changes in the law on the Presidency and the election of its members. Stjepan made it clear I had his special thanks for having persisted in the struggle for national equality.

As president of the Democratic Socialist Alliance (DSS), in its role of representing civic interests on the broadest possible basis, I held several pre-election consultations in the summer of 1990 with presidents of the founding committees of the nationalist parties. Accompanied by Ismet Grbo, secretary of the DSS, I met with Radovan Karadžić of the SDS; and, the next day, with Davor Perinović, president of the founding committee for the HDZ. We talked of the practical issues that were an open topic during the creation of these parties: the need for satisfactory conditions for their work and suitable accommodation for their headquarters. Here they had our concrete support: we spoke with Zlatan Karavdić, Speaker of the Bosnian Parliament, to request a speedy solution of these difficulties. The SDS was the first to settle on a location, which turned out to be a very good office in the former Parliament Members' Club. The HDZ and SDA had to wait longer for a home - only once the elections were over did they obtain their own quarters, in a building belonging to the Alliance of Workers of Bosnia and Herzegovina. It could here be suggested that there was a certain bias in favor of the SDS, demonstrated over this issue of office space. However, this was more of a coincidence. Karavdić, as Speaker of the Parliament, wanted to help at least one party, and the SDS request was the first to come to his attention.

As a part of these consultations, the DSS made a proposal to all the political parties planning to compete in the forthcoming parliamentary elections.[11] We suggested that all parties, given the ongoing crisis of the Yugoslav federation, should formulate a

---

[10] Stjepan Kljuić, a well-known Sarajevo journalist, replaced Davor Perinović as President of the HDZ in August 1990. This change was made at the direction of Croatia's President Franjo Tuđman for reasons that have never become entirely clear, but Perinović was dismissed shortly after the public revelation that his father was a Serb and a Serbian Orthodox priest.

[11] The elections were scheduled for November 18, 1990, and held on that date.

common basis on which to preserve and build Bosnian society and its historically multiethnic character. The DSS presented a Declaration advocating three core principles: the sovereignty of Bosnia and Herzegovina; the common life and equality of its nations; and respect for the institution of parliamentary democracy. The idea underlying the Declaration was that all political parties competing in the elections should pledge themselves to uphold enduring values that would rise above the individual, partisan interests of each. Thus the Declaration was something of a defensive blueprint against the growth of political forces opposed to the unity, multiethnicity and historic uniqueness of Bosnia. It also provided a litmus test of what would happen, and how it would happen.

The Declaration readily won support from the SDP and several other social movements. Their support for the Declaration shows that the bloc of democratic-social-liberal, social-democratic, and leftist forces stood firm from the beginning on behalf of a united and sovereign Bosnia and a common life for all its nations. I now visited various other party leaders, hoping they too would respond favorably.

My first conference was with the leadership of the SDA. This was in July 1990, and the SDA headquarters were in a building opposite Markale Square in the center of Sarajevo. Here I met with Alija Izetbegović and Adil Zulfikarpašić. Izetbegović, as president of the party, was occupied with another set of talks, and entered at a later stage into my dialogue with Zulfikarpašić, who was then deputy president. Zulfikarpašić received me cordially, with obvious readiness to discuss the issues I had raised. Both declared themselves in favor of the initiative, describing it as being "of great interest" and "highly acceptable," and both were willing to engage in promoting it. Izetbegović was subsequently to give it his public support. At this time, the attitude of the SDA was straightforward. They saw in our Declaration the possibility of strengthening the foundations for preserving Bosnia, while reforming and reconstructing the state on contemporary lines. However, during the developments that led to divisions in the governing coalition of the national parties, and during and after the war, this issue was to remain one of the thorniest questions for the survival and development of Bosnia.

Davor Perinović, then the President of the HDZ, was also enthusiastic about the initiative, and offered several suggestions.

But the Declaration was destined to end in failure, for it turned out that the SDS was against participating.

After preliminary discussions with the parties, a meeting was organized, attended by all parties except the SDS. All who came declared themselves in favor, and later confirmed this position publicly, in statements given at press conferences. But the SDS still did not want to join – at all events, we received, on one occasion, the answer that the SDS still had not developed a position on the issue of Bosnia's sovereignty, and therefore could not accept the Declaration at this moment in time. In fact, as later became clear, they were already opposed to its principles as a foundation for constituting the government and developing the country.

Since SDS support was lacking, the other parties' enthusiasm waned. Eventually the SDA, HDZ and the SDS drew closer together, with one overriding aim: to destroy the current Communist government and seize power for themselves, while evading discussion of any of the questions on which they currently disagreed. Thus they abandoned the Declaration.

I saw more evidence of the SDS position in a conference with Mr. Karadžić during this period, which took place in Nedžarići in August 1990, in an ugly, dilapidated house, visibly decaying. In a lengthy meeting, we talked about the development of Bosnia, about the country's current position, and, at my suggestion, about inter-party cooperation. I noticed that Karadžić was obsessed with the idea of forming Serb municipalities, a question which he raised repeatedly during my visit. I told him squarely that this could only happen in places where there was an absolute Serb majority, and there were very few such places in Bosnia - a negligible number - while regional social organizations could not be based on this type of national concept. I also warned him that advocacy of such a concept would lead sooner or later to conflict between the Bosnian nations. Karadžić countered by pointing to Milići, and a few other places with a Serb majority. On this question we remained totally at odds.

Then Karadžić said to me – in answer to my question of whether he was cooperating with political parties in Belgrade – that he wanted neither alliance with the Communists nor with the Socialist party of Serbia, which was the bastion of the Communist movement. He claimed his focus was on new democratic forces, particularly the leading intellectuals of the Serb nation. (Here he mentioned Dobrica Ćosić.)[12] At this stage Karadžić was planning a profile for the SDS that would require its members to be democrats rather than Partisans or Chetniks. This was an intriguing formula, designed for public consumption, by which he hoped to demonstrate that he stood for the future, rather than for past sources of division.

However, during our talk I mentioned a problem I had noticed as a member of the inner circle of leaders in the Bosnian Republic. I had visited the initial meetings of several regional founding committees, notably those of the SDS, as an observer. I told him how, in my home area of Živinice, an SDS founding committee had gathered in front of the church at Gajevi. I had heard late at night on the radio that its elected leaders included people whose parents or grandparents had served in the Chetnik forces, and who were themselves Chetniks. I warned him that freedom of political association together with the revival of ideas from the past could lead to an SDS-generated Chetnik revival in Bosnia. He replied categorically, even angrily, that there was no question of this ever happening. He claimed that they were forming a party to carry the flag of democracy, not to bring back the Chetniks or Partisans. Our conversation ended there.

This was one of the talks that showed me that Karadžić, as the creator and leader of his party, was preoccupied not only with the idea of "Greater Serbhood", but with the idea of national regions, national homogenization. In other words, he was ambitious of creating a whole political system and interest-based social structures founded primarily on nationality. This would progress from the creation of new Serb municipalities, to the creation of whole new regions: ultimately leading to the creation of a separatist Serb Republic.

During these consultations it became obvious that the emerging political forces were far from agreeing that Bosnia was, above all, a

---

[12] Ćosić was a noted Serbian writer who was expelled from the League of Communists of Serbia in the 1970's. He became a hero to many Serbian nationalists. On June 15, 1992, the federal Parliament elected him President of the vestigial Yugoslav state proclaimed on June 27, 1992 after Slovenia, Croatia, and Bosnia had declared their independence.

historically unique country with historic borders and historic unity, a multiethnic population, and the values of a multiethnic society. Unless the programs of all parties competing for power should solidly buttress these values, this could not be a stable society. A return to these original principles, and to ideas like that of forming a Bosnian Front, was necessary for the secure development of this country. Building a consolidated position required a broad-based democratic approach, with the inclusion of all civic associations and individuals. It would have to engage all forces that could potentially support the three fundamental historic prescriptions for Bosnia: sovereignty, common life and equality of the nations, and the institution of parliamentary democracy.

Although fearing a divisive trend, I personally felt that the national parties would not in themselves necessarily be a cause of social tensions, nor of conflict or war between the nations of Bosnia. I believed that the national parties, like other parties, might be mono-ethnic in structure but could also be democratic and progressive in their ideas. I thought they had the potential to reach agreement on the historic question of the common and individual growth and development of the three nations. I was in favor of anything that meant full democratization, even if this meant nation-based plurality: the formation of political parties along ethnic lines.

Unfortunately, what followed instead was the alienation of the three national parties. Instead of drawing closer on the key ideas of social reform, they grew further and further apart on the grounds of national difference, due to their nationalist programs. This alone led to the destruction of Bosnian society from within, the destruction of its state organs, especially the security and defense components, although these differences were not in themselves decisive in causing war. The deciding factors were the expansionist projects drafted in Belgrade, and later adopted by Zagreb in 1993, once the war had started.

But the question still stands of whether the formation of national parties actively worsened the social and political situation in Bosnia, and led to war. It is left for historians to provide an objective view, with the help of the distance left by the passage of time. The emergence of such parties was not automatically a cause of hostilities, the forces that produced war. Rather, the causes of war lay in how these parties related to one another, and how the ruling parties exercised their powers in Parliament: for it was this that produced open conflict. This was the route down which the SDS traveled, for example, in radicalizing its political program of national segregation, homogenization and ethnic cleansing to the bitter end. The SDS was determined to carve out an ethnically pure territory and take no account of Bosnia's real borders. The final issue is of these parties' attitude to partnership. Collectively they failed to build a strong coalition founded on political agreement.

## II. ANTE MARKOVIĆ'S FAILURE

When Ante Marković took over the Federal government and started introducing his economic reforms, the standard of living began to rise. Along with purely economic reforms, Marković came up with the idea of forming an association of reformist forces as a distinct political party. This was to be the League of Reformist Forces of Yugoslavia (SRSJ – *Savez reformskih snaga Jugoslavije*), encompassing all of Yugoslavia. He hoped this party would counteract the hard-line forces within the League of Communists and also a force for counteracting nationalist ideology. It would do so by following the route already taken in the Czech Republic, for example, of finding legal, peaceful, reform-based political solutions to problems accumulated over the ages (found in abundance within the former Yugoslavia). He could have tested out this idea in any of the Republics of Yugoslavia, but he was eager to try it out in Bosnia.

The Socialist Alliance had normally organized celebrations in honor of major historical events, in particular the Day of Liberation, the Day of the Uprising of Bosnia and Herzegovina, (29 July).[13] Thus we organized celebrations as usual, in Kozara, on 29 July 1990. Marković agreed, in response to our invitation, to come and speak at the Kozara rally. We met him in Prijedor, the day before. He had arranged for a general consultation with industrialists from the Banja Luka region, and public officials from the local municipalities. I found it a stirring, inspirational debate. He put

---

[13] July 29 was celebrated in the socialist period as the anniversary of the Partisan uprising in 1941 against German, Italian, and Ustasha occupation.

the economic questions facing everybody into a political context. These problems included the fall of the dinar against other currencies, the rapid decline in foreign currency reserves, and the precipitous drop in industrial production throughout Yugoslavia. He pointed out the problems raised by reform, especially of ownership – the process of privatizing socially owned property, or, rather, the creation of several different types of property. During this debate in Prijedor, Marković went twice to the loudspeaker. Both times his speeches gave the impression of a man with a firm concept, a solution, and the strength and the confidence to carry them out.

After this, although we had not previously asked him to do so, Marković met separately with the delegates of the Socialist Alliance. We told Marković about the political situation in Bosnia, the ongoing formation of political parties, and the process of pluralization. We also told him of the Socialist Alliance's transformation into a party, the DSS. Marković himself then described to us the essentials of his idea for forming a political party, which at that time were not yet widely known. He aired these the next day at the rally. His vision was of a reformist party, liberal-social in character, which would build a model society through liberal and social-democratic reforms. This model society would, without war, without conflict, convert Yugoslavia into a market economy and parliamentary democracy, following the trend of European integration.

We then told him of our own view, that such a reformist party would have greater success if united with other political forces that were forming parties based on similar concepts, in order to have as broad as possible an approach to creating the new order. For us, such cooperation was paramount in the quest to achieve reform. We felt that this force would have more success at the elections if not represented just by a single party but by an association of like-minded forces in Bosnia and in Yugoslavia. Marković favored the notion, and we expressed the readiness of the DSS to become a future member of such an association. We told Marković of the structure and components of our organization in Bosnia, and our estimate that we then had around 100,000 members - a number later confirmed by the first multi-party elections.

At twilight we went on foot in a column to Mrakovica, where Marković was to spend the night. The next day he gave a speech at the traditional rally of the people of the Krajina on the Day of Uprising. The journey from Prijedor to Mrakovica, and the charming Kozara valley, took place in an atmosphere of intense excitement. All along the road, everywhere you looked, people had strewn masses of flowers on the road in honor of Marković. It seemed the people who had come out in such numbers to greet Marković were keyed up to the heights of anticipation. They displayed unbounded confidence in him and his ideas, as was confirmed the next day by the gigantic popular rally. From the small hours of the morning the crowds started to gather on the Mrakovica plateau: it was later estimated that there were around 100,000 people present. This rally deserves to go down in history as having shown the authentic will of the people to accept the concept of reform, and the man who brought them this concept.

Marković now gave his famous speech in which he publicly declared, for the first time, that he was forming his League of Reformist Forces (*Savez reformskih snaga*, the Reformists). Having made this announcement, he went on to talk about all that would follow the formation of the party, and how it would take part in the first multi-party elections in Bosnia. Additionally, both before and after the rally, in his accommodation in Mrakovica, Marković met with a multitude of people who had journeyed from Croatia as well as from throughout Bosnia, to greet him and show their respect. One of his colleagues brought in a huge notebook and began collecting the signatures of the many supporters of the new party. Zlatan Karavdić, the Speaker of the Parliament, came to represent Bosnia; while, as president of the body that sponsored the rally, I was there as a host.

After his speech at Mrakovica, Marković started the work of founding the Bosnian Reformists, coming frequently to Sarajevo to meet with the members of the founding committee. Džemal Sokolović, professor of the Sarajevo Faculty of Political Science, was elected as the first president of the Bosnian League of Reformist Forces of Yugoslavia. Later, however, Nenad Kecmanović was elected, and led the Reformists at the elections.[14]

---

[14] Nenad Kecmanović was a long-time activist in the Socialist Alliance of Bosnia and Herzegovina and the Rector of the University of Sarajevo. In 1989 he was an unsuccessful candidate for a position on the Presidency of Bosnia and Hercegovina.

Now we come to the question of why Marković, when still pursuing the course of forming the League of Reformist Forces in Bosnia, failed to ally his party with a wider association of movements, and why he refused to include some of the more respectable political forces of the time, including the SK – SDP, the group that had previously been the League of Communists. I think he made a grave mistake, and that he was led to do so, against his own will, by various people who were promoted with his full support to the leadership of the Reformists. Those responsible were, in my opinion, Kecmanović, Sokolović, and later Dragan Kalinić and others. Although the majority of them had been activists in the SK or had enjoyed its confidence as editors of magazines, deans of faculties, or directors of firms, they were now anxious to escape its approaching collapse. They thought to escape by isolating themselves from it and claiming it belonged to the past, even though they themselves were a part of that past. They made the same mistake in dealing with the DSS, the Bosnian Liberal party, and several other parties which tried to promote reform but also to foster and preserve all that was positive in Bosnia's experience under the socialist system.

I personally experienced this narrowing-down of the Reformist forces. While its leaders were being elected, we of the DSS instructed our activists in regional locations, who were often highly influential, to help the Reformists establish themselves. But once this was done, the Reformists were ordered to have nothing to do with either the DSS or the SDP. They initiated a certain defined hostility, later developed more fully in the attitude officially adopted by their leaders toward the coalition of the SDP and the DSS. Nenad Kecmanović, in particular, was suspicious of the coalition of leftist forces.

Thus instead of Marković's idea proving stronger than that of the national parties, in practice his policies fatally divided the democratic, reformist bloc, rendering it less effective with the voters, as the election results were to demonstrate. However, Marković had the best of intentions. His was a historic and redemptive idea for the reform and the transformation of Yugoslav society, without blood, without drastic revolution, and without any return to the past. Marković felt his idea would find its greatest support in Bosnia, as indeed it did. Bosnia's institutions and leaders, new and old, along with their calls for more radical reforms, advocated for the survival of Yugoslavia - including Izetbegović in his first speeches as the president of the founding committee of the SDA, and later as party president. Thus, Marković had the support of all Bosnia, which hoped his idea would gain historic dimensions and prove triumphant. He long retained this support: Marković himself was born in Bosnia, at Konjic. Apart from his birthplace connections with Bosnia, he shared the views held by Bosnia's then united people, its social and political forces, on reforming the Yugoslav Federation and creating a new, plural society.

Tragically, due to the narrowing of this concept, and for other reasons that are plainer now than they were then, there was fierce resistance to the League in Croatia (Marković himself was a Bosnian Croat) and still fiercer resistance in Slobodan Milošević's Serbia. Marković found more support in Macedonia, and was joined by a number of colleagues from Slovenia (Živko Pregl, for example) who favored the League. Later events, however, including the short war in Slovenia, demonstrated that the most significant opponents to Marković's idea included the Yugoslav National Army (JNA – *Jugoslavenska narodna armija*) Command, which had already been won over by Milošević. The JNA had no interest whatsoever in Marković's fight to reform Yugoslav society, and he lost still more political power thereby, as the outcome was to show. Marković himself underestimated the strength of the movements for sovereignty in the various republics - movements that subsequently came to enjoy the support of the European Union.

## III. THE ELECTION COALITIONS

The DSS entered into a coalition with the SDP for the election campaign, and together we held pre-election rallies in the majority of Bosnian municipalities.[15] I managed to be personally present at rallies in 60 municipalities, and Nijaz Duraković of the SDP visited all 109 municipalities of Bosnia. The preparations were jointly carried out on what could be called a high political and professional level, and in most places we gathered impressive crowds of local supporters. Examples are the pre-election rallies in Teslić, Mostar, Goražde, and the final pre-election rallies in Sarajevo and Brčko. At that time a change could be felt in the political mood of the public, parts of which were moving away from the concept of civic interests and towards the desire for national homogenization. The first seeds of the latter concept were sown in Bosnia by the "spontaneous gatherings of the people" in Serbia. These seeds found fruitful soil in those municipalities where Serbs were in the majority, in Gacko, Drvar, Vlasenica, and several others. The same process followed the formation of the HDZ in Croatia, in Bosnian municipalities with a Croat majority, particularly those of West Herzegovina.

The growth of nationalism could already be felt, despite the efforts of the former Socialist Alliance to transform itself into a democratic party within which new processes and new interests could develop. For example, near Sanski Most, when we were

---

[15] "Municipality" is the typical translation of the word for the local unit of government, "*opština.*" Many *opština*'s, however, were rural districts with their headquarters in small towns and thus were not "municipalities" in the sense that they were urban areas.

discussing the projects and goals of the party the Socialist Alliance would become, an old woman of Bosniak nationality asked if we could hang a portrait of Alija Izetbegović in the conference room. (At the time Tito's portrait still had pride of place in all our offices.) Izetbegović was by then a leading figure in the movement to create a Bosniak national party, the future SDA.

It became obvious that the political arena of Bosnia was undergoing radical division. Monopolies were starting to appear and grow, inherited from the power bases of the SK and the like. Some time after the Socialist Alliance had become a party, for example, we started holding debates in West Herzegovina. We found in several municipalities, notably Čitluk, that people had plenty to tell us privately after the meetings that they had been reluctant to reveal in public. They told us they saw no hope in their region for the future of a reformed League of Communists, a reformed Socialist Alliance, or any other such party for that matter. The only party that could succeed, they said, was the HDZ, which was already holding its promotional campaign in Croatia. The spirit of this party, and all it carried with it, was easy to recognize everywhere it spread. Its presence was evident not only in the municipalities of West Herzegovina but in every settlement, however small, from the banners, slogans, and the manner in which people had started to think. One civic leader who took part in a debate we organized told us explicitly that in his region, only one party could win the elections, the HDZ. This was to be confirmed by subsequent events.

There was the time when Nijaz Duraković and I arrived together in Ljubuški for a pre-election rally, hosted in an auditorium. This was not a suitable environment for holding a public rally, given the presence of hard-line groups of HDZ supporters. The latter were politically extreme, and had little tolerance for the cultivation of political interests that were other than their own. We could sense their hostility, from the atmosphere and other indications, as soon as we entered the hall. In the event, a local worker delivered the most notable speech. He talked about the most important values of a society like Bosnia, and the values of the society that we wanted to build: modern and plural, with a market economy capable of integration into the community of the peoples of Europe. The meeting thus ended on a positive note in spite of numerous attempts at provocation. However, there was a constant sense of tension, suggesting strongly that the outcome might not have been so favorable.

We saw something similar in areas that were traditionally Serb. On a visit to Drvar to promote the Socialist Alliance's transformation into a political party, the local president of the Socialist Alliance told us before the rally that he had had immense difficulties in persuading people to come, since there was considerable local resistance to the concept. In fact, the only really successful public rallies were the kind then being widely publicized in Yugoslavia as "spontaneous gatherings of the people", held under the portraits of Slobodan Milošević.

Thus the process by which the population was to be polarized and homogenized on the basis of nationality had already begun. The Socialist Alliance, in its new incarnation as the DSS, was working together with the now-reformed League of Communists under its new double title, the League of Communists-Social Democratic Party (SK- SDP). Together, these two parties battled in the new political free market for seats on the municipal and city assemblies, and in the Bosnian Parliament.

Duraković, my colleague from the Faculty of Political Science and President of the SK - SDP, took on the nationalist parties directly at a pre-election meeting in Bugojno. He replied vigorously to a contemptuous speech Perinović of the HDZ made somewhere near Prozor. Perinović had bitterly denounced everything connected to the past and the Communist movement. Nijaz's answer was that if the embryo national parties were to follow their present course, of stressing the differences between the nations, and seeking to resurrect past sources of division, then the birth of such parties in multinational Bosnia could lead to war. He spoke as if he foresaw what was to follow at the start of 1992. Yet I would add that no individual parties could be solely answerable for the developments that were to come, and the use of force to adjust inter-ethnic relations. A historic process is at issue, and degrees of responsibility remain open to question.

I would compare this rally with that held the next day in a sports hall in Bileća, in West Herzegovina. Ivo Komšić and I were there together, Komšić on behalf of what was now the SDP, myself for the DSS. Throughout the rally, while we were on the podium, a group on the platform kept yelling "This is Serbia" and hurling stones in response to every statement they differed with. Somehow I got through my own speech without stoning, although I told them frankly that Bileća was a place where Serbs and Bosniaks lived together, and that an area where Serbs live may be Serb to some extent, but is not Serbia. This, and some other points, angered them further, and they were at their most aggressive during Komšić's speech, not only because he responded to them more toughly than I did, but also because Komšić himself was a Bosnian Croat, who saw Bosnia as an integral part of his own destiny. We left this meeting full of painful impressions. Our viewpoint was clearly in trouble in this region, and we guessed that it would fail to win any support – an accurate forecast. It should be noted that the group who entertained us with stones were, or at least they represented themselves to be, part of Vuk Draskovic's Serbia-based Serb Renewal Movement (SPO – *Srpski pokret obnove*).

In contrast, I have a vivid memory of the welcoming atmosphere in the cities of Goražde, Brčko, Teslić and Tuzla, as one of the most beautiful things about Bosnia, as something that lived on in this country undimmed by the passing of the centuries. I would almost say the same of the city of Banja Luka as it was then. These were, first of all, very impressive rallies, with tens of thousand of people present and enthusiasm pouring out on all sides in support of the ideas for which we spoke: social reform, market economy, parliamentary democracy. Most memorably, they demonstrated unexpected support for the historic uniqueness of Bosnia. We said clearly that we were fighting for a unified and multiethnic Bosnia within its historic borders, and we spoke of the significance of the values of common life and tolerance as the preconditions for peace in Bosnia. We also talked of the equality of all nations living in this country, and the mutual values that had developed over many centuries of life together.

At our final pre-election rally in Brčko, I believe there were between twenty and thirty thousand people present – forty thousand according to the hosts of the gathering. It was the end of October 1990, and it could already be sensed that people were afraid something was going to overturn this peaceful life in Bosnia, the product of centuries of inter-ethnic tolerance. They had witnessed party rallies that incited fear and hatred of other nations, rallies that voiced the prospects of war. "Sell your cow and buy a gun," Karadžić famously declared at a pre-election rally in Banja Luka. He had already begun calling on all ordinary people to start thinking of war, claiming that as there was no political consensus or agreement on the political future of Bosnia, the time for war had come.

This was the death sentence for the political growth of the people, especially for the Serbs of the Krajina, which in the Second World War had been mostly antifascist and Partisan. Their attitude was already affected by events in Croatia: Karadžić harped on the experiences of Croatia's Serbs in order to swing the mood of the Serbs of the Bosnian Krajina. The effect was further augmented by the unscrupulous behavior of the SDS in attempting to smear all leftist democratic forces. In Banja Luka, propaganda materials appeared, distributed to homes and throughout apartment blocks, announcing, "We will not betray you - the League of Communists and the leftists will betray you! The Ustasha knife awaits you again." An abrupt change in the political mood resulted, and the SDS won the heavy majority of votes in this region at the elections. Nevertheless, the DSS got one of its own members from the list of regional candidates into the Bosnian parliament: this was Goran Popović, then director of the Vitaminka firm in Banja Luka, a young man who wanted economic progress. During the war he was a member of the independent club of members in the Parliament of the Republika Srpska, the group headed by Milorad Dodik. A long time later, after the signing of the Dayton Peace Accords, Dodik told me that Popović had become a member of the SDS.

At the start of the campaign, the SDP and the DSS formed coalitions in the majority of municipalities. The Liberal Party headed by Rasim Kadić ran independently; the Muslim Bosniak Organisation (MBO – *Muslimanska bošnjačka organizacija*), created after a split within the SDA between Zulfikarpašić and Izetbegović, also ran independently, as did the Reformists. But during the campaign, the three nationalist parties, the SDA, HDZ and SDS, reached an agreement, never fully made public, to support one another in the final vote. They decided to cooperate for the sake of one basic goal: to keep the democratic, liberal and leftist parties out of power. They could agree on this without any difficulty, as long as they did not enter into any of the fundamental political questions about Bosnia's future. They simply agreed to join their flags and win the elections. They also agreed that the followers of one party would vote for the candidates of the other two parties, and vice versa. Thus all would vote for all.

This enabled an unprecedented landslide victory, and mysterious gains of voter confidence. For example, HDZ candidates of Croat nationality, despite their use of disturbing symbols from the past, won astonishing triumphs in traditionally Serb regions.[16] Franjo Boras won as many votes in Drvar and Sekovići as he won in West Herzegovina. Fikret Abdić of the SDA won votes in traditionally Serb areas such as Kladuša, and Nikola Koljević won as many votes in Croat-majority Listić as he did in Banja Luka.[17] The nationalist parties had merely instructed their sympathizers to vote for all of them. After the elections, a man from the town of Ključ in the Bosnian Krajina told me that there were polling stations where the election commissions told ordinary voters as they took their ballot papers that they could vote only for SDS candidates, not for the SDP or DSS. When people challenged this, they were told that the three national parties had agreed to support each other in the elections, and this meant they could only vote for Plavšić and Koljević. It was an unscrupulous battle for votes, which took no account of democratic principles, and the results are well known.

Thus a pre-election collaboration developed which continued, in the shape of a so-called partnership, once Parliament was constituted. The Parliament speakers were elected on the basis of this partnership, as were the Presidency and the Government of Bosnia.[18] The three national parties achieved full agreement right from the start, whether tacit or open, on winning the power struggle

---

[16] The HDZ employed symbols such as the checkerboard "Šahovnica," which to many Serbs was a reminder of the Ustasha regime and its atrocities against them in the Second World War.

[17] Nikola Koljević, a candidate of the SDS for the Presidency, was a Professor of Communications at the University of Sarajevo and a well-known Shakespeare scholar. Together with the other SDS candidate, Biljana Plavšić, he was elected to the Presidency in November 1990. He resigned in April 1992, departed Sarajevo for Pale, and became the Vice President of the Republika Srpska. In 1995 he initiated the Dayton Peace Agreement on behalf of the Bosnian Serbs. He died in January 1997 of an apparent suicide.

[18] The term "government" in the Bosnian context refers not to the entire apparatus of administration but only to a body consisting of the Prime Minister, Deputy Prime Ministers, and various Ministers. It is thus closer to the European concept of a Council of Ministers or the American Cabinet.

and defeating the democratic bloc. They formed their election coalition on this basis, and with its help they won the elections. They won so decisively that only a small slice of the pie was left for the opposition. Thus Parliament was shaky on its legs right from the start, or, rather, was forced to limp on one leg only, as there was no significant, electorally established, opposition.

When the three national parties entered into their pre-election coalition agreement, they raised none of the historic questions for the survival and development of Bosnia, nor did they form any political understanding or consensus on these issues. They put this off for later, and by so doing, won the elections. Several convincingly worded statements from the leaders helped accomplish their victory. Best known is that of Stjepan Kljuić - that Bosnia would become Switzerland once it had a market economy, parliamentary democracy and pluralism. Karadžić meanwhile stated that the SDS would wipe away all shadows from the past. He declared that Serbs would be neither Partisans nor Chetniks but democrats, and would bring about general economic prosperity through democratic growth. At no rally did Karadžić ever say that his party would go to war for the sake of Greater Serbia. Izetbegović, meanwhile, became known for moderate statements and for upholding the essential values of Bosnia's past, with the basic concepts that would lead to progress and reform. It should be remembered that at the beginning he even advocated for the survival of Yugoslavia, and its transformation into a genuine federation.

However, the leaders avoided addressing any of the fundamental political questions, inevitable though these proved to be when they formed their post-electoral coalition. Instead they entered Parliament without adopting any position on their coalition agreement. All the crucial questions arose, as they were bound to do, in Parliament. They were unable to agree on what direction Bosnia should take at this historic moment when Yugoslavia was disintegrating, the socialist order was collapsing in Europe and the world, while national ideologies and movements were marching at full strength in Serbia and Croatia. At the same time the forces for national homogenization were already marshalling their strength in Bosnia, while the leaders of two of the national parties, the SDS and the HDZ, had already become virtual affiliates of the Belgrade and Zagreb regimes respectively.

Debates were held in Parliament on these very points, precisely because the parties had failed to clarify their political positions and the political program of the coalition. From its first post-election session, the Bosnian Parliament rapidly deteriorated into several disparate cliques. The politicians in these cliques had been able to agree on winning the elections, but they disagreed absolutely on all questions concerning the future of Bosnia. The SDS, HDZ and SDA became each other's opposition, particularly the SDS and the SDA. This in turn led to growing political conflict, squabbles, fights, and ended in the final breakdown of the Parliament in 1991. In Parliament it became obvious that there was a lack of clearly formulated political goals towards which the victorious parties could work. The result was political warfare and what could be called the fight for national homogenization, the reduction of politics into the issue of partitioning national territories. These disagreements ultimately led to negotiations mediated by the European Union and the internationalization of the Bosnian question.

When the EU began its attempt at mediation in Bosnia, it was these three parties that represented the country. Each of them, the HDZ, SDA and SDS, had a different political position, and their divergence created a prototype for Europe and the world's view of Bosnia as a country of three conflicting nations, a view that endured until 1995. Meanwhile, under their leadership, Parliament tottered, its sessions more and more resembling pitched battles. During 1991, there was no agreement on any one major question to buttress the coalition's government. There is no country in Europe or the world where three victorious regimes can coexist without any common political program. This of course opens up plenty of questions about the leaders of these parties: what sort of vision, if any, did they have? The clashes enabled Belgrade to use the SDS, and Zagreb the HDZ, all the more easily for the purposes of their envisaged Greater States. These purposes were finally exposed when war broke out, first by the aggression of the JNA, in the guise of the Republika Srpska Army, and later in the Croatian Army's support for local Croat forces in the Bosniak-Croat conflict of 1993.

We are left with the inevitable question of whether the nationalist leaders, or rather some of these leaders, had agendas that they deftly avoided declaring at the start of the struggle for power. There is also the question of whether the other leaders – those who never stopped promoting the unity of Bosnia - knew about these hidden agendas, and, if so, how much they knew and why they passed them over in silence. It is clear that at no point did the SDS ever accept the idea of a sovereign Bosnia as an independent state, internationally acknowledged within its historic, recognized borders - one of the most strategic issues confronting Bosnia during the dissolution of the Socialist Federated Republic of Yugoslavia. The HDZ, on the other hand, spoke out publicly on behalf of a sovereign Bosnia, at least until the military conflict broke out between Bosniaks and Croats in 1993. Meanwhile the SDA always stood for the idea of a united and sovereign multiethnic Bosnia – and continues to do so to this day – as did the opposition forces - although these parties differed on whether that Bosnia should be liberal, liberal-Bosniak, reformist, social-democratic or democratic-socialist.

But when it came to this most fatal, crucial, question for the future of Bosnia, the SDS consistently advocated remaining within rump Yugoslavia. A program was already in existence to achieve this goal by carving up the country, forming national territories inside Bosnia and incorporating these into the Republika Srpska or into the Serb regions of the Associated Republics of Yugoslavia. This was the deadlock where the concepts and interests of the three national parties met each other head-on. I personally believe that their views were, in fact, fully known to one other when they formed their election coalition, but were ignored, by mutual consent, by the leaders themselves. Open political battle was not fought until nearly a year after the parties had taken power.

The next question is, could their divisions on this question have been otherwise resolved - did this really have to lead to war? When talks were taking place on the destiny of Yugoslavia, some of the final negotiations between the leaders of the socialist republics were held in Sarajevo. Afterwards, Milošević visited the headquarters of the SDS and met with Karadžić, and the latter subsequently visited Milošević in Belgrade. These visits and talks occupied the front pages of all the leading newspapers in Serbia and featured as the main news on the television and radio. It was clear that the SDS was building its political position on the principle of affiliation to the political interests of Belgrade, and that the HDZ, in spite of the independence for which it fought in the time of Kljuić's leadership, could not refuse to do the will of Zagreb. During the speeches he made in Parliament on the future of Bosnia, Karadžić openly claimed that Milošević was authorized to represent the interests of all Serbs, including those of Bosnia.

The nationalist parties, around this time, declared they stood for all members of their individual nations: the HDZ alleged it spoke for all Croats, the SDS claimed to represent all Serbs, and the SDA asserted it was the voice of all Bosniaks. These parties systematically excluded members of the opposition from any rule in government at any level. A new model for government had been set up, based on national homogenization, national division, and the fight for national territory.

## IV. THE TRIUMPH OF THE NATIONAL PARTIES

After the results of the elections were announced, a major press conference was held in the Bosnian Parliament. Representatives of all political parties that ran in the parliamentary elections gave statements. Ismet Grbo, then secretary of the DSS, was our representative at this conference. When advising Grbo on his speech, I suggested he should point out that the elections had passed peacefully, and were an expression of the democratic will of the Bosnian people, in spite of the considerable problems with the elections themselves. The DSS wished the victorious parties success in the execution of government, and hoped their rule would uphold the interests of the citizens and nations who had freely elected them. As one of the parties that had, albeit very modestly, passed through the elections, the DSS would cooperate in any program of government that would assist the common and general advance of Bosnia, its transformation into a modern market economy and plural democracy, and that would, in all ways and circumstances, foster its identity, its sovereignty, and its multiethnic structure.

Several days after the publication of the first election results showing the victory of the three national parties, Grbo and I visited their presidents. Our first visit was paid to Karadžić in his office in the former Club of Members of Parliament. We congratulated him on the election results, but our session with him was cut short, since he was constantly called away to take telephone calls from several municipalities in the west of the Bosnian Krajina, where the ethnic structure has since been so radically altered - towns such as Grahovo, Drvar, Livno, Glamoc. He was overwhelmed by a variety of problems, and these preoccupied him. He showed no particular emotion at his victory in the elections, nor did he have much to say. But it was noticeable that he was already obsessed by the course events might take in Croatia particularly. He mentioned the problems of anti-Yugoslavism and the swing in the popular mood against the JNA. Of course, this was just a courtesy visit, and was soon over. We did succeed, however, in saying that we expected the parties which had won power to act responsibly in approaching the problems facing Bosnia, and that they would resolve them in a spirit of mutual solidarity, trust and tolerance, in the interests of peace and progress.

Next we visited Alija Izetbegović, in the offices of the SDA, which was then in the municipal building of Stari Grad, Sarajevo. We congratulated him, wished him success in his future work, and added our hopes for cooperation between our parties in Parliament. Izetbegović said in response something that made a deep impression. He said that the future of democracy in Bosnia, and of Bosnia itself, must lie in modern European social democracy. Matters had fallen out otherwise, but this would remain the only viable solution for the future of Bosnia. Thus, his answer to our congratulations on his victory was to wish that responsibility for the political future of Bosnia had gone to the parties that we ourselves represented: the DSS and our coalition partner the SDP. I feel that in saying this Izetbegović showed himself both clear-sighted and honest regarding the development potential of the political structures of Bosnia, given its ambitions to join the community of European states. It was a totally spontaneous comment, but it suggested Izetbegović was already well aware that the victory of the three national parties, did not necessarily mean prosperity for Bosnia and its people. While our visit may have prompted Izetbegović to make this statement, subsequent events were to show he had already considered the nature of modern democracy and its rules. He realized that contemporary democracy in Europe, at its most advanced, has nothing to do with ethnic homogenization or the confinement of political interests to ethnic membership.

It seems likely that Alija Izetbegović's theory on Bosnia's future lying with social democracy was essentially about finding a solution in contemporary European methodologies for developing a democratic market economy. In itself his theory implied awareness that government founded on the concept of ethnic parties would turn out to be a dead end. Of course, this did not take account of the war and the goals of the Serb nationalists in particular to build Greater States. But the status quo was indeed due to become a cul-de-sac in which no internal democracy could be built nor any joint consensus formed on the future development of Bosnia. What system of government would be necessary for peaceful and successful social progress in this country, remains an open question. Izetbegović's promise at the beginning of 1997, that he would transform the SDA into a civic party, is just an indication that he was even then still seeking a solution that could be implemented by contemporary European processes for the development of society and democracy.

The third visit was paid to Stjepan Kljuić, who was, as we say in Sarajevo, a good *raja* (colloquial term for friend) of Grbo and myself, from long before. Our conversation with him was far more relaxed and optimistic. He announced that Bosnia, under its new government, would develop a flourishing economy, leading to all the benefits enjoyed by Swiss society. Kljuić was in fact repeating his main message to the voters in the elections.

These were our first post-election communications with the leaders of the winning parties, and a further encounter took place in Parliament itself, after the constituent session, once preparations for nomination of the government had been carried out. The HDZ had the candidacy for Prime Minister, and Kljuić, as a genuine democrat, consulted with other parties regarding the candidates. Jure Pelivan was proposed for Prime Minister, and we all supported his nomination. This was a concrete case of action by consensus, unique in the history of the multiparty Parliament and government.

After the elections, there was, naturally, much discussion and examination of the work of all parties, including those in the opposition: I had a direct view of this process within the DSS and the SDP. All parties analyzed the election results and assessed their own performance. In the DSS we worked further on profiling the party and building up and modernizing our program and statutes. We continued to envision it as a democratic party of socialists, reaching full consensus on this point at an advisory session with the presidents of the municipal level branches in February 1991 in what is now the building of the Federation Parliament. We also agreed with the branch presidents - apart from those of Sarajevo - that the DSS and the SDP would be integrated, thus creating a single, stronger social democratic option for this country. The integration process started in the Tuzla region, and proceeded in Mostar, Banja Luka, Bihac and Zenica, until only the Sarajevo region was left. In Sarajevo the principals could not agree, with one group opting to form a separate independent democratic party of socialists. Later, during the war, this was transformed into the Civil Democratic Party (*Građanska Demokratska Stranka* GDS), led by Ibrahim Spahić.

In this post-election period we also discussed how to promote agreement among the political parties on Bosnia's sovereignty and unity, its historic uniqueness, and its relations with the other republics of the former Yugoslavian federation. The SDP presented a declaration on these issues in Parliament in 1991, while Miro Lazović, president of the SDP Club of Members, promoted this declaration´s concepts on several occasions. It finally entered the parliamentary procedure for adoption, but because of poor relations within Parliament, and disagreements between the ruling parties, it went nowhere.

During 1991, the public was following the parliamentary debate closely. One of the many ideas to emerge was that a historic agreement should be created between Bosniaks and Serbs in Bosnia, to remove all danger of war from disputes likely to result from the dissolution of Yugoslavian society. The biggest debates relating to this issue had already begun in Parliament on whether Bosnia should remain within rump Yugoslavia or follow the route to independence, sustainability and sovereignty. The MBO and its leader, Adil Zulfikarpašić, were the first to promote the idea of a Serb-Bosniak agreement. Before it entered the public arena, a meeting was held in a restaurant in Grbavica at which the representatives of several parties were present, including Mr. Zulfikarpašić and Professor Filipović as the MBO leaders.[19] We from the DSS gave our support to the idea in principle,

---

[19] Muhamed Filipović, like Adil Zulfikarpašić, was a Vice President of the SDA when the party was first formed. He withdrew from that party and joined Zulfikarpašić in forming the Muslim Bosniak Organization. That party drew little support either in the 1990 elections or since, but it remains as of this writing a small party allied with non-nationalists and moderate nationalists in opposition to the SDA, HDZ, and SDS. Filipović remained highly visible as an outspoken and widely published member of the Academy of Sciences of Bosnia and Hercegovina throughout the 1990's.

but right from the start we recommended that all care should be taken to prevent this idea leading to fresh conflicts with the Bosnian Croats. However, we were told that the initiative was flexible regarding potential inclusion of the Croat nation, and therefore should not produce conflict.

Later the initiative was publicly promoted, and grew to considerable stature before descending into oblivion. It failed principally because it did not have sufficient support from the largest ruling party, the SDA. The latter lacked the readiness of the democratic opposition to see the concept as providing potential motive power for building consensus on the political future of Bosnia. The concept of an inter-ethnic agreement was aimed at avoiding war and preventing the use of force to define the relationships of the three Bosnian peoples, Serb, Croat, and Bosniak. It will certainly have some space to itself in any historic analysis of events in Bosnia. But it is mentioned here as an attempt by one of the opposition parties, the MBO, to offer a peaceful, democratic, political solution to the question of relations between the peoples.

I was not involved in the work of all Parliament sessions, but attended a number of them in the capacity of president of a parliamentary party who needed to follow directly the Parliament's activities at close quarters. I did not myself take part in the debates, as I felt that speaking in Parliament is for its members, not for guests – and it was as a guest that I was invited to attend the sessions. I shared in what the people of Bosnia were experiencing by way of their TV screens, including the realization that, from the start, Parliament's work went badly. The parties had only agreed on winning and dividing power, not on dealing with the political problems facing this country. Parliament was now a field of deadlocked political battles. The squabbling and irresponsible rhetoric grew worse from day to day. Representatives of the three nationalist parties, the SDA, SDS, and HDZ, were jockeying with one another for position, but also attempting to persuade the public that each was the sole representative of its own particular nationality. Parliament had become the arena for honing political conflicts, and thus contributed directly to the deterioration of the general political climate. In my opinion, the Bosnian Parliament was reduced, in part deliberately, by those who dominated it, to a mere mirror for the mood of the political parties, and, as the effect spread, the mood of the public at large. In Parliament the seed was sown for political division in Bosnia and for inter-ethnic conflict over the country's future status. Once the issue of Bosnia's political future was squarely on the Parliament agenda, the tensions rose from day to day, ending in an irreparable breach between two concepts, one demanded by the SDS, and the other jointly by the SDA and HDZ.

This conceptual division came to its climax in October 1991 during a long night of intense debates in the Parliament of Bosnia and Herzegovina. I myself left around nine that evening, during a break, and went home to my house in Breka. Parliament continued working late into the night, with many bitter words exchanged by the leaders of the SDA and SDS. During that same night, individuals from both parties struggled to draw closer together, to try and find some common ground, but Karadžić reduced all to an ultimatum: that, if the SDS proposal was not accepted, war would follow, and in that war the Bosniak nation would disappear. This threat heralded the coming genocide, later to be committed against the Bosniaks of eastern Bosnia and the Bosnian Krajina. The sole option offered by the SDS was that of joining all Bosnia to rump Yugoslavia, or rather, to "Greater Serbia." The SDA and HDZ, on the other hand, advocated for the sovereignty, independence, and sustained development of Bosnia. The two latter parties were supported in their stand by the opposition, which during and after the pre-election campaign argued for a united and multiethnic Bosnia, for common life and equality of the nations. The opposition parties formed, in fact, the strongest defense against the advocates of ethnic division.

That same night the leader of the SDA, Alija Izetbegović, delivered his answer to the ultimatum: if the choice lay between peace and the sovereignty of Bosnia, the Bosniak nation would choose sovereignty. Once this statement had been made, Parliament passed a Declaration of Sovereignty. The SDS delegates promptly walked out. They then formed their own independent parliament and declared the Republika Srpska as a separatist entity. [20]

The DSS and the SDP took part in a working seminar in November 1991 held at Palić, near Subotica in the Vojvodina, and

---

[20] At an assembly in Sarajevo, SDS Serbs proclaimed the Republika Srpska on December 21, 1991.

attended by presidents of social democratic parties from all over former Yugoslavia and abroad, as well as various independent intellectuals. Grbo and I were there to represent the DSS, and Zlatko Lagumdžija came on behalf of the SDP.[21] At this two-day seminar we discussed the crisis in Yugoslav society, and how it might be peacefully and democratically resolved. When the question of Bosnia came up, Lagumdžija, Grbo and I all stressed the specific nature of this country, its significant historic identity, and the need for a solution that would enable its independent development in the post-communist era. Then the well-known demographer and academic of the Serb Academy of Arts and Sciences, Milos Macura, made a speech. His message was that wherever the Serb nation is ethnically present, a Serb state will be created, regardless of the cost in victims and bloodshed. In 1992, when I experienced the beginnings of what we were to endure in Sarajevo and in Bosnia, I remembered the statement of Professor Macura, and how he had already committed himself to the position enshrined by the infamous Memorandum of the Serb Academy of Arts and Sciences.

In fall 1991, a delegation of opposition party leaders approached Alija Izetbegović, then the Chairman of the Presidency. The SDS had announced its separate referendum on the future of Bosnia, held in the form of a plebiscite of the Serb nation. This referendum was held on the 9th and 10th of November, and the results favored Bosnia's remaining in rump Yugoslavia. Our delegation - Duraković, Komšić, Kecmanović, Grbo and I - talked long and hard with President Izetbegović. We hoped to persuade him to somehow pre-empt this step by the SDS, which we considered an unconstitutional act in defiance of Parliament's authority. After a long discussion, however, President Izetbegović said finally that there was nothing left to be done, and that he saw no possibility of taking further steps to prevent the SDS from holding their referendum. He then suggested that we ourselves should try to do something, but we finally agreed amongst ourselves that we could do still less. By this referendum, the SDS ensured support for its aim of using force to bind Bosnia to Yugoslavia.

---

[21] Zlatko Lagumdžija was Vice President of the SDP during the electoral campaigns of 1990 and became its President during the war. He is a Professor at the Economics Faculty of the University of Sarajevo. He has led the SDP as its President in all elections since 1996.

As the president of a party, and a public official of Serb nationality, I myself came under strong pressure from the SDS leadership, more precisely from Momčilo Krajišnik, to join the celebrated February 1992 session of the Serb delegates, declared to be the parliament of the Republika Srpska.[22] I did not respond to this call, although plenty of pressure was used. As for other opposition members, Nenad Kecmanović and Dragan Kalinić from the Reformist party were present at this session, together with the DSS delegate for Banja Luka, Goran Popović. I consulted my party colleagues, and everybody, including Ismet Grbo, the Party Secretary, said that the decision was mine alone. I decided not to go. After this, all the communications I had previously maintained with the SDS club of members ceased.

These episodes reveal how strong, clear and well-developed were the SDS intentions and strategy. In the case of failing to reach a parliamentary agreement, the SDS already had a reserve option ready. This was to withdraw from Parliament, declare the Republika Srpska, adopt the constitution of the new government, and if necessary fall back on Pale.[23] It was, in fact, the sequel to earlier efforts to form autonomous Serb regions in Bosnia. As the historic consequence of its departure from Parliament, the SDS, in obedience to the will of Belgrade and with the support of the JNA, decided to achieve its political aims through the use of force.

Abandoned by one of the ruling parties, Parliament dispersed. In practice, the parliamentary collapse was no more and no less than the final death of the pre-election coalition of the national parties. This development of events in Parliament was clear and predictable, given the lack of consensus between the parties on any point of government. Parliament had largely consisted of a group of people who, finding themselves exposed to the public eye, were finally forced to declare themselves on the question of whether

---

[22] This session of the Serb self-styled Parliament, meeting on the night of February 27-8, 1992, only hours before the Referendum on the independence of Bosnia and Herzegovina, approved a Constitution for the RS. *Oslobodjenje*, 29 February 1992, p. 24.

[23] Pale, a mountain village near Sarajevo with excellent skiing facilities and several hotels, effectively became the separatist Bosnian Serb capital during the war. Under the Dayton Peace Agreement it remained in the territory of the RS.

Bosnia should exist independently or remain part of a diminished Yugoslavia. Given the absence of even the most rudimentary agreement, the result was total parliamentary crisis, which had a serious impact on the mood of the people of Bosnia.

## V. THE CIVIC PARLIAMENT – PROTEST AGAINST THE WAR

Many ordinary people realized that Parliament was foundering and that the conflicts within it were spiraling out of control. This led to popular revolt. To a great extent this was spontaneous - the idea of a "citizens parliament" grew from the gathering of crowds around the Parliament building.[24] A founding committee was set up, formed from groups of Sarajevans who demonstrated outside and inside the building. The broadcast of their first public statement mobilized others in greater and greater numbers. The protesters were not only Sarajevans, but people from all over Bosnia. I was present throughout, both as the president of the DSS and as a citizen of Sarajevo. I myself stood on the raised plateau in front of the Parliament building, in the immense crowd that formed there. That same evening, late into the night, I went to the loudspeaker and called on all people of good will to fight for the preservation of our common life in Bosnia and the preservation of peace as the vital precondition for our survival and our way of life. I told them – and I found myself growing emotional at this point – that when all battles were over, the concept of living together would triumph.

Other opposition party leaders spoke that evening and during the days and nights that followed, together with many artists, intellectuals, professionals, media personalities and public figures generally. But this was, as I see it now from the distance of time, just an inchoate popular effort, lacking organized leadership. It was the Bosnian people's spontaneous resistance to what they saw

---

[24] Citizens assembled in growing numbers in front of the Parliament building in late February 1992. It is to these demonstrations that Pejanović refers.

coming - to what had, indeed, already arrived. Patrols mobilized by the SDS were out barricading the roads with stockings over their faces, blocking the groups that came from the direction of Dobrinja and Novi Grad.[25] The people understood that a completely new situation had arisen: Parliament had fallen, and there was open conflict between the ruling parties. One party – the SDS - wanted war, and had an organized force to make war with, inherited from the military might of the JNA. The people realized that all Bosnians were in danger of their lives. By the second or third day of this "parliament of citizens," snipers´ bullets around the Parliament building were starting to destroy the mood of the gathering. As far as we knew, the shooting was from the Holiday Inn hotel, where SDS snipers had their nests.[26]

But before the final end of these demonstrations, it was perceived that these surging popular energies should be channeled, that they should be used to try and prevent war. People from the informal Organizing Committee talked with the commander of the JNA in Sarajevo and with the leaders of many political parties. But there was no program of defined ideas and no organization to execute them. Several of us realized the problem, and I myself, after consulting with Salih Foco from the MBO and several others, offered the Organizing Committee a list of names of people I knew, whom I could personally recommend for helping to form some kind of committee for national safety. I thought they could implement the developing will of the great masses of people who had come to Parliament, to demand that peace should be restored, that our common life should be ensured, that war should be prevented. I believed that this was more than a fight for power, or for the destruction of the current government. It was a genuine campaign to prevent war, to prevent the use of force to back political conflict. This is why I was among those who proposed members for a government of national security.

---

[25] These barricades were erected by SDS loyalists on March 2, 1992, the day after the referendum on the independence of Bosnia and Herzegovina.

[26] On April 6, 1992, the day that Bosnia's independence was formally recognized by the European Council, the anti-nationalist demonstrators in front of the Parliament building came under fire from paramilitary troops loyal to Radovan Karadžić quartered on the upper floors of the Holiday Inn Hotel across the street from Parliament.

The names were announced to all present, but many of the people on the list, outstanding academics and public officials, and, in my opinion, Bosnian patriots, had not been consulted and were not ready to accept. The body was never constituted, and so no shape was ever given to the citizens' initiative – which, properly channeled, could certainly have influenced not only those in power, but also the JNA and perhaps even the international community.

There are many different estimates of the significance of these demonstrations, including the theory that this was a campaign by hostile forces seeking to destroy the current government. But this was certainly not the motive of the miners and other workers who traveled in such numbers from Tuzla, Kakanj, Zenica, Banovići, and elsewhere. Their motive was solely to put a stop to the already obvious intention of the SDS to start a war. Had the proposed government of national security been formed, this might have exerted special pressure on the international community and may even have procured international arbitration for a solution for Bosnia. This would have prevented what was shortly to become full-blown aggression against Bosnia, open aggression by a military force inherited from the JNA and led by a political party. One thing is certain: The SDS would have been impotent, and would never have dared to put its concepts in motion, had there been no Yugoslav National Army at their backs.

I saw this citizens' parliament as a spontaneous effort by the people to express their feelings: it was their protest against the events that were leading so rapidly to war, to slaughter, and the destruction of our common life. Later, the theory arose that an Army-based splinter movement of the League of Communists - Movement for Yugoslavia (SK-PZJ – *Savez komunista – Pokret za Jugoslaviju*) was behind these protests and had instigated the idea of forming a citizens' parliament.[27] I had no knowledge of this, and can neither confirm nor refute this theory, but according to my own findings, and in my personal opinion, this was a genuinely spontaneous civic protest. The informal Organizing Committee, which led the first

---

[27] The SK-PZJ was a political group that grew out of political activists in the JNA. Many of its members were former JNA officers. Thus the notion that this group instigated these demonstrations is a conspiracy theory. The SK-PZJ would have encouraged the anti-nationalist demonstrations only to provoke the SDS into acts of retaliation.

march on the Parliament building, was inspired by the several young people who put themselves at the head of the column of demonstrators.

In the early days of the war, from April to June 1992, various parties came together to form an opposition bloc in Bosnia. All opposition parties: the SDP, the Reformists, the DSS, the MBO, and the Liberal Party, gathered to form a central committee with the aim of taking joint action to prevent war. The chief initiator was Professor Muhamed Filipović, the most senior of the party leaders. We gave joint press conferences, issued joint statements, and held several round tables on preventing the escalation of war. But by the end of May, the city was being shelled on a regular basis. Immediately after the broadcast of one of our joint press conferences, in which we condemned the bombardment and those who were behind it, deliberate shelling gutted the headquarters of Radio Sarajevo in Danijela Ozme Street.

Conditions for our work deteriorated rapidly. Some of our activities during this time should be highlighted, such as our efforts to explain our view of the situation to the international community, and to halt the escalation of the conflict. There were also our attempts to communicate with the parties in Belgrade. A delegation of the Bosnian Reformists, including Kecmanović, Sejfudin Tokić, and Josip Pejaković, visited Milošević to plead for a peaceful resolution. We also supported the Bosnian government's suggestion that, due to the besieging and shelling of Sarajevo, and the slaughter of civilians, the SDS should be declared a terrorist organization, and deprived of its status as a political party. At the same time we sketched out our idea of establishing joint cooperation between all interested parties in order to defend the legitimate state of Bosnia and its organs.

Once checkpoints and blockades were erected throughout Bosnia, the Bosnian Parliament was no longer able to meet. In accord with provisions of the Constitution, if emergencies prevented meetings of Parliament - as between 12 and 14 April 1992 - the Presidency of the state, in consultation with the political parties, could decide what course of action to pursue. The Constitution foresaw that until conditions could be established for re-summoning the Parliament, the Presidency itself could temporarily undertake Parliament's functions. [28]

---

[28] As will be seen in subsequent pages, the Parliament met a number of times during the war. However, shifting front lines and ubiquitous checkpoints

The truth is that, in this new situation, there was much doubt and uncertainty within the government about what do and how to do it. Opposition groups therefore assisted in speeding up the Presidency's decision. Professor Muhamed Filipović, the Vice President of the MBO, originated this initiative. His proposal had several points. The first was that the Constitution should be implemented and fully respected; the second was that Bosnia as a state, a historic entity, and a democratic society, could and should be defended on the principles of legitimacy and democracy. This became the framework of the debate, which was finally held in the smaller chamber of the Parliament building. The majority of the remaining parliamentary parties agreed with the initiative, and so the decision was made that the Presidency should take on the offices of the Parliament.

This was an inevitable and rational decision. As the war unfolded, it became clear that this had also been a historic decision to take responsibility for the destiny of the country, to defend the centuries-old values of its society, and to defend the Bosnian state as a community of equal peoples. It was, in my opinion, a decision of lasting worth. On this foundation, for nearly three years, the Presidency managed all defense activities, all recruitment, and all campaigns of the patriotic forces. The Presidency also represented the country during the peace negotiations, starting with the International Peace Conference in Geneva.

Meanwhile, these were hard days for the citizens of Sarajevo and for all citizens of Bosnia. The Serb members of the Presidency had resigned, and the Presidency was in a state of semi-paralysis, although it did not cease to function.[29] When the shelling began buildings and monuments in the center of the city were destroyed. The killings had also begun, and the first blood was spilt on the

---

made this infeasible in the first months of the conflict. Sessions were often held with many delegates from outside Sarajevo unable to attend, and always in the absense of the SDS delegates who had been elected in November 1990.

[29] The two SDS Serb Presidency members, Nikola Koljević and Biljana Plavšić resigned on April 6, 1992, the same day that Bosnia's independence was recognized by members of the European Council. As recorded in Chapter VI, their departure posed a dilemma on the manner in which the resulting vacancies should be filled.

streets of Sarajevo. It was hard to bear such sights. An oppressive atmosphere, of tension and fear, lay on the city of Sarajevo and on our country. What response could we make to the destruction of the city by bombardment, and the killing of its civilian population? We presidents of the opposition parties, working together at our center in Danijela Ozme Street, were adjusting ourselves individually and altogether, to face this reality. I gave an initial talk to the public, recorded by the TV Sarajevo journalist Sulejman Vlajčić. My topic was how to view the daily and nightly efforts to destroy Sarajevo and its people. I condemned both the intention and the act of destruction and killing and called on all patriots in Sarajevo to organize themselves into units for territorial defense. Defending the city was for me, above all, a moral necessity.

We also conferred among ourselves on our relations with the party that had so recently left Parliament, the party that had formed part of the government up to yesterday, and was now the organization behind all these crimes. Every representative of the opposition parties - and I vividly recall the presence of Professor Muhamed Filipović, Nenad Kecmanović, and many others – agreed to the state organs' proposal that the SDS, because of its criminal aggression, its destruction of Sarajevo and slaughter of civilians, should be excluded from public life. Everybody supported the decision.[30] This was when death dogged every step in Sarajevo, and this was our answer to those who sat at the head of this party, committing such unprecedented crimes against their city and their civilian neighbors of all nations: Croat, Bosniak, Serb, Jewish, Albanian, Slovene, and Macedonian.

---

[30] This decision, among other things, barred SDS delegates from participating in sessions of Parliament, something they had no intention of doing anyway since they no longer recognized the legitimacy of the state of Bosnia and Hercegovina.

## VI. SECRET MISSION TO KRAJIŠNIK

Every new step taken at this time on behalf of the concept of a peaceful, multiethnic Bosnia was a source of optimism for the people of Sarajevo. They were still living in hope, though shells were already tearing the city apart. There were still ambitions to stop the conflict before the launch of full-scale warfare. One source of hope was the possibility of finding replacements for the two places in the Presidency left empty by the resignations of SDS members Biljana Plavšić and Nikola Koljević. According to all regulations of the Constitution and election law, these places could be filled by those Presidential candidates of Serb nationality who had received the next highest number of votes in the elections of 1990. Next in line, therefore, was Nenad Kecmanović, who had received 500,783 votes, some 55,000 votes fewer than Professor Koljević. Next came myself, as the recipient of around 335,392 votes.[31] Thus we were the two who, in accord with the Constitution and the election laws, should and could become new members of the Presidency in the situation created by the resignations of Plavšić and Koljević.

Naturally this was discussed with the remaining members of the Presidency and within the bloc of civic opposition parties which we represented, Kecmanović as the Reformist candidate and myself as candidate of the SDP-DSS coalition. There were plenty of debates on this issue, both public and private. Most of my own talks were with the members of the Presidency, but at the same time I consulted with all presidents of the opposition parties, especially the SDP, which had supported my candidacy during the elections.

---

[31] Zoran Tomić and Nevenko Herceg, *Izbori u Bosni i Hercegovini* (Mostar: 1998), p. 72.

During this period of suspense - a time of great expectation, uncertainty and fear - Professor Filipović came to my house in Breka, and, finding me busy, suggested that we should meet up a little later and start working together. There was much to discuss: not only our drive to form a central committee for the opposition parties, but also the ongoing talks over initiating proceedings for our entry into the Presidency. Professor Kecmanović, after his departure for Belgrade in summer 1992, wrote at length about this period, for the Belgrade magazine *NIN* in particular, describing what he personally witnessed and experienced and the people with whom he spoke. My own memories are also clear, and I remember every episode in detail. With almost every step we took, people were asking eagerly whether we had yet decided to join the Presidency and whether we would try to save this country from war and collapse. The idea that our joining the Presidency could mean the redemption of this country and the survival of its essential ideal of multiethnic, common and equal life for the Bosnian peoples, inspired a new public mood in favor of democracy and patriotism. People were optimistic that we would help find a solution by political agreement and political means, without killing or bloodshed. In this, the thinking of ordinary people was close to mine. I had accepted the arguments of the bloc of opposition parties, which were all in favor, but Professor Kecmanović and I each had to make the decision individually.

He and I met and talked together, but the decision was not an easy one to take. Personally, I was fully aware of all that was facing us, although up till now I had not allowed myself to believe that our way of life could be so valuelessly destroyed by war. This was now an encounter with raw reality. I had in mind the fact that a single organized political force, the SDS, had started the war - a party that not only won a majority in the elections and within the Serb nation, but which seized for itself the right to represent the interests of all Bosnian Serbs. A model of life and values had been created in which the SDS was the global representative of the Serb nation. Historically this could not correspond with the truth, nor could one party represent a whole people - especially when other parties also had candidates who were members of the Serb nation, who had personally received mandates in the elections, and who saw the whole Bosnian question very differently. But within the

Serb nation the civic option, and all parties that supported it, such as the SDP, the Reformists, the Liberal Party, and the DSS, remained in the shadows.

Given the advanced state of the conflict, many in my place might have decided against entering any position of responsibility, on the grounds that they had not themselves chosen war, and that taking office in the midst of political division rapidly deteriorating into warfare could help nobody. Faced with such a choice, a man falls back on his own nature, what he himself would be ready to fight for. I felt that this was a decisive time for Bosnia, and that I should do for my country what I believed in, which was to fight for peace. I told Kecmanović I would act on the basis of my own convictions, of the ideas of the party to which I belonged, and of the civil opposition bloc of which I was a member. I believed that our double accession to the Presidency made sense and that it should, when the time came, happen in unison. Thus Kecmanović and I decided to join the Presidency together. Later our decision was severely tested, in many situations.

There was one day when I made my way through the city to Vaso Miskin Street, to a certain office (in a building opposite the Cathedral), to drink coffee with a friend I was particularly fond of. This was my neighbor, the economist Vehbija Karić – he was later killed in this same office, by a shell, as the tragedy of the war unfolded. There were many other Sarajevans present that day, who, over coffee and drinks, wondered whether this state of affairs would last, whether the vacancies in the Presidency would be filled, whether Bosnia would once again have a legitimate leadership, whether war and the risk of further war could be avoided. But war was already upon us. My coming intensified the debate: everyone wanted to question me, and share with me their own thoughts on the topic. Many said they not only wanted, but recommended Kecmanović and myself to join the Presidency.

Vojo Milijaš, well-known secretary of the City Committee, and later director of the Economic Bank, thought that while I currently bore no responsibility for what was happening, entering the Presidency would mean that Kecmanović and I must answer for all further developments. Secondly, he felt that the Serb nation, in demonstrating its political will at the elections, had knowingly put its trust in the two people who had received the most votes. Since these two had now exercised their powers by resigning, our accession to the Presidency could be in some way illegal, especially given the expectation that the whole nation could be represented through one political party. Vojin's comment aroused a storm of contradictions, but this was a group where all could freely declare their views, and nobody attempted to impose their own.

I went on to the Youth Center in Skenderija. There I found many Sarajevans gathered on the ground floor. I saw my close friend Senad Sečerović, then secretary of the SDP for the city of Sarajevo – he was killed in May 1992 in front of the Sarajevo Army Command building - and several others who were good friends. While we were talking over coffee, the main theme was the entry of Kecmanović and myself into the Presidency. I remember that most people there appealed to me not to wait any longer but to take the decision and help save this country and its people. I remember how Sead Fetahagić, who was skilled in chambers at persuading other lawyers, said "Pejanović, the times are such that without your decision there will be no progress. We see you as the last hope for matters in this country to go differently." All this, coming from good friends and good people, put brick upon brick in the decision slowly rising in my mind.

Kecmanović and I consulted further with the leaders of the opposition bloc, regarding the basic program and principles on which our accession to the Presidency would be founded. These discussions went on for several weeks. On one occasion we visited President Izetbegović together and conferred with him in his private office. We told him that our decision would soon be made and listed our various political demands. Kecmanović and I had also, in our many talks together during May 1992, come to the conclusion that it would be useful to visit Krajišnik and Karadžić to talk over the current situation. This was, at that time, neither war nor peace. There was scattered shelling of the city, and terrorization of its people, but the citizens of Sarajevo had not yet started any mass movement to escape.

After some preparation, we selected a day for going to Lukavica, where, we were told, Krajišnik would be waiting to meet us. We went first through Grbavica, then on via the former police academy at Vraca. The Serb forces had undertaken to guarantee our safety from this point. We went by car over Vraca and further on to Lukavica, stopping at Tilava. In the office of the community council at Tilava, in the late evening, we met with Krajišnik as agreed. We had a long and weary conversation with him, lasting around three hours. All the crucial questions were raised, principal among those being how to stop the war machine already now in motion, and how to return to Parliament and reach a solution through political consensus rather than war. Kecmanović and I were united in our conviction that the use of force was not the way to solve questions between the peoples of Bosnia. In principle, Krajišnik was not against this view, but he had his questions about our position, and of course he had his own views. As he saw it, the SDS had already tried everything and there was no other option left, since the SDA and HDZ - which was how he termed the Bosnian Muslims and Croats - had refused to accept the position of the SDS on any essential point.

During the conversation, we readily got down to fundamental issues. But these were all points on which the SDS would not make any concessions whatsoever. Their position was that Bosnia could not become independent, since this would mean the end of the Serb nation in Bosnia. The SDS claimed that a plebiscite decision to join Yugoslavia had been passed by the people, and they were determined to fight for this decision. We gave Krajišnik the argument which remained the defining point of our own program: that solving the Bosnian question through political consensus would uphold the equal rights of all nations, including the Serbs, in the constitutional establishment and in all aspects of society. The goodwill of the Serb nation was the key to solving relations with Bosnia's neighbors and for interethnic relations between the peoples with whom the Serbs had co-mingled in Bosnia for centuries. We talked about the possible cooperation of the Serb nation with other nations in a united state, and with the state's neighbor countries, where the Serb, Croat and Bosniak nations, along with others, were all present. But on this issue we remained absolutely opposed.

Krajišnik put his next question in a radical form. He asked whether, in accord with the thinking of the SDS, ethnically pure territories could be defined that would belong to the Serb people only. Krajišnik presented this as a problem in the context of both the whole territory of Bosnia and of Sarajevo. The discussion ended with our agreeing to talk over this demand with everybody in Sarajevo who might be capable of offering a solution. We told him we would discuss it with President Izetbegović, along with the proposal that Izetbegović and Krajišnik should meet one more time, in the hope of making some progress toward a solution. Krajišnik's effort to explain the problem consisted of saying, "Here, you two are educated people, so come on, work out how many Serbs there are in Novo Sarajevo, Novi Grad, Ilidža and Vogošća, and then decide how these municipalities should be divided into Serb municipalities, Bosniak municipalities, and municipalities of other nations." He was clearly hinting at the relatively small proportion of Croats in Sarajevo.

It was obvious that the SDS, quite apart from its project for achieving all goals by force, was firm in its belief that only a unified ethno - territorial base would enable the lives, government, and society of the Serb nation to be organized as intended. Carving out territory with a mono-ethnic makeup, and placing it under the rule of the SDS, was the heart of the party's position. We argued that anything of this sort was impossible in Bosnia, and especially in urban Sarajevo, given the mixed nature of its municipalities. We also told him what he already knew well, that every tower block was as varied as a leopard's hide, that every floor on every building had a mixed ethnic structure. But ultimately this argument could not help. The SDS could only see a solution in ethnic division.

Meanwhile in Ilidža, as in Lukavica, forces were being mobilized, guards were posted, and the blockade of the city was continuing. Every now and then shells were fired. In our forthcoming accession to the Presidency, and in our efforts to seek a solution to this crisis, Krajišnik perhaps saw something that should not be opposed. Thus, while he did not actually support our way of thinking and our decision to join the Presidency, he did not challenge it. He even said that the political knowledge, experience, and good public standing of Professor Kecmanović and myself might enable us to be more effective than the two who had been, until lately, members of the Presidency.

The evening was far advanced. We were all hungry, and Krajišnik showed himself a good host. One soldier standing on guard before the building brought bread and tinned fish, and Krajišnik, Kecmanović and I ate together. Once we left the building, however, everything we saw made my heart sink. People were lost, troubled, did not seem to know what was happening, while at every step we saw guns and other weapons on display. As we returned towards Sarajevo - by way of a road that was being mended and extended with funds contributed by a civic initiative to the municipality of Novo Sarajevo - it seemed clear that the worst could be expected.

Depressed, we returned to Vraca - to find it was already impossible to get back into the city, for night had fallen. It was arranged that we would spend the night in the police academy. Before sleeping, we talked with the men standing guard, who had been tasked with looking after us. We discussed whether it would be possible to stem the tide of war and find a political solution. Although they were strangers, they showed respect for us and for our efforts, and we all entered freely into conversation. Kecmanović has already written about how I said that night, after a long and serious discussion, that the solution lay not in the use of force but in a political agreement, and that the most valuable thing to be defended was peace itself. At this, one of the guards said, "The Serb nation has no other choice but to take up arms." Nenad told me, "Hey, Pejanović my friend, what can we do to pull ourselves out of this? I can't see daylight anywhere. This has already gone too far, and can only lead to years of war."

The next day we made our way to Ilidža, and found ourselves in the Hotel Serbia, where the SDS leadership had their headquarters. Krajišnik was waiting for us, while Karadžić had just given an interview to the BBC. At one point in our talk with Krajišnik, Karadžić appeared and greeted us theatrically. He had no time for conversation; he merely said, "Here we are, as you see. I don't want blood to be shed here, or a single life of the Muslim nation to be lost. I don't want to insult the dignity of the Muslim nation. The best man at my wedding was a Muslim. I have been through a lot with my Muslim friends. But, you see, their leaders don't want to accept our ideas; they don't want an agreement." Karadžić, in fact, saw all responsibility as lying on the other side - yet all gun-barrels were even now aimed at Sarajevo, and the first shells were burning the city. We had no chance to disagree with Karadžić or to have any exchange of views with him. He simply said his piece, and left.

We finished our final talk with Krajišnik, and returned safely to Sarajevo. On our return we described to Izetbegović where the difficulty lay, and a meeting between Izetbegović and Krajišnik followed. However, our initiative of visiting Lukavica bore no fruit, nor could it have. For two days following our return from Lukavica, Kecmanović and I went over various statistical and demographic data and convinced ourselves, who knows how many times, that mathematics alone made the re-distribution and re-grouping of the population in such a mixed territory impossible. It could be done only through the criminal eradication of whole communities. This was a difficult reality to face, and it is interesting that Krajišnik still showed regret and conscious doubts regarding the step the SDS had taken in withdrawing from Sarajevo.

We spoke to everybody directly involved in seeking a solution, especially President Izetbegović. Kecmanović personally informed President Izetbegović about our encounters, and I too spoke to Izetbegović and to several other members of the Presidency. But the point was that we had not succeeded in making any change to the SDS leaders' way of thinking, nor could we persuade them to come back to Sarajevo, return to Parliament, and try to find a political answer - instead of retreating to the forest and bombarding the city.

One of the topics at our two meetings with Krajišnik, was our proposal that he and Izetbegović should meet. This meeting did actually take place, several days after our return from Lukavica and Ilidža. It was in the Parliament building at Marjindvor, held at night in the prevailing conditions of broken telephone and power lines, interrupted communications, and a blockaded city. This meeting brought with it the hope that some rapprochement could take place on refraining from the use of force. But there were no results - this was just another failed attempt. What I do know is that Krajišnik, in this conversation with Izetbegović, continued to insist that Sarajevo should be divided on ethnic lines, and on this there could be no agreement. He reiterated the problem in the form already presented to Kecmanović and myself: how to transform part of Sarajevo to Serb Sarajevo. Yet this, like partitioning the rest of Bosnia, was clearly impossible without war.

This meeting was the last that took place between the representatives of the SDS and the SDA before the full military onslaught commenced from the surrounding hills. It will be remembered as the last attempt to solve the problem through dialogue. Izetbegović has described this meeting, and how, before they parted, Krajišnik gave Izetbegović his fountain pen. For the rest, I only know that this meeting was prepared and conducted in conditions of full blockade, and was necessarily secret.

After returning we also held further consultations on our accession to the Presidency. One session was with Stjepan Kljuić; another was with Fikret Abdić, who were then both members of the Presidency. Kljuić told us of the Presidency's position, which was that the procedure for filling the vacant positions within the Presidency should be initiated on the basis of the election law, which meant nominating the new members of the Presidency in accordance with the election results. We told Kljuić that we had already consulted as much as possible on the issue, and we begged him to inform the Presidency of our conditions, which were the demands of the opposition bloc. We said the same to Fikret Abdić, and I had an additional talk with Ejup Ganić, also a Presidency member. With Ganić I discussed how the Presidency would start the procedure for filling the vacancies, and I informed him that Kecmanović and I accepted this procedure, but that prior to our entry into the Presidency, certain conditions must be met.

There were four conditions. The first was that none of the members of the Presidency, while holding this office, could hold any other public office, and particularly could not be the leader of a political party. At this time Izetbegović was both the Chairman of the Presidency, and the president of the SDA. Our second request was that procedures should begin for the formation of a new government, which would be broadly based on the principle of a union of patriotic forces. It would be a government of national safety that would, by its structure and the strength of its members, act a factor for cohesion, for resistance to aggression, and for finding a solution to the Bosnian question.

The third condition was more of an initiative, but with the force of a demand, and this was that the Presidency should pass a platform document laying down the goals for which the Presidency was fighting at this time, now that armed aggression - which the SDS could easily wage, thanks to the inherited might of the JNA -

was the order of the day.³² Our fourth, and perhaps most sensitive request, was that the Presidency, which already was carrying out the function of the Parliament, should approve all vital decisions only with the consensus of all members. These points were accepted by all the Presidency members and were given out as the political program that would accompany our accession to the Presidency. A friend from my student days told me that in the Dobrinja settlement of Sarajevo, there was widespread celebration of this event when it finally took place - everything there was to drink got downed.

As for our visit to Lukavica and Ilidža, and our talks with Karadžić and Krajišnik, we gave full information on this subject to everyone we spoke with about joining the Presidency. Our basic motive for going had been the hope of bringing the SDS back to the negotiating table. On this we received support from everybody we spoke to, both from the opposition parties and from the members of the Presidency. Of course, from the point of view of our personal security, it was a sufficiently risky expedition, for once we were past the Vrbanja bridge, and especially during the journey to Vraca from Lenjina street, we were in no-man's land, an area which was already the target of military action.

I have said that appointing a new government was one of the points demanded by the democratic opposition as a condition for the accession of the two new members of the Presidency. We took part in several discussions on how this new government should be formed. Our final position was that, due to the exceptional circumstances, the government should consist of acknowledged experts, people whom all parties could support. With this view, we talked to all parties that stood for the defense of Bosnia. These were the five opposition parties, the SDP, MBO, Reformists, the DSS, and the Liberal Party; and the two ruling parties, the SDA and HDZ. It proved easy to agree on the structure of the government and on seeking out top quality candidates for its members. We were

---

³² In May 1992 those units of the JNA in Bosnia were withdrawn to Yugoslavia, except for those personnel who were born Bosnians. Careful advanced planning assured that the vast majority of troops stationed in Bosnia were natives, so over 80% of the JNA troops remained. This army was renamed the Bosnian Serb Army (BSA, its acronym as used by the international community). On May 12, 1992, General Ratko Mladić was named the commander of this force.

occupied longer by the question of which candidate should be nominated for the position of Prime Minister. However, we of the democratic opposition succeeded in gaining support from the majority of the Presidency's members for our proposal that the current Prime Minister, Jure Pelivan, should be replaced. We hoped for a candidate of greater abilities, an expert, political and academic, to lead our government of national security. We wanted a government of experts that could unite parties and nations in the defense of Bosnia. After consulting, we agreed that the Prime Minister's post should be offered to the Dr. Bozidar Matić, a member of the Academy of Sciences of Bosnia and Herzegovina.

Kecmanović and I approached Matić twice. We had our first, long interview with him one evening in his home in Breka. Matić asked about the program of the government, and he stressed the need for political unity to support a program with goals that included ending the war, rescuing the economy, and joining with those forces in the international community that supported an integral and multiethnic Bosnia. During this first meeting Professor Matić neither refused nor accepted our proposal, but he asked for time to think and consult. When we next spoke, he said that he preferred not to accept the office, but he did not exclude the possibility of further talks. More followed. I know that Professor Matić talked to Professor Filipović, who spoke both in the name of his party and in the name of the democratic opposition bloc. There was also a meeting between Kljuić and Matić, and then between Kljuić and Izetbegović and Matić. I was not involved, but was told later, including by Professor Matić himself, that an insufficient level of agreement had been reached and that he would therefore not accept the office.

As far as I could understand, in addition to everything else including his own personal dilemma, what finally made up his mind was being asked why he had not accepted earlier when the HDZ originally proposed him as a candidate for Prime Minister. This reminded him of what had originally turned him against standing for office. He felt that he could not accept being proposed as a candidate by the HDZ or any other party.

Thus the post of Prime Minister again fell to Pelivan, and Stjepan Kljuić supported his nomination. In planning for the session at which we would nominate the Prime Minister - for this was a competence of the Presidency - Kljuić argued that Pelivan had achieved results in spite of everything. Kljuić asserted that Pelivan was a man who could reconcile and unite the moderate forces in the Croat nation with the more extreme elements, such as those in Western Herzegovina. On this note, the session was held. However, at the session itself, most of the opposition thought that we should try to find a new solution. There was a debate, and in the end the matter was put to the vote.

In the first round of voting, neither the opposition nor Izetbegović and Kljuić, who had mutually agreed on giving Pelivan the mandate, had the majority. A break was called for, late at night, and during this break Izetbegović and Kljuić withdrew in order to talk alone. When they came back, they had formed a new agreement that enabled them to create a majority. In the next round of voting, Kecmanović and I were left isolated, as not only did both Izetbegović and Kljuić vote for Pelivan, but also Franjo Boras, who cast an absentee vote through the Presidency's Secretary, Mile Akmadžić. Both Abdić and Ganić supported Izetbegović. We were thus outvoted, and Pelivan was chosen. With the top levels of government all ranged against us, we could not succeed in our choice of a Prime Minister who would back the civic option favored by the opposition.

However, Zlatko Lagumdžija, Hakija Turajlić and Miodrag Simović were chosen as Deputy Prime Ministers. Lagumdžija, a well-regarded economist, was one of the leaders of the SDP and the opposition in general. Hakija Turajlić was a known economist with wide experience in management and was regarded as one of the best businessmen in the firm Energoinvest.[33] He was also known for his democratic behavior and ability to cooperate, especially for persuading everyone through his own self-denial and hard work. His death at the hands of the BSA in Stup was one of the great losses that the government was to sustain during the war.

In my opinion the new government was the strongest of the war period. Its other members included Professor Nikola Kovač as Minister for Education; Jusuf Pusina as Minister for Internal Affairs; Žarko Primorac, as Minister for Finance; Uglješa Uzelac as Minister

---

[33] In 1993 Turajlić was killed by members of the BSA while sitting in a UN armoured personnel carrier at a Serb checkpoint while travelling from the airport into the city center.

for Reconstruction, Professor Mustafa Beganović as Minister for Health; and Ranko Nikolić as Minister for Justice. There were many notable economists, experts, and public officials in this government. All were people of integrity who stood personally for the idea of a multiethnic and democratic Bosnia. Thus, the structure of the government itself compensated for what we had wanted to achieve through its Prime Minister.

We in the opposition were sorry that Professor Matić, whom I exceptionally admire, and with whom I cooperated throughout the war on a multitude of issues, had not been firmer in his initial readiness to accept the office of Prime Minister. The proposal of Matić for Prime Minister was an honest and valuable attempt by the democratic opposition within the wartime regime, which was in effect a rule of seven parties: the SDA, HDZ and the opposition bloc. The league of democratic forces genuinely desired a unified, expert government of national safety: Kljuić and Izetbegović, however, only partly supported our idea. They were more interested in the competition for party positions within the government, and therefore both favored giving the mandate to Pelivan in the name of the HDZ. Later, in 1993, when clashes within the HDZ were accompanied by major changes in the leadership of the state, and Kljuić came under pressure from his party to resign, a government was formed with a new Prime Minister – Mile Akmadžić. This government, and further governments until the election of Silajdžić as Prime Minister, lacked the political and expert authority that the war demanded.

# VII. THE PRESIDENTIAL PLATFORM AND ITS DESTINY

The Platform of the Presidency was a document developed in the early days of the war with the aim of providing basic answers to the questions of war and peace: how to safeguard Bosnia's character and integrity, its plural culture, and its democratic growth.[34] We needed to establish a unified concept of what kind of Bosnia we were fighting for. The opposition bloc insisted on this as part of the package for our accession to the Presidency: as soon as Kecmanović and I became members, it was settled that the document would be drafted. An initial debate was held on what this document would signify, and what its goals should be. We all agreed it would be a platform for the work of the Presidency in wartime and would seek to answer the fundamental questions of the state's destiny. These were the issues of preserving its integrity, sovereignty, independence, and the equality and constitutionality of the three nations, which, along with numerous other nationalities, live together in this country. The document would also address the perennial question of what political structure would most fully implement the principle of the equality of the Bosnian nations.

The Platform should also address the questions surrounding the formation of armed forces for the defense of Bosnia: the character of these forces, their structure and ideological basis (for until now, Bosnia had never, as an independent sovereign state, maintained a standing army). Finally, the Platform was supposed to define the Presidency's attitude to the crimes now being committed by the extremists of the Bosnian Serb Army (BSA).

---

[34] The Platform of the Presidency was adopted on 26 June 1992. *Službeni List Republika Bosne i Hercegovine*, I (2 July 1992), 237-8.

It was suggested that a working group should form to draft this Platform, which should primarily consist of a representative from each nation: Kljuić on behalf of the Croats, Kecmanović for the Serbs, and Fikret Abdić for the Bosniak nation. The group met one afternoon and agreed that first a working text should be prepared for consideration at an upcoming session of the Presidency. Kecmanović undertook this task. However, he felt unwell that day, and begged me to prepare a first draft. I devoted a whole day to staying at home and drafting a text, which was presented for discussion at the next Presidency session.

President Izetbegović played a big part in the editing of this draft, making additions in several places, in particular inserting definitive terms for the aggression and crimes then already current. After receiving these first suggestions, we reviewed the text of the Platform in full. The Platform was then adopted, presented to the public, and printed. Public expectations of the Platform were high, It was well received as the product of special historic circumstances, and because it gave answers to the questions then being asked about the defense of a unified, multiethnic, democratic Bosnia.

What was especially of value about this Platform was that all members of the Presidency, from all nations, showed a high degree of accord over its contents. I remember best the part of the Platform that regulated a long-standing question - the status of Bosnia. The document gave us a vision of this country, defining it as a citizen-state of its constituent peoples, Bosniaks, Serbs and Croats, together with members of other nations. Listing the names of the constituent nations was the suggestion of Mariofil Ljubić, then a deputy member of the Presidency and acting Speaker of Parliament.

The Platform asserted that the internal structure of Bosnia should be neither a unitary state nor partitioned into regions on an ethnic basis. Instead it should be structured on those criteria which are accepted in contemporary European states: local and regional self-government based on communities that had developed over history and formed according to geographic and economic, as well as ethnic, criteria. These two premises were especially significant, for all peace negotiations held later started from this view of Bosnia, as opposed to the preference of ethnic criteria.

Finally, this Platform was drawn up at a time of political evolution, and incorporated a certain measure of theoretic-constitutional development, and it remains as a historic, seminal document. In the decisive battle for a multiethnic Bosnia, it provided the political and ideological foundation on which patriotic, social and political forces united to defend this country. As more peacetime passes, the fundamental principles of the Platform will be what we return to and use for building the political future of our country. From this perspective, I can claim that the people who then sat in the Presidency had, individually and collectively, a clear vision of this country's future, and their ideas accorded in full with contemporary concepts for the development of democracy in Europe. I should add that to me personally belongs the honor of having drafted the first contents of this Platform – perhaps eighty percent of the final text.

Part of the Platform dealt with the creation of armed forces, and with defining what these would be fighting for. It established that the goal of the battle was the defense of Bosnia as a sovereign, independent, multiethnic and democratic state. The Platform also laid down that the armed forces of Bosnia should be constituted as the Bosnian Army, in which service would be voluntary, and which would consist of all citizens of Bosnia, members of all peoples and nationalities.[35] When the Platform was issued, the commandant of the Territorial Defense, Sefer Halilović, had just been appointed. Halilović had demanded on several occasions that the publication of the Platform be speeded up, so that work could begin systematically on building the army. He was adamant that this could not begin until the political goals of the defense had been defined. I myself was further included in drafting the sections that related to the defense of the state and creation of the armed forces.

Two other significant initiatives came to fruition during this period. President Izetbegović held a conference with religious representatives, in which I did not take part, and which I know of chiefly from the press reportage. However, Kljuić and I worked together with Deputy Prime Minister Zlatko Lagumdžija to organize

---

[35] The defense of Bosnia was assigned to two separate forces, the Army of Bosnia and Herzegovina (ABH), which took its orders from the Bosnian Presidency and central government, and the Croatian Defense Council (HVO – *Hrvatske vijeće obrane*). The latter in principle proclaimed its loyalty to Bosnia and Herzegovina but was in fact a force financed and directed by the Republic of Croatia.

a meeting with the members of the Bosnian Academy of Sciences. This was held in the working conference hall of the Presidency, was attended by a great number of academics, and lasted several hours.[36] During its first half the guests gave their views of the situation and the possibility of further widening the front of patriotic forces for the defense of a multiethnic and united Bosnia. Much support was expressed for the Presidency's efforts, including all that had been done to strengthen the defensive front on a broad, multinational, basis.

There was also much talk on how the Academy as an institution could be actively included in some of the processes of defense, given the harsh conditions that then prevailed. People were blockaded into their houses and cellars, without electricity and without water. There were already problems with food, and the problems of winter, severe cold and shortage of fuel, were on their way. It should be remembered that many members of the Academy were elderly. The idea was mooted that a number of academics, if not all, and the institution as a whole, should remove from the city, to a friendly country which could provide suitable conditions for their work - the Adriatic coast of Croatia was suggested. However, this idea was never taken further, and the academics stayed to share the fate of the other citizens of Sarajevo. Many of them found this particularly difficult, for they were people whose age and physiological and psychological state put them at a disadvantage for coping with the Sarajevo inferno, while their work was severely restricted. It was suggested that the government and appropriate ministries should do something to enable the Academy to continue some kind of work in wartime: first the Army, then the Ministry of Culture and Education, and then the government as a whole, offered the most concrete help. It was agreed that the army should vacate the Academy's offices so that the academics could meet regularly, while the next step was to make sure their telephones were working and that they had the technical and material preconditions for their work.

This conference had a positive public impact. Subsequently,

---

[36] Members of Academies of Arts and Sciences in the various countries of the former Yugoslavia bear the title of "Akademik." Membership is largely honorary, and most academics also hold positions as professors at various university faculties.

however, the solving of individual problems dragged on. I worked on various operational aspects, together with Zlatko Lagumdžija, and at a subsequent meeting with the academics we assessed what had been done to fulfill the terms of the original agreement. We had been able to meet most of their needs. I remember a subsequent encounter; I think it was in 1993 - with the academic Arif Tanović, who came to the Presidency to seek my help. Lacking electricity, he had long been unable either to read or work. According to him, some other user in his neighborhood was being treated as a priority. I wanted to help as much as I could, so I called Edhem Bičakčić, then the head of the electrical utility company, and begged him to find a solution by which Tanović could occasionally receive electricity. Bičakčić agreed to this, and was able to find a temporary solution.

One of the positive results of the conference was the fact that the academics were now in direct communication with the Presidency. Members of this group, by virtue of their ideas and loyalties, stood at the forefront of the battle for a multiethnic and united Bosnia. If something should be specially noted from that first meeting, it was the proposal of the academics, especially those who had long specialized in Bosnia's history, that our efforts to stop the war and build a lasting peace in this country should focus more on the role of the international community and the participation of international factors in ensuring the growth of an independent Bosnia. Avdo Sućeska, for example, argued from history that the uniqueness and unity of Bosnia, from the time of the Ottoman Empire until today, had always rested on the will of the great powers. Due to relations with Bosnia's immediate neighbors, this principle was still valid, especially in this historic time of building Bosnian sovereignty.

Before the vacancies in the Presidency were filled, and while I was still just a citizen living in Breka, one evening in May 1992, during a powercut, a neighbor of Professor Ekmečić came to me.[37] She sought me out on behalf of Ekmečić's wife, who wanted me to know what had befallen the family. That very afternoon her

---

[37] Milorad Ekmečić was a Professor of History at the University of Sarajevo. He lent his considerable authority as an intellectual leader in Sarajevo to the Serbian nationalist cause on the eve of the war. He left Sarajevo in May 1992 and has since lived in Belgrade.

husband had been beaten by members of the armed forces, and this abuse, and the ransacking of the house, took place in front of his family, who were now deeply traumatized and suffering from shock. The Professor himself had been taken away, they did not know where. Two more neighbors soon came to me: Professor Ante Markotić, and Dino Kusturica, a businessman. They, like Ekmečić's wife, begged me to find out what had happened to Professor Ekmečić, where he had been taken, what was going on, and what could be done for the family. None of us had a working telephone at the time. I suggested we try the local Community Center of Podhrastovi, and we went there together.

I found several of my acquaintances, and they helped me to find a phone. I called Kljuić in the Presidency and told him of the request of the Ekmečić family. He was with Colonel Karić at the time, and the reaction was immediate. By the next day, we knew what had happened to Ekmečić. He had been taken as a hostage by Bosniak soldiers who planned to trade his freedom for the safe passage of a convoy of children of all nationalities, who had been prevented from leaving Sarajevo by Serb nationalists in the suburb of Ilidža. He was returned home and put under protection. We did not try to investigate further, as I had no opportunity to do so at the time. We had simply done something humane for a man and a neighbor.

Later I found out that Ekmečić, thanks to diligence on the part of the SDS and its influence with the current UNPROFOR, left Sarajevo under full protection. I subsequently heard from various people that the government should not have let him leave Sarajevo but instead should have ensured his safety like that of every other citizen, and used his presence in the city as a propaganda tool against the SDS bombardment and destruction of the city. I also heard that on reaching Belgrade, Ekmečić was active in spreading the idea of the Greater Serbia state, while what he wrote about wartime Sarajevo and its people was negative in the extreme. I never had a chance to verify this, but I am sure that he did not know what was done to help his family. However, if he does know, perhaps he does not care to admit publicly that there was plenty of concern for him, that he left the city safely, or that I myself was involved in his rescue, at the request of his family and neighbors, especially his two fellow professors. I also want to stress that what I did for him had nothing to do with my feelings about the man himself, but was simply to help his family.

With Professor Leovac, it is a very different story. Unlike Ekmečić, whom I did not know personally, although I knew his work, I knew Professor Leovac from my student days at the end of the seventies. At that time he was President of the Sarajevo Committee for Ideology and Education of the League of Communists. That was in 1970, when the University was undergoing reform. I had another reason for knowing him: he was an exceptional teacher, and his lectures were unforgettable. My brother Ranko studied in the foreign language department at the Philosophy faculty, so I heard plenty of stories from Ranko and his friends about Professor Leovac.

When we joined the Presidency at the beginning of June 1992, Kecmanović and I began finding out, from friends of the families involved, that many intellectuals had been arrested and taken away, often to unknown prisons, first however being beaten in their own homes. The distinguished Sarajevo doctor, Trifko Guzina, and several other people, brought us the case of Professor Leovac, for example. Nenad Kecmanović and I tried to find out what had happened to these people, why they were taken, and where. Everybody who had information was willing to help. We particularly sought information from the Commandant of the Territorial Defense, Sefer Halilović, his assistants and deputies. Much of our help came from Zaim Backović a Territorial Defense staff member in charge of security issues, who after the war entered the Federation Parliament as a representative of the Party for Bosnia and Herzegovina.

On the practical level, so to speak - the level of ordinary life and events - Nenad and I received the best information about the city prisons from Ismet Bajramović Ćelo.[38] He agreed to come and visit us in the Presidency, and his behavior was correct, honest and well intentioned. As for the subject of our conversations, I can only say that he did not in any way seem obsessed by nationalism, but

---

[38] Ismet Bajramović gained notoriety as a gangster particularly skilled at terrorizing those who posed a threat to him. He was publicly named as the murderer of a Serb attending a wedding at the Old Orthodox Church in Sarajevo in March 1992, an event repeatedly cited by Karadžić and his followers as proof that Serbs were unsafe in the city. He was never prosecuted in connection with that killing. He rose to become a commander in wartime. During the year 2000 he was arrested by police of the Sarajevo Canton, denied bail, and tried for a murder committed earlier that year.

purely dedicated to the city's defense. He always managed to say at some point: "You know, President, I am a Sarajevan, I respect everybody. We are searching for people who are cooperating with those who are shelling us, but we want to protect everyone who is a decent citizen, regardless of nationality."

Finally, one morning, we heard that Leovac was imprisoned in the Hotel Zagreb – a prison about which we knew nothing, despite being members of the Presidency. Professor Leovac was released and allowed home. He soon gave a public statement in which he condemned the use of force by the BSA and the SDS. His words were a direct challenge to the policy and actions of the SDS. Everyone felt that Professor Leovac had spoken out of integrity, despite the fact that he had formerly been the president of the SDS Advisory Board. He tried now to distance himself from his party's policies, maintaining that during the Advisory Board's peacetime activities, there had been no question of using force and that he himself had never been informed of the intention to use it.

Having made his position plain in public, he now asked to meet with me, through Nikola Kovac, the Minister for Sciences, Education and Sport: Kovac visited me one day and suggested I should receive Professor Leovac. I reserved the whole day for the visit, for in spite of everything, I respected Leovac as a distinguished professor. My cooperation with him as a student in the seventies had left good memories: I remembered him as a zealous party worker.

I received him with the greatest respect, and we had our talk. I suggested we should lunch together, since it was time for the Presidency's lunch of humanitarian aid. Leovac accepted, while, to our satisfaction, Nikola Kovač joined us. Professor Leovac was very frank. He first made it clear that he had divorced himself from the path the SDS had chosen, and he condemned the use of force, the sacking of towns, the shelling of Sarajevo, and the killing of civilians. He read out to us a statement he had written on a card, which he wanted to publish, and on which he wanted our thoughts. I suggested he should add a sentence on how he favored conducting politics by political means, as he had done through the Advisory Board as its president, and adding his condemnation of the appalling crimes against civilians that had resulted from the present conduct of politics by violence. He agreed, and added just such a sentence to his statement.

Leovac then asked to leave Sarajevo – not to go to Pale, but to Serbia, where he would have better conditions for living and working, in particular for nursing his already shattered health, ruined by the war, and the stress of his imprisonment. Professor Kovac and I thought long and hard about his request, and said we would talk to President Izetbegović about it. We then phoned Izetbegović, and suggested the two should meet. The President immediately agreed, and, after lunch, Leovac went to see him, accompanied by Professor Kovac. I did not join the meeting, but I know that it lasted a long time. Afterwards, with the full protection of the legal organs of government, Professor Leovac left Sarajevo.

I was not able to follow his career in Serbia during the war, although I know that he was active in Belgrade. While, to a certain extent, he remained close to the SDS, nevertheless, by staying in Sarajevo after his party had left for Pale in order to make war on Sarajevo from the hilltops, he showed his moral revulsion against the campaign to achieve the Greater Serbian state by dividing Bosnia. However, as one-time president of the SDS Advisory Board - and therefore a leading mind of the party – he must bear some general responsibility for its actions, from which history can never fully free him.

I not only knew Professor Branislav Đurđev, one-time President of the Academy of Sciences and Arts for Bosnia and Herzegovina and Dean of the Philosophical Faculty in Sarajevo, I also know how it was that he left Sarajevo to die in his birthplace of the Vojvodina. I was, in fact, personally involved in his evacuation. It all began when he asked to visit me in the Presidency. He was already very ill, and was having great problems in procuring the medicine his treatment required. His son and daughter in law were looking after him: she in particular was diligent in her care for him. I received him together with the Minister of the Interior, Jusuf Pusšina, for I wanted us all to talk together. We heard about Professor Đurđev's critical health and his desire to leave Sarajevo for Novi Sad in Serbia – Sremski Karlovac, where he had family who would look after him and enable him to carry on his work.

I informed the Presidency of this conversation, and there was full support for helping him. A second talk followed, but this time he was very different - excited and agitated. I asked him if he wanted to give a public announcement. He said that he did, and journalists were invited in to report on it. It turned out that his house had been ransacked and he himself beaten by members of the city's armed forces, which were then not consolidated but were operating in small, uncontrolled groups. In spite of this, he wanted to say what Bosnia meant to him as a country and what he had gained from working here as an academic since his student days in Sarajevo. All his work had focused on the past and growth of Bosnia, which he saw as the homeland of everybody living in it. For him, this country historically confirmed a model of tolerance, of life together. He was glad he had been able to live and work in such a place, and would always fight for such a Bosnia, even now when the harsh conditions of wartime were driving him from Sarajevo.

We agreed at this second meeting that he should be helped to leave, together with his son and daughter in law. Later I heard from several people that, while in Novi Sad where he eventually died, he wrote articles affirming the lasting value of Bosnia and its people. He openly praised those who had helped him, including myself, for what they had done to prolong his life – since undergoing extremes of cold and hunger in the harsh Sarajevo winter would certainly have cut it short. Looking back, these were hard times for all patriotic people. The wartime conditions were bitter, and Đurđev in particular could not cope because of his health. The city of Sarajevo wanted to show its respect for him, and his contribution to educating several generations in Sarajevo and in Bosnia. Today, a street in Sarajevo bears his name.

Before the war I knew nothing of Milan Vasić, former Professor of history at the Philosophy Faculty, although I had heard of his work. In July 1992, I was approached by his wife, Professor Lejla Vasić. She came to me primarily because of the problems she was having, in spite of being a born Sarajevan, and from a well-known Bosniak family, as the wife of Professor Vasić. Self-styled "authorized" forces, toting guns over their shoulders, had come to her door, threatening her, calling her a Chetnik, and asking what she was waiting for, here in Sarajevo. The next step, of course, was a campaign to seize her apartment. Lejla, a proud and brave woman, approached not only myself, but also the academic Ljubo Berberović, a colleague in the Faculty of Natural Mathematics;

Professor Muhamed Filipović; Seid Huković, the president of the Academy of Arts and Sciences; and others.

I myself played a positive part in resolving her future. I told her that I would see her immediately whenever she asked for me, and for several months we remained in close contact. With the help of personnel in the Central Security Service of Sarajevo, I helped her to travel out to Grbavica to meet with her husband, Professor Milan Vasić. As soon as they were able to meet, they understandably decided that they must be together again. On her return she asked to leave Sarajevo in order to be with him. She offered the excuse that her husband had traveled from Sarajevo out to Mrkonjic Grad just before the war to visit his sick father, and that the start of the war and the blockade of communications had trapped him there. With the support of various people, I helped Professor Lejla Vasić to leave Sarajevo. I did not want to go into what professor Milan Vasić was doing to promote the SDS, or whether he was doing so of his own accord. My motive was simply to help Lejla as a professor of the university, a loyal wife, and a good human being. Lejla herself made no difficulties about going. She only asked for the home library of her husband to be protected, but in this I could not help her. She came safely to her husband, and today they live in Banja Luka.

When I visited Banja Luka for the first time since the war in 1996, I finally met Professor Milan Vasić. He was then working as professor of the University and dean of the Philosophy faculty in Banja Luka. He was waiting for me in the OSCE (Organization for Security and Cooperation in Europe) headquarters, where I attended a meeting with representatives of the Banja Luka-based opposition parties. After a good conference, Vasić introduced himself to me. He passed on greetings from Lejla, and begged me to come and stay with them. I could not accept the invitation, as I had no time - lunch was arranged in the OSCE, to be followed by the journey back to Sarajevo. "Why don't you stay and lunch with us?" I said to Professor Vasić, and he accepted. We ate together with our delegation and our Banja Luka hosts.

Talking to Vasić was simply human, a testimony to something which has survived in our land of Bosnia in spite of so much killing. I remember the Professor asked me how he could get to Sarajevo and if someone could help him rescue his library, which had been left in his apartment. He confessed near the end that he could not organize his academic work in Banja Luka as he had done in Sarajevo before the war, for he lacked adequate books, libraries, literature, atmosphere, and colleagues. He wanted to carry on with his work - he was a well-known historian and Turcologist. I suggested he should write to Seid Huković, as the President of the Academy, about his intentions, and that this would certainly be well received. I also suggested he could join Miodrag Živanović and the other people who frequently traveled to Sarajevo with the OSCE. I welcomed the prospect of his return to Sarajevo as a professor of history. From these confessions of Professor Vasić, I realized afresh that no other city of Bosnia could replace Sarajevo as an academic and cultural center; and that Sarajevo must and should remain the seat of the leading educational institutions of Bosnia.[39]

---

[39] Vasić chose to remain in Banja Luka as a Professor of History at its University. He became Deputy President of the Academy of Arts and Sciences of the Republika Srpska, which was founded in autumn 1996 at the Hotel Bistrica on Mt. Jahorina just outside Sarajevo.

## VIII. THE BOSNIAN ARMY AND ITS FIRST COMMANDER, SEFER HALILOVIĆ

Units of the Bosnian Army started forming in June 1992, while the Territorial Defense still consisted of police units under the Ministry of the Interior.[40] Units formed spontaneously or were organized in Sarajevo and other cities of Bosnia, even where there was total breakdown in communications between Sarajevo and these other places. At the very start of executing my Presidential mandate, I became chairman of the Advisory Board for the Protection of Constitutional Order, on which sat a representative of the Ministry of the Interior and a representative of the armed forces. Together we tried to deal with the constant problems of the defense of Sarajevo and the whole country. I was therefore deeply involved in the creation and development of the Bosnian Army. The foundation for recruiting armed state forces was the Platform on the work of the Presidency. This had, in essence, defined the character of Bosnia's army. Its concept was of recruitment based on the patriotism of the citizens and peoples, for the sake of defending their peace and freedom, and a multiethnic Bosnia as an internationally acknowledged state. This was the first, most fundamental step.

The second step was constitution of the leadership of the Bosnian Army, and the third was defining the Army's relationship with the

---

[40] On April 15, 1992, the Presidency ordered that all armed forces in Bosnia and Herzegovina be consolidated under the unified command of the Territorial Defense Forces (TO – *Teritorijalna odbrana*). This day has been celebrated since 1992 as the "Day of the Army," but in fact units that were referred to as the Army of Bosnia and Herzegovina were not formed until June. In April the term "armija" was still associated with the JNA, which was then initiating hostilities against the civilian population.

Presidency as the High Command, specifically over issues such as mobilization. I enjoyed excellent cooperation with Sefer Halilović, then Staff Commander of the Territorial Defense, as we worked to create the Army. Our relationship dated back to our work together on preparing the Platform, and our concepts of the Army were virtually identical. Sefer Halilović was persistent in his vision of the Army as a multiethnic and multinational force of all citizens and all peoples.

At this period there was a very high percentage of Serb and Croat involvement in the Territorial Defense Staff and its affiliated units, especially in units of cities such as Sarajevo, Mostar and Tuzla. General Jovan Divjak, a Serb, commanded the army units defending Sarajevo. Membership in the armed forces was 12-15% Serb, and 15-18% Croat in the affiliated units. There were units in the field that were up to 20% Serb and over 20% Croat. There were also Croat unit commanders, in Gradačac for example. In Sarajevo and Tuzla Serbs held lower and middle command posts. For a long time the Serb Momčilo Đurić was the commander of an operative anti-aircraft defense unit in Tuzla.

To begin with, Sefer Halilović, together with Jovan Divjak and the Croat Stjepan Šiber, implemented the concept of a Bosnian Army primarily founded on multiethnic components. Željko Knez and Anđeljko Makar, both Croats, were in command of the Tuzla Second Corps. In units throughout all territory controlled by the Bosnian Army, there were a great number of Bosnian Croats and Serbs who commanded platoons and companies or were deputy Brigade and Corps commanders. Serbs and Croats were in the leadership of the Sarajevo First Corps throughout much of the war. The Serb Zlatko Petrović, for example, was an assistant commander of the First Corps for legal issues until almost the end of the war. Zlatko was the son of the well-known general Stanimir Petrović of the Sarajevo army command. Today Zlatko Petrović practices as a lawyer in Sarajevo, and is one of the activists of the Serb Civil Council.

In July 1992 a rather sharp dialogue took place between Minister of Defense Jerko Doko and myself. We were both with Presidency member Fikret Abdić at the time: we had dropped in to congratulate him on the festival of Bajram. As we talked, the topic arose of Serb participation in the Army, and the form this should take. Doko said that we were mistaken in not forming a separate Serb "Council of Defense," a Serb counterpart to the Croatian Defense Council (HVO – *Hrvatsko vijeće obrane*). He was far from being alone in this feeling. Various Serb members of the Army had already approached Divjak and myself on this subject. To me they had raised the possibility of forming special units inside the Army, which would consist of Serbs only and would act as a separate but allied structure, comparable to the role of the HVO.

I told Doko of my concept of the Bosnian Army as a common army for all people who accepted Bosnia as their historic destiny and who accepted common life with other nations, and he and I remained absolutely divided on this issue. I kept to my own position, both ideologically and politically, from the start of the war onwards, for I consider that the organization of the state represents the organization of society, and the army is one of the most significant elements of the organization of the state as a whole. Looking at Bosnian society as a whole, as an internationally recognized legal entity, the growth of this society and the progress of its security and defense, it did not seem possible that its army could be segmented into ethnic components. If it were to be, the division would constitute a permanent source of inter-ethnic tensions. Therefore I have always been an advocate for armed forces that mirror the ethnic structure of Bosnian society in full.

In 1994 several Serb political activists in Tuzla raised the idea - which remained only an idea - of forming a Serb battalion of Serb units, inside the Tuzla Second Corps. The idea was not to divide this battalion from the unified system of command, but simply to form units with a clear Serb majority to attract a greater number of Serbs to the ranks of the Bosnian Army. Grave problems had already arisen, of lack of support, and mistrust, which prevented young people from having more confidence in the army. Instead they were leaving, or were reluctant to join. The Tuzla initiative was discussed with Izetbegović and Rasim Delić, commander of the General Staff of the Bosnian Army, and somewhere between Delić and Izetbegović the initiative was stopped. The excuse which Delić made to me and to several of my colleagues was that this would lead to still greater problems in preserving the unity of the Bosnian Army, especially in the territory of the Second Corps, for at that time there were growing demands from the HDZ for all units of the HVO to be operatively combined and placed under HVO command. This however, never happened in the territory of the Tuzla Second Corps, where command and operations remained unified during the war. In the face of these arguments, we dropped the initiative.

I think we were misunderstood, for the idea was not to divide a military unit from the unified structure, but rather to create units which would have greater strength to attract the Serb population, not only in the Federation, but more widely in territories under the command of the BSA. Serbs would thus be more readily persuaded to remain in their homes in the wake of Bosnian army offensives, and even to join liberating units in which Serbs were the majority or whose commanders were Serbs. This strategy was proven by the Partisans to be effective. It was precisely in the Tuzla region, during the Second World War in 1943 and 1944, by the decision of the High command, that a Muslim brigade was formed at Bukovik in Brčko and a Croat brigade at Husino near Tuzla. These units, including their commanders, were mostly, though not exclusively, Croat and Muslim, with Croat and Muslim titles and badges. In many villages of the Tuzla region, and in other areas of Bosnia, these brigades acted as a magnet for attracting ordinary people to the Partisan units.

Before Sefer Halilović became Commander of the Army, the Presidency attempted to offer the staff leadership to three famous generals of Titoist Yugoslavia: Džemil Šarac, Mirko Vranić and Milan Ačić. Šarac had been a colleague of Tito and within the JNA was Secretary of the Committee of the Association of Communists of Yugoslavia. Before retirement he became Deputy Secretary for National Defense of the Socialist Federated Republic of Yugoslavia. From the start of the war in Bosnia he held by his dignity as a soldier, standing firm in support of freedom, peace, the equality of nations, and a multiethnic, democratic and united Bosnia. Mirko Vranić was head of the former Sarajevo army command, which covered Bosnia and Herzegovina together with part of Croatia and of Montenegro. He too had a reputation as a Bosnian patriot and a man of personal integrity. Milan Ačić had also been part of the Sarajevo command, and was formerly head of the famous school for officers in Bileća. He was a man of high moral stature, who stayed on in Sarajevo from the start of the onslaught against the city, and never surrendered to the idea of ethnic division.

Kecmanović and I, together with other members of the Presidency, proposed offering these men the leadership of the

Bosnian armed forces at the time of their expansion from the territorial defense. When we discussed this with Izetbegović, he approved the idea, and it was settled that Kecmanović and I would hold preliminary negotiations with Generals Šarac, Vranić and Ačić. Our first meeting, held in the Presidency Building, lasted several hours. We explained the concept underlying the creation and development of the Bosnian army and our hope that these generals would undertake its operative leadership. The proposal was that Džemal Šarac should be Commander in Chief, and Generals Vranić and Ačić deputies. The generals, at this meeting, supported the basic concept, and added some ideas about Partisan methods of conducting war and recruiting troops, from their own knowledge and experience. But they all, particularly General Šarac, took the view that their ages were not suited to operational posts in the Army, especially in wartime: they stressed they had all "reached the eighth decade of their lives." According to them, this would sooner or later turn out to be a flawed solution. Regardless of their experience, they no longer felt capable of heavy day and night work and operational tasks.

We tried to persuade them: I personally pushed hard for their acceptance. We begged them not to take a final decision at the first meeting, although they had already visibly done so. It was agreed that, in a few days, we would discuss their decision further. They did, however, consent to serve on an advisory board for defense issues. They insisted the Bosnian Army should be patriotic, multiethnic and antifascist and that it should employ methods of combat based on the Partisan experiences in World War II. They called for an accurate estimate of the forces in the Bosnian theatre of war, and they urged that the Bosnian Army lean heavily on the rich political and military experiences of the Partisans during the war for national liberation of 1941 to 1945. They proposed to write a memorandum to the General Staff of the Bosnian army on these topics.

Several days after the first meeting, we talked again, and it was clear that their original decision was final. We regretfully informed Izetbegović and other members of the Presidency of the outcome. We had failed to persuade these three generals to undertake the leadership of the Bosnian Army, but in the face of their reasonable arguments, there was nothing we could do. Our next proposal was that Sefer Halilović should be appointed Commander in Chief of the Bosnian army. The Advisory Board for Defense was constituted, and started its work: Generals Ačić, Šarac and Vranić as members of the Board made valuable contributions, although they were present at only two sessions altogether. The chairman of the Board was Izetbegović, as Chairman of the Presidency, while I too was a member. Several sessions were held, and at one I deputized for Izetbegović. At the start of 1994, however, on the initiative of Izetbegović, the structure of the Board was transformed. In its new configuration, it consisted of the commanders of the various corps, with Izetbegović again chairing, so the three elderly generals and I no longer participated. Instead, it narrowed to a purely advice-giving body. This new Board proved itself of use, but its structure confined its potential for consultation with those who had experience of both the theory and the practice of a defensive war.

One of the ideas for developing the multinational character of the Bosnian Army was that of creating a Board of Morale, which would consist of well known public figures from all three nations: Serbs, Croats and Bosniaks, who would contribute to strengthening the public image of the Bosnian army, and attracting people to the ideas the army supported. This board would also have a component for information and propaganda. Kecmanović and I worked hard with Sefer Halilović to implement this idea. Sefer considered it vital for the development of the Army Staff. We proposed to Sefer that we would discuss it with Zdravko Grebo and Bogić Bogićević, but we were forced to talk to Ivo Komšić by phone, since he was in Kiseljak at the time, and Sarajevo was already under full siege. Thus the notion of including well-known personalities was left unrealized, and we did not return to it. The rapidly unfolding aggression, and the consequent preoccupation of Sefer Halilović and his staff with daily operational tasks, helped prevent this idea from ever achieving a solid foundation.

Later, in a humbler form, something similar was brought about, when Ivan Brigić joined the Morale Board. But as time passed, it appeared that our original concept of a board founded on Bosnian patriotism and a multinational society was narrowing. Somewhere during 1994, Ivan Brigić stopped working on the staff. This abandonment of the multiethnic structure of the Morale Board resulted from the attitudes of the ruling parties, the SDA and the HDZ, both of which put their confidence solely in people of their own nations and their own parties.

In June and July 1992, many personnel of Serb nationality working in various firms and industries were placed under suspicion, and some were temporarily imprisoned. They were held in what came to be called the "wild" prisons, set up by local units. I learned of one such prison, in a basement of the Otok settlement, from a friend who was actually incarcerated there. This was Milenko Banović, director of one of the factories of Klas, the bakery firm, in the Paromlinska area of Novo Sarajevo. Milenko was taken, together with Dragan Podinić, also a Klas director, to this prison in Otok, and left there for several days before being transferred to the central prison in Sarajevo. It was by way of messages from mutual Bosniak friends that I learned Milenko was in prison and needed our help. Milenko had been a youth activist in Novo Sarajevo municipality when I had worked there at the end of the seventies and the beginning of the eighties. He was successful, young, distinguished for his activities in the SDP, and consistently upheld the values of tolerance and coexistence.

We organized ourselves to find out what was happening to Milenko Banović and Dragan Podinić. Commander Sefer Halilović himself was deeply involved in the search. The two prisoners were traced and eventually released from jail. The day of their release, they came to see me in the Presidency. A session was ongoing, and they had to wait for a long time, but Banović was persistent. By chance, Sefer and I came to my office together, and there we found Banović. He did not look traumatized. In fact he was ecstatic at having been released from prison, and at seeing me once more. After several minutes alone with him, I suggested to Sefer that he should meet this young man who had just experienced a stay in jail. When Sefer entered, Banović was more than pleased to meet him, and an atmosphere of trust was readily created. Banović was very ready to talk, and even suggested that he should show us his back, which was blue with bruises, and the skin broken from blows.

Having told us of all he had survived in this "wild jail" in the basement at Otok, Banović went on to describe his stay in the central jail. He said that for him it was a new lease of life, the moment when an authorized representative of the security services came to him in jail, introduced himself, asked to talk, and explained what he wanted to talk about. At this point in the story, Banović suddenly stood up, and we saw he was almost weeping. He explained: "I saw that here at least was the proper service of a proper state, and that I was recognized as someone with a name, a surname, my honor, and my dignity. The fear and the uncertainty were over."

Interrogation inevitably served only to prove that Banović and Podinić had never played a double game, had never helped create chaos by raising the prices of certain goods, had never transferred particular goods to parts of the city under control of the Serb army, and were not secret SDS activists. However, in those days, few bothered to make distinctions, and as a result many patriotic Bosnians suffered from uncontrolled "security checks" just because they were Serbs. Many good and honorable people, including others like Banović, ended up in the "wild jails." Fortunately, these jails were soon transformed into organized prisons under the control of legal government organs and professionals, and, eventually, came to bs properly run.

Milenko Banović's life and work, as the war went on, showed him to be undeterred in spite of his difficult experiences at the beginning. Throughout the war he remained the director of Sarajevo's pasta factory, and continued in this position after the war. He is known to have helped many desperate people and communities: everybody knew they could always go to Banović for a kilo of pasta. He eventually took part in the first forum of citizens of Serb nationality in Sarajevo. Banović was one of those who always remained steadfast: a good neighbor, a patriot and a pro-Bosnian.

Episodes such as these influenced Sefer Halilović's thinking, and he subsequently set in motion the formation of a military police, a judiciary and appropriate legislation. Toward the end of 1992, the Presidency and the Board for the Protection of the Constitutional Order held several sessions and issued appropriate orders regarding criminal prosecution of those in military units. In 1993 a state-run structure for the functioning of the security system was established, accompanied by the gradual closure of all temporary prisons. Thereafter the security services were consolidated, although the process did not always go smoothly. The result was proper development of the security services of the Ministry of the Interior and the Army, the formation of a military police on the principle of ordered command, and the establishment of a military judiciary.

The biggest challenge for the Bosnian defense forces was ending the siege of Sarajevo. This was seen as a high priority for two particular reasons. One reason was that ending the siege would create the possibility of uniting forces in Sarajevo, Tuzla, Zenica, Mostar, Travnik and other regions, enabling closer cooperation between military units within a unified territory, partly under the ABH and partly under the HVO. The other was to stop the unprecedented, inhuman torment and killing of the citizens of Sarajevo. Tens of thousands of Sarajevans died from shells, and many more lost their lives from hunger, cold, exhaustion and trauma.

One of the options for unblocking Sarajevo was military, but on the political front, new moves were expected from the international community. It was hoped that the latter would finally start doing more than it had done up till now and that the siege of Sarajevo would be lifted by outside military intervention. This did not happen. Many people believe that Mitterrand's visit to Sarajevo in June 1992 was decisive in excluding all possibility of foreign intervention, by ensuring that the European Union and the rest of the international community would not enter upon such an undertaking. Any military action to relieve the city had therefore to rely wholly on our own forces. The problem was that the forces inside Sarajevo were numerous but poorly equipped and were especially lacking in artillery. I was not involved in the detailed preparations of plans for ending the siege. These were made by the Headquarters of the General Staff, military experts, and various Corps representatives, often in consultation with President Izetbegović.

But the first attempt to unblock Sarajevo from inside failed. The question remains of how realistic was the assessment that this could be done with inside forces, and whether it took account of all the consequences that would await any attempt at a breakthrough, given the advantageous positions of the besiegers, carefully prepared before the war by the professionals of the JNA. It is possible - and military experts might one day shed light on this - that the ABH attack from Mount Igman was too poorly synchronized with the action of the HVO, which at that time possessed greater technology. There may also have been inadequate levels of political decision-making and coordination. But from this perspective in time, when the desires and emotions which then prevailed are set aside, it is clear that this campaign was more the result of overeagerness than of hard-headed military strategy, and that there were too many obstacles to its successful completion. The troops that attempted a breakout at Poljine suffered heavy losses, and further attempts were abandoned. With greater synchronization between the forces inside Sarajevo and those in Tuzla and Zenica, and better training and equipment of the units, more might have been achieved. As it was, the campaign ended in failure.

The Presidency, in its constitutional role as Commander of the Army, managed the Army's personnel policy in the General Staff headquarters and all larger units. In 1993, when tensions were growing between the HVO and the ABH, Halilović's leadership as Commander in Chief came into question. At issue were certain actions of the ABH in central Bosnia, or rather, ABH responses to actions of the HVO in central Bosnia and in Herzegovina. Halilović also several times issued what must at the least be described as provocative statements – declaring, for example, "We will march the Army straight through Neum and into Ploče!"[41] This naturally made matters worse, and a campaign against Halilović started in the Croatian press. This was also an anti-Bosnian campaign aimed at diminishing the role and the strength of the ABH. Several new problems arose, including difficulties with local commanders in Sarajevo and other places, who did not respect the principles of military hierarchy and order of command. Most significant of all was the rapid decline of the relationship between Sefer Halilović and President Izetbegović: it was the latter who finally put in motion an initiative to dismiss Halilović.

Izetbegović and I talked about this frequently. At the beginning, I personally did not support going so far as to dismiss him. However, the direction events had taken seemed to have left dismissal as the only option. The strongest argument of President Izetbegović was that relations with the HVO and Croatia could not improve as long as Halilović remained Commander in Chief. The second reason was the poor cooperation between Halilović and the Minister for Internal Affairs, Jusuf Pušina. This did not have the same political

---

[41] Neum is a small resort town on the Adriatic Sea that is Bosnia's only outlet to the Adriatic Sea. Ploče is a small coastal town northwest of Neum that is part of Croatia. The notion of marching through Neum on the way to Ploče would necessarily involve an invasion of Croatia by the Bosnian Army.

weight as the first reason; it did, however, open the question of dismissing Pušina.

A highly charged situation resulted, with Izetbegović insisting that both dismissals must be decided on together as a package. After several debates I unwillingly accepted that Halilović must be demoted, although this was not yet confirmed. With still greater reluctance I accepted the idea of dismissing Jusuf Pušina. Later on I and other members of the Presidency came in for criticism from the opposition parties, who demanded why we had agreed that Pušina should be dismissed along with Halilović. However, the poor relationship between Pušina on once side, and Izetbegović and Ejup Ganić on the other, had led to the demand that the ABH's problems with the Ministry of the Interior be resolved by a double dismissal.

The discussions lasted long, and there was much dragging of feet. But because of the difficulties in the operative management of the ABH, other members of the Presidency and I finally agreed to place the issue of these dismissals on the agenda of the Presidency. Later we realized that Pušina should have kept his position, for he contributed enormously to the consolidation of the services of the Ministry of the Interior by forming operational units, special units, and the security service. Particularly well known is the special unit of Dragan Vikić, which, in alliance with units of the Bosnian army, played a vital role in the military campaign, especially on the heavily contested front lines in Sarajevo, in the neighborhood of Žuči and toward Ilidža. Like Halilović, Pušina had the general confidence of all citizens of all nationalities. Both Pušina and Halilović always stoutly defended the idea of a civic, multiethnic Bosnia. But, matters so fell out that the decision had to be taken, and this was the form it took.

The public reacted badly. Both Halilović and Pušina demanded full explanation of their dismissals. They know best what was at issue between themselves and Izetbegović, but taking everything into consideration, it does seem that the most important reason behind their dismissal was Izetbegović's conviction that relations with the HVO and Croatia could only improve if a new man headed the ABH. Greater cooperation and alliance between the units of the army and the Ministry of the Interior also required new cooperation, and therefore new personnel. The circle was now closed, and we again found ourselves forced to seek a new commander for the army. Izetbegović revived the idea of talking to General Džemal Šarac on becoming Commander in Chief, and asked me to take it on myself to discuss this question with the General. I did so, but General Šarac simply repeated what he had said a year ago in the summer of 1992, that he could not, because of his age, responsibly undertake difficult operational tasks.

After this, Izetbegović held various private consultations about possible candidates for the post of Commander. When he spoke to me, my first idea was the commander of the Fourth Corps, Colonel Arif Pašalić. However, after a second round of consultations, Izetbegović proposed Rasim Delić for commander. Delić had not been much noted as a candidate in the first round of consultations, but this suggestion was finally accepted, along with the proposal that Sefer Halilović should remain in the post of Army Chief of Staff.

The arguments for Rasim Delić were that he had been operationally involved right from the beginning of the defense, had studied at the highest professional level, and was competent to take on the heaviest duty in the Army. Thus he was nominated to succeed Halilović. When it came to the handover of duties, however, relations between Delić and Halilović were not exactly conducive to cooperation. Halilović in practice withdrew entirely from the leadership of the Army, resulting in what I felt to be a totally unnecessary situation for the Army, for Sefer Halilović, and for the Presidency.[42] Together with two other Presidency members, Nijaz Duraković and Tanja Ljujić-Mijatović, I later revived the issue of Halilović's status. This would ultimately be solved by his promotion to General, which in a way put a seal of approval on his role in the Bosnian Army.

Because of Halilović's bitterness over this unexpected demotion and his lack of cooperation with Delić – though it is difficult to say to what extent Halilović was responsible for the latter - Halilović withdrew, convinced that his contribution and work were insufficiently appreciated. But these events had resulted from the exceptional times we lived in, when policy moves which left individuals embittered were sometimes made as a result of wider

---

[42] Halilović was very bitter about his dismissal and has repeatedly accused Izetbegović of treachery and withholding vital supplies from the army when he was commander. Sefer Halilović, *Lukava strategija* (Sarajevo: 1996).

currents. In my opinion Sefer Halilović was and remained a solid personality, a fine professional, a man who took a firm stand in the fight for a unified and multiethnic Bosnia in which all citizens and nations would be equal. He often spoke in all sincerity of how the Bosnian army must sooner or later win the battle against Chetniks and Ustashas, and how Bosnia would then see the day of its final freedom dawning.

Later in the war, in January 1995, several other members of the Presidency and I grew alarmed about the state of the army. The particular occasion that aroused our concern was Izetbegović's visit to the Third Corps in Zenica, or rather its Seventh Muslim Brigade, which was celebrating the anniversary of its foundation. The public display of Bosniak and Muslim symbols was ethno-religious in the extreme. Presidency members Stjepan Kljuić, Tatjana Ljuić-Mijatović, Nijaz Duraković, Ivo Komšić, and I met on several occasions to discuss our shared anxiety on this topic. By conducting the inspection as President of the Presidency and, as such, the key representative of the collective high command, Izetbegović, in our opinion, invited extremely contrary interpretations of this event, to say the least. We finally issued a press statement clarifying our concerns, which aroused strong reactions locally and in Europe and the international community.[43] We received unaccustomed attention from the journalists of foreign agencies, who bombarded us with demands for comments and explanations, which we refused to give. We kept to our original statement, which we felt was clear enough.

Izetbegović and Ejup Ganić issued a counter statement that appeared as an article in *Oslobođenje*. The day following their announcement, a political editorial appeared on the second page of *Oslobođenje*, written by Nedžad Ibrišimović, suggesting that those of us who had protested against Izetbegović's public display were conspiring to persecute followers of religion in Bosnia, as in the

---

[43] The announcement signed by five Presidency members decried the imposition of ideological views and the "Islamization of certain units of the Army of Bosnia and Herzegovina" and affirmed that the army should be "secular, multinational, and beyond the influence of political parties." The declaration is discussed in Roger Cohen, *Hearts Grown Brutal* (New York: Random House, 1998), p. 408.

days of religious crusades. He went on to suggest that prejudice against religion was the reason why the socialist system had lost its place on the world's historic stage. It was a provocative commentary that strongly suggested a desire to radicalize the issue. It declared that we were jeopardizing freedom of worship, freedom of faith, the free celebration of religion in the Army. The article clearly endorsed the defensive reaction of Izetbegović and Ganić.

I feel our original message gave no motive for such a reaction. It merely warned that the use of religious badges and symbols in official displays of an ABH unit would inevitably, in a multinational country and a multinational institution, lead to negative consequences for potential recruits from other nations. Our sole aim was to call attention to this phenomenon and enable public debate. We were forced to raise this issue because we felt strongly that President Izetbegović had failed to appraise the situation properly when carrying out the inspection. We stressed that faith is primarily an individual issue. While full religious freedom was guaranteed to the members of the Bosnian Army, military life and the organization of army units should not be religion-based, and this applied particularly to the Bosnian army.

Subsequent events, however, suggested this whole episode was really about the manipulation of power. The day after the statement of Izetbegović and Ganić made its appearance, the Army's General Staff met and issued a statement, as did the Ministry of the Interior, then headed by Bakir Alispahić. Both statements expressed unlimited support for Izetbegović and Ganić, thereby deliberately revealing where the centers of power lay and showing where the loyalties of the army and police would lie in any unplanned crisis. This led to an internal division in the Presidency, which could have had disastrous consequences. A session was held, at which we agreed that the Presidency, in the interests of unity, and should respect the basic principles that had been laid down for the defense of a multiethnic Bosnia. We also accepted that the President of the Presidency (Izetbegović), as chairman of the Advisory Board for Defense Issues, should assume further responsibility for the operations of the Bosnian Army. Thus a compromise was found which ensured that the armed forces would be managed jointly and in unity.

We had issued a clear warning about this new phenomenon and had demonstrated that there were mixed feelings about endorsing this phenomenon publicly as a civil right. This placed a useful check on any tendencies to intensify mono-national development of the Bosnian Army. Public display of religious symbols and religious membership, and the formalized use of traditional religious greetings in the ABH had already been the subject of several debates in the Presidency sessions. These debates led to the passage of various regulations on the Army's structure, and on the use of formal greetings in the Army. We ourselves could not agree on the latter issue. The opposition elements of the Presidency (Kljuić, Duraković, Komšić, Ljujić-Mijatović and myself) were convinced that civil, secular principles should underlie all official communication in the Bosnian Army, since the latter was a public institution and must therefore be universally accessible. But when the religious option failed to pass, Izetbegović said, "Fine, let's have it on paper, then, that the official term of greeting remains secular, but that people are able in private personal communication to use the greetings they use in everyday life – "Merhaba" instead of "Zdravo" (hello); "Selam Alejkum" instead of "Dobar Dan" (good day). The natural result was, of course, that the parallel use of such greetings increased.

By bringing this issue up repeatedly at the sessions of the Presidency, we warned of this phenomenon and of the need to define our approach to it. But when we saw that this only affected the surface, and that in a way that gave rise to many queries from ordinary people, we were driven to state our views publicly. At the same time, however, we did what we could to prevent this from becoming a matter for political division and crisis in the work of the Presidency. I think that the warning we gave was in itself sufficient, both psychologically and morally, to prevent this from becoming a wider-spread phenomenon, although such practices contributed significantly to reducing Serb and Croat participation in the ABH. The manifestation of support by the General Staff for President Izetbegović and Ganić, in the face of our statement, showed too that influential personnel in the Staff embraced party ideology. Their statement was the act of party members rather than people in service of the state: they should not have displayed affiliations to any party while acting as officers of an Army representing all the peoples of Bosnia.

## IX. KECMANOVIĆ GOES TO BELGRADE

One night in June 1992, Nenad Kecmanović was driving home from the Presidency to his flat in Ciglane. Due to the constant shelling, all driving had to be without lights. Near the city center, Kecmanović had an accident in which he suffered an injury to his spine. He subsequently recovered, although still in pain, and started coming back to work. One Sunday he and I met to discuss the whole situation, which in those days seemed hopeless. Shells rained down on the city, and the death-count rose every day. People were deeply depressed, and distrust for Serbs had grown. We two were constantly faced by the questions of what we should do, and what could we do, to change this state of affairs. We finally came up with the notion that it was worth taking a trip to Belgrade to try and get the attention of people there. We were counting the most on Milan Panić, a man who spoke out publicly for stopping the war and finding a peaceful solution.[44]

I myself suggested to Kecmanović that he should travel to Belgrade. He and I called Izetbegović to tell him we needed to confer. He soon invited us over, and we found ourselves together in his private office. Every meeting between Izetbegović, Kecmanović and myself always lasted longer than planned, because

---

[44] Milan Panić is a naturalized American citizen of Serbian origin and President of ICN Pharmaceuticals, a New York stock exchange listed company based in Costa Mesa, California. In June 1992 he challenged Milošević for leadership and ran against him for the office of President of Serbia in December 1992. After losing this election, Panić was ousted as Federal Prime Minister and returned to California, but he frequently attempted to rally opposition figures in opposing Milošević. Robert Thomas, *The Politics of Serbia in the 1990s* (London: Hurst and Co., 1999), pp. 122-135.

of Izetbegović's particular relationship with Kecmanović. The two always had plenty of topics to prolong their conversations. There was some kind of magnetism between the two of them - my impression was that each found the other deeply entertaining. We now told Izetbegović of our idea that Kecmanović should travel to Belgrade, and if possible try to set up a meeting between Izetbegović and Panić. Izetbegović agreed, and preparations for Kecmanović's journey started.

Of course, all this was necessarily kept confidential. None of the other Presidency members knew about our talks. Kecmanović waited for UNPROFOR to organize the journey, and meanwhile business went on as usual. During one Presidency session Kecmanović and I were sitting next to each other, and in the middle of the session a message was brought from Kecmanović's office. He told me in a whisper that his trip to Belgrade was confirmed, and that same afternoon he set off. His only request to me was to try and find the time to help his wife Nataša, who would remain in Sarajevo. Everything carried on as normal until the next day, when we saw Nenad Kecmanović meeting with Nikola Koljević, on the Pale television evening news.[45] Of course Serbian television made a huge event out of this, claiming matters had reached such a crisis in Sarajevo that Kecmanović had come to stay permanently in Pale. This was confirmed by the statement of Jovan Tintor, a leading SDS activist from Vogošča.[46] Tintor added that Pejanović should have left Sarajevo when Kecmanović did, but that a payment of three million German marks in exchange for his departure had been refused. This was typical of the propaganda featured on Pale television.

The next day numerous party officials in Sarajevo gave statements, all of which took the form of personal attacks on Kecmanović. Almost everyone believed that he had simply gone over to Pale - nobody knew that he was on his way to Belgrade, on a vital mission agreed in advance with Izetbegović. Since I was the only other person who knew of this mission, I gave a statement to the media, in which I tried to speak mildly and to protect Kecmanović. I could not publicize all the reasons for his journey to

---

[45] Koljević was at that time the Vice President of the Republika Srpska.

[46] Vogošća is a suburb of Sarajevo that came under control of the SDA early in the war.

Belgrade, stating only that time would show his purpose. As a result, I let myself in for some hard questioning, strong criticism, and plenty of misinterpretation.

Kecmanović arrived safely in Belgrade, and I heard from his wife that he had started treatment in Belgrade's Clinical Center. I finally managed to talk with him on the telephone. He told me the doctors felt he must stay in bed for further treatment, that his condition was graver than had been realized, and that it was uncertain how long this treatment would last. I explained to Kecmanović that many people felt the treatment should be continued outside Belgrade, due to political circumstances. Kecmanović replied that the doctors advised no movement at all. I accordingly gave this news to the public, President Izetbegović and the other members of the Presidency. Meanwhile, Kecmanović remained in Belgrade, with questions coming in from all sides as to how this had happened, what it meant, how long he would stay, and whether he was coming back.

Subsequently, however, media interest declined. It was believed that the treatment would soon finish, and everybody waited to see what Kecmanović would do. Following a long silence, Kecmanović announced, via the Belgrade media – the easiest channel to use - that he had ceased to be a member of the Presidency. This created a new situation for everybody in Sarajevo: it was painfully new for me. The day after Kecmanović's announced his departure from the Presidency, Zdravko Grebo, with whom I worked closely on various activities in my student days, came to see me in the Presidency. He came specifically to tell me - although his visit was, in itself, the strongest message - "Hold on: I know you will hold on." The same day Kljuić, who had worked with me so successfully on so many issues, especially when it came to protecting the rights and interests of the individuals who approached us, also came. Kljuić was more direct: "Don't you end up leaving us too."

In this new situation, I did a lot of thinking, but never about resigning. I always came back to the idea of the multiethnicity of Bosnia as its historic destiny, greater and stronger and more enduring than the total sum of the people who live in Bosnia now. These thoughts helped at certain moments to dismiss any idea of resigning. My position remained the same, and I turned to the task of finding a candidate for the Serb vacancy in the Presidency.

Kecmanović, at the time of joining the Presidency and during his work there, stood plainly on the side of those who stood for a multiethnic, united and democratic Bosnia, and was equally clearly against the forces that carried out the ethnic cleansing, genocide and division of this country. But by his departure to Belgrade, and by remaining there while the war continued, he chose a position that was neither that of Sarajevo nor of Belgrade. It was a fine position: it enabled him to await the outcome of events, and then become re-involved without any loss to himself – meaning that he never lacked a feather to fly with.

Kecmanović actively followed events, displaying his continuing intellectual involvement by writing numerous articles in *NIN* and other Belgrade papers, giving interviews, statements and talks. I had no opportunity to keep track of his work, but he was well known before the war as a skilled political analyst with an excellent critical reputation as an ideologue of civil society. He was a stern critic of Communist ideology, but also of nationalist ideologies. In fact he chose to ride the middle of the political see-saw, suggesting by his speeches and articles that he was neither wholly for, nor explicitly against, the Pale leadership. Thus he ensured for himself a comfortable position in Belgrade, the support of many organizations, and solutions to all his problems, existential and social.

Kecmanović was of importance in Bosnia as a successful intellectual, an unrivalled expert at navigating political currents - as in fact he demonstrated by staying in Belgrade to await the outcome that eventually arrived in the form of the Dayton Peace Agreement. To me, however, he remains a supporter of the ideology and values of civil society, and in this context he can still be a man of the future, helping build up these values in the Bosnian Serb nation and in Bosnia itself.

In Sarajevo itself, there are many who blame him bitterly for the way in which he spoke and wrote of the city in wartime - for example, his long article expressing the opinion that Sarajevo should be razed to the ground. It is up to him to explain himself publicly, when he comes back to his city - which he certainly can never remove wholly from his heart, nor from his memories, for he was a good neighbor and good citizen, warmly welcomed wherever he went. He himself, however, has denied this fellowship with his neighbors.

Prior to his departure for Belgrade, Kecmanović and I worked together in the Presidency, and in general our collaboration was friendly and successful. But, even at the beginning, Kecmanović showed apathy and a lack of willpower, especially from noon onwards. This became particularly marked following his accident. He used to drop into my office with a "What's up, Pantelija?" - as if he wanted somehow to lean on me. He would sit down, light a cigarette, and stare at the wall, with comments like "This is going nowhere", "This can't be endured any longer," and "If these people of ours in the hills keep on at it, they'll destroy everything in the city." It was hard to cope with the tasks of wartime amid so much destruction. His children had left Sarajevo, but his wife was still in the city, and it was not easy to deal with the trauma of the siege. He and I were fully agreed on most of the important issues such as preparing decisions for Presidency sessions, and offering our assistance to all citizens, particularly those of Serb nationality. We worked together on the cases of the many Serbs who came to our offices, doing what we could to protect them, to help them leave Sarajevo, or whatever else they asked for.

One of our more memorable meetings was with a larger group of fellow Serbs, a meeting in which President Izetbegović took part. This followed the episode in which Zoran Cegar of the special police organized the mass detention of Sarajevo Serbs in Koševo Stadium, in response to threats that Serb Army forces would kill his relatives who were living in a suburb under Serb control. His action aroused terror in the city. Panic-stricken people came crowding in to see us, and Izetbegović himself helped receive them. Altogether, we spent a great deal of time and energy on direct communication with ordinary people, offering them our help, resolving their security issues and other difficulties.

In the strongly nationalist perceptions of the SDS, Kecmanović and I were insufficiently national people, "reserve Serbs," in their jargon. But if we were compared, he was, in specific ways, distinctly more national-minded than I was, though he never wanted to reveal this publicly. We based our role, and the public interpretation of that role, on the genuine truth that we were advocates of a policy that promoted the view of all citizens as individuals, in the context of human rights, including the right to national equality. As Serb members of the Presidency, we not only represented the Serb nation but all people who had voted for us. (Kecmanović had won around 500,000 votes, and I had received approximately 335,000, and in both cases our votes came mostly from ethnically mixed urban centers, from members of all nationalities in Bosnia.)

At the end of 1992, in Geneva, where I took part in peace talks as a member of the Bosnian delegation, I gave an interview to a *Nezavisna Borba* journalist, Gordana Suša. She asked what I thought about Kecmanović's departure, his resignation from the Presidency, and his retreat from the fight for a multiethnic Bosnia. In answer I stressed the values that Kecmanović upheld while a member of the Presidency - history will show what kind of values he supported after leaving. Gordana Suša said, "He doesn't talk like this about you. He doesn't have the same feeling of goodwill towards you that you still have for him." I replied that each of us had our own reasons, our own motives to answer for.

History will define not only the totality of events, but also the role of key people in these events. I should emphasize that Kecmanović, when performing the duties of a Presidency member, did so responsibly. We cooperated very successfully, particularly over the concept of defending a multiethnic Bosnia, its unity, and its democratic and secular character. We worked closely on the effort to restore peace by finding a political solution - Kecmanović used to joke about me because of the solidity of my conviction that a political solution was the only possible exit from the pan-Bosnian drama.

Milan Panić did finally come to visit Bosnia in July 1992.[47] He met with Chairman of the Bosnian Presidency Alija Izetbegović in what was then the UNPROFOR headquarters in the PTT Engineering building in Alipašina Polje. When we were preparing for this visit, I asked President Izetbegović to ensure that, in addition to his own official meeting with Panić, a group of Sarajevo Serbs, including myself, could meet with Panić separately. This was agreed.

---

[47] With this visit, Panić "proved that he had a mind of his own. On 20 July, only a few days after his appointment as Federal Prime Minister of Yugoslavia, he traveled in a UN-provided aircraft to the besieged city of Sarajevo to demonstrate his dedication to the cause of peace. After a meeting with the Bosnian President Alija Izetbegović, he made a thinly-veiled criticism of Slobodan Milošević, condemning the cheap politicians who have played on nationalism and created a civil war." Thomas, *The Politics of Serbia*, p. 123.

The group that met with Panić consisted of the President of the City Forum of Sarajevo Serbs: Dragutin Braco Kosovac, myself, and several others.

We arrived at the PTT building early in the morning. The conference between Izetbegović and Panić, arranged by the UNPROFOR commander, Canadian general Louis McKenzie, went on for a long time. When it was over, Panić finally came to where we were waiting. As soon as he entered, after greeting us all, he handed round pieces of white tape, asking us all to put them round our arms as a symbol that we supported peace, not war. This was surely pleasant enough, but we found it somewhat odd. The talk itself was very brief.

Braco Kosovac described to Panić the situation in the city and in Bosnia, and then told him of the proposal by the Civic Forum of Serbs from Sarajevo for ending the war and finding a solution through negotiation. Kosovac condemned the evil the Serb bombardment was wreaking in Sarajevo, the havoc, the burned buildings, and the killings by snipers and by shells. He spoke of the meaninglessness, the wholesale tragedy, of such a war. As if to underline his comments, throughout Panić's visit shells were falling steadily on the PTT building itself – tokens of the resentment felt by the Pale commanders and politicians at Panić's visit to Sarajevo and his meeting with President Izetbegović. It was a situation both tragic and ridiculous. Replying to Kosovac, Panić declared that he stood for stopping the war, for a halt to all military activities on all sides, for seeking a peaceful political solution, and for ensuring the unity and equality of all peoples in Bosnia. It was obvious that he possessed the will for peace but that he lacked the power to bring it about.

I then spoke to Panić separately, and begged him to do something to ensure the presence of Orthodox priests in the territory under the control of the Bosnian Army, since by then all priests had left, except for the Zenica priest, Miroslav Drinčić, and the retired Sarajevo priest, Krstan Bijelica. Panić listened, and promised to see what he could do with the Holy Synod of the Orthodox Church, and to talk with His Reverence the Patriarch Pavle.

With that the meeting ended, leaving us dissatisfied. It was followed by a press conference, while I remained in the PTT building. I tried, as I had been begged to do, to persuade General McKenzie to do me the favor of allowing Kecmanović's wife Nataša to travel to Belgrade to see her husband, taking the plane on which Panić would return. Nataša had come in my car to the UNPROFOR building, a fact that many journalists had criticized, creating an uncomfortable situation. My appeal to General McKenzie did not go well. Naturally, he justified his refusal of this request by citing "reasons of security" – always the easiest excuse when any of the UNPROFOR representatives did not want to or could not find a solution.

The press conference was held, and everybody's statements published, including the unforgettable comment of Izetbegović to the effect that Panić was a bright and breezy character but that his overall effectiveness was not encouraging. My own impression was that Panić did not want his involvement in the Bosnian war to be in any way dishonest or underhand. On the contrary, he spoke openly, and I believe that what he said was genuine, but his power was insignificant in relation to that of the Belgrade, Yugoslav, and Serbian regimes of Ćosić, Milošević, and the JNA General Staff. This visit turned out to be just another episode in the struggle to begin negotiations, but had no influence on further developments in Bosnia.

After Kecmanović's departure from Sarajevo, his position in the Presidency went unfilled for several months, as did the question of Serbian representation in the Parliament and the issue of appointing a Speaker. Momčilo Krajišnik had been Speaker until the departure of the SDS from the Parliament. Thereafter, his deputy, Mariofil Ljubić took up the post. In this capacity, Ljubić served as a member of the expanded wartime Presidency, which consisted of the Presidency's elected members, the army Commander in Chief, the Speaker of the Parliament, and the Prime Minister of the government.

First, the issue arose of how vacancies on the Presidency should be filled. The basic principle adopted at the time of the departure of Plavšić and Koljević in April 1992 had been to accept the constitution and the law on elections, which specified that the candidate with the next highest number of votes would be the legal successor. This provision led to the selection of Kecmanović and myself as representatives of the Serb nation. Nijaz Duraković was the next Bosniak in line after Izetbegović and Fikret Abdić, and the next Croat on the list was Professor Ivo Komšić. I personally recommended that this principle should continue to be respected, and this was accepted in all further personnel changes in the Presidency.

However, it was not feasible to follow this principle strictly after Kecmanović's resignation. Đorđe Latinović and Nikola Stojanović, who were actually next on the list of presidential candidates with the highest number of votes in the 1990 elections, had left the territory controlled by the Bosnian army – in fact, as far as we knew, they were in Serbia. We therefore could not negotiate with them about their willingness to act. So we turned to Tanja Ljujić-Mijatović, a member of the Bosnian Parliament, as the next candidate in line according to the 1990 election results.[48] At the same time we advised that a Serb candidate should be proposed for the post of Parliament Speaker, with the recommendation that, in these current wartime circumstances, the Serb nation should be treated with equality in the execution of government. The proposed candidate was Miro Lazović, SDP parliamentary delegate. These two initiatives ran in parallel, since the proposal of Lazović for Speaker had already been submitted.

Resistance to the nomination of Lazović for Speaker came from the HDZ: not openly, but in the form of deliberate delay. Finally, at the end of 1992, the HDZ issued an ultimatum, demanding that Stjepan Kljuić resign from the Presidency. Under strong pressure, he eventually obeyed, and so a Croat seat on the Presidency fell vacant. Ejup Ganić telephoned from Sarajevo while I was in Geneva, to tell me of the HDZ ultimatum. I opposed yielding to it on the grounds that this was purely a party ultimatum. The elections had been general, and although the parties had the right to put candidates forward, the candidates themselves were ultimately chosen by all nations and all citizens. The deciding factor, however, was Kljuić's own choice. He held out for a long time, but threats were made against his daughter, who was then in the United States. His decision to resign cut short all debates about the possibility of rejecting the HDZ ultimatum.

After Kljuić's resignation, the HDZ suggested Miro Lasić, one of the HDZ party leaders, to fill the vacancy.[49] I neither supported

---

[48] Ljujić-Mijatović had not run for the Presidency. Votes were cast for her as a candidate for a seat in Parliament.

[49] Lasić also had not run for the Presidency in 1990.

nor rejected this proposal, but I demanded that acceptance of Miro Lasić's candidacy should be linked to election of a Serb Parliament Speaker – specifically, Miro Lazović. A stalemate followed, with the HDZ insisting that the election of Miro Lasić should be placed on the agenda, and myself pushing for acceptance of Miro Lazović's candidacy. The result was a dramatic Presidency session which lasted late into the night. The danger loomed of total breakdown. But after several long breaks, during which we consulted among ourselves, we found a compromise solution. Mariofil Ljubić agreed that Lazović should be nominated for Speaker; the rest of us agreed to Miro Lasić's candidacy for the Presidency, and at the same time we demanded election of the second Serb member of the Presidency, proposing Tanja Ljujić-Mijatović as candidate. Late that night I requested that Nijaz Duraković should join the presidency on behalf of the SDP.[50] We conferred with him, and he accepted. Next, we talked to Tanja Ljujić-Mijatović herself, and she, too, accepted our proposal. On entering the Presidency she proved energetic and decisive in supporting the goals for which the Presidency as a body was fighting: a multiethnic, democratic and unified state of three equal nations.

This, then, was how the various vacancies were filled. Ljujić-Mijatović took Kecmanović's place, and Miro Lasić took the place of Stjepan Kljuić. Some time after this came the famous collective departure in 1993 of all HDZ personnel from their positions in the state organs of Bosnia, the Presidency, and the government. This paralleled the start of military conflict between the ABH and the HVO. Franjo Boras and Miro Lasić handed in their resignations and left Sarajevo, as did the Prime Minister, Mile Akmadžić, and many Croat ministers. Bosnian Croat citizens in Tuzla, Sarajevo, and other cities that had struggled to preserve their multiethnic character, disagreed with the unilateral decision of the Croat

---

[50] Duraković received 558,263 votes for the Presidency as a candidate of the SDP, coming in third among Bosniak candidates behind Fikret Abdić and Alija Izetbegović. Ejup Ganić, an SDA candidate and a Bosniak originally from the Sandžak region of Yugoslavia, was the leading vote-getter in the category of "Others." He ran in that category based on having declared himself a "Yugoslav" in the most recent census. His victory in the "Others" category meant that the Presidency initially had three members who were identifiably Bosniaks and members of the SDA.

representatives. Several influential Croats came to visit me, including many well-known public and political activists, to protest. Meanwhile Ivo Komšić had arrived in Sarajevo, and had formed the Croat Peasant Party.[51] This was profiled as a political option for the Croat people and advocated a multiethnic Bosnia, common life for all nations, and resistance to the politics of national division, the politics that produced ethic cleansing and the expulsion of whole populations.

The Presidency members had to find a way to fill all the vacancies left by the departure of so many Croats. Activities began on several fronts, in some of which I was directly involved. One night Ivo Komšić and I went to the Ministry of the Interior to find Jozo Jozić, who, as the chief of the State Security Service, had the technical capacity to reach Zagreb by phone. We called Stipe Mesić, explained the problem, and listed possible solutions.[52] Stipe Mesić supported our continuing to lobby for joint government in order to defend the values of Bosnian society and the Bosnian state. He was firm in his belief that this could be achieved only by the election of Croats to the highest organs of the state. Subsequently, returning from abroad via Zagreb, I met with various opposition leaders, and talked to Dražen Budiša about the mood of the Croats who had remained in the cities, and who supported a common life for all nations and the unity of the Bosnian state. Budiša, as is well known, always advocated that the Bosnian Croat people should solve their destiny in Bosnia together with its other nations. Next came the initiative that Ivo Komšić should join the Presidency and that Stjepan Kljuić should also join, effectively returning to the position that he abandoned in late 1992, under HDZ pressure.[53] This was

---

[51] Komšić announced the formation of the Croatian Peasant Party (HSS – *Hrvatska seljačka stranka*) of Bosnia and Herzegovina, or more correctly is re-establishment from the period before the Second World War, on April 15, 1993. *Oslobođenje*, 16 April 1993, p. 16.

[52] Stipe Mesić was then the Vice President of the Republic of Croatia. Before the war he had been a member of the Presidency of Yugoslavia. In January 2000 he was elected President of Croatia in the first election after the death Franjo Tudjman on December 10, 1999.

[53] Komšić received 353,707 votes for the Presidency as a candidate of the SDP in the 1990 elections, coming in third among Croat candidates behind Kljuić and Franjo Boras.

accepted at a Presidency session. Both men were nominated and began to carry out their constitutional duties. Thus the Presidency was complete and fully functioning once again.

We faced a similar problem toward the end of 1992 when Presidency member Fikret Abdić moved his political base to Velika Kladuša.[54] Once Abdić had created the Autonomous Region of Western Bosnia, and entered into political conflict with the Sarajevo government, the issue of his status grew more and more urgent. The final outcome came at one of the wartime Bosnian Parliament sessions. With the SDA holding a majority in Parliament after the departure of SDS delegates, a vote of no confidence in Fikret Abdić was passed, and he lost his status as member of the Presidency.

In the debate on how to fill this vacancy, the SDA first claimed publicly that the place belonged to them, since Abdić had been their candidate – a claim similar to that made by the HDZ after it had ordered Kljuić to leave the Presidency. This repeated itself when the SDA came into conflict with its own candidate; not only was a vote of no confidence passed against him, but his candidacy was in fact withdrawn. It was debated whether his replacement should be the candidate with the next highest result in the 1990 elections, or whether the party should make its own nomination. The first of these two options was the clear constitutional course to follow, as we opposition representatives – Kljuić, Ljujić-Mijatović and I - pointed out. To begin with, however, the various talks were unsuccessful. Then the SDP and other parties got involved, and the process became long and tortuous. Miro Lazović, Bogić Bogićević and Gradimir Gojer from the SDP were especially active throughout these talks. They argued that the election law should be implemented, and the Constitution respected. Gradually, the SDA abandoned its position, and the principle of appointing the next highest vote-getter prevailed. Nijaz Duraković was chosen as the new Bosniak member of the Presidency, and the Presidency was complete once more. All Bosnian supporters of civil democracy felt a sense of relief at this demonstration of respect for constitutional principles. Nor did people hide their satisfaction that the new arrivals were people who had always stood firm in defense

---

[54] Fikret Abdić had been a very successful director the enterprise Agrokomerc prior to his entry into politics.

of the idea of a multiethnic, united and democratic Bosnia, a state of equal citizens and nations.

At about the same time, Alija Izetbegović's term as President of the Presidency expired. According to the constitution, in normal conditions a new President of the Presidency, elected internally by the Presidency members, should be appointed annually with the possibility of extending the mandate by one more year. The maximum length of the mandate, therefore, was two years, and this period was exhausted by December 1992.

The question then rose of wartime chairmanship of the Presidency. According to the interpretation of the Constitutional Court, when there was a declared war or when an immediate danger of war existed, the President of the Presidency should remain in this post until the cessation of the danger or conflict. It was therefore understood that the President's mandate would automatically be extended. Alija Izetbegović was currently Chairman: this was uncontested, and the extension of his term was an uncontroversial solution. However, the solution had to be ratified by a session of the Presidency and published. During preparations for this session, I think I was among the first of the Presidency members to be consulted by President Izetbegović. At that time the Presidency consisted of two Bosniaks (Izetbegović and Abdić); one member from the category of "others" – (Ganić, as a Yugoslav); two Serbs: Tanja Ljujić Mijatović and myself; two Croats: Franjo Boras and Stjepan Kljuic; and three other members by virtue of their positions: Parliament Speaker Miro Lazović; Commander in Chief Sefer Halilović; and Prime Minister of the Government Jure Pelivan.

In an open conversation with Izetbegović on this topic - which I cared about deeply - I offered two options. One was independent of the constitutional regulation, which was clear; I was, however, in favor of the development of democracy in wartime, which, to my way of thinking, meant taking steps towards changing the President. I felt this would be a significant stand for democracy, as it would show how, in the harshest struggle for Bosnia's survival, the Presidency had the internal strength to cope with electing a new Chair. President Izetbegović, however, made no comment. I next speculated on whether re-election, if it took place, would produce another Bosniak President or someone of a different nationality. I told him I saw this as a time of intense hardship for the Bosniak nation. It was still not known what the full situation was and how many Bosniaks had been killed or driven from their homes. There were still concentration camps in the Krajina: thus the survival not only of a multiethnic Bosnia, but also that of one of its peoples, was in question. I felt, therefore, that if we decided to make any changes, the new President should also be Bosniak.

President Izetbegović opened the question of how much support the other two Bosniaks in the Presidency, Abdić and Ganić, could expect to receive from the Bosnian people and from the Islamic countries: the latter were then supplying the most concrete aid to the Bosnian resistance, morally, politically and materially. Izetbegović commented that Abdić was unknown in most Islamic countries, although Ganić was somewhat better known - he had already visited several Islamic countries, including Libya, and had been well received. The nature of the comment, however, suggested that, in his opinion, neither Bosniak could win sufficient confidence at home and support abroad, particularly from the Islamic countries that were making such an important contribution to the battle currently being fought by the Bosniak and other nations to preserve a multiethnic Bosnia.

By this I understood that President Izetbegović was fully aware of all implications but was ready, in fact anxious, to continue as Chairman. We parted without any precise agreement. Before the Presidency session, however, I had a talk with Ganić, at his request. He used this opportunity to test my position, and did not conceal his interest in becoming President of the Presidency. At the session itself, however, we all agreed to accept the constitutional regulation that the current President, Izetbegović, should continue to act as President of the Presidency. This was purely a consequence of war - there would otherwise have been no constitutional possibility whatsoever of extending the mandate. Izetbegović remained President of the Presidency until well after the Dayton Peace Agreement of 1995.

## X. HERCEG-BOSNA – A NEW POLITICAL FACT

On the political scene of Bosnia, during 1992, a new reality appeared which crucially altered current political and military trends: the Croat nation's novel construct known as "Herceg-Bosna."[55] Herceg-Bosna was created as not only a political and military but also an economic structure. It produced a great psychological and ideological impact especially on the unity of Bosnia and its central institutions. Politically, it was based on the rule of the HDZ, and its first appointed seat of power was Grude.

What was the concept of Herceg-Bosna, and what was its ultimate goal? Herceg-Bosna was based on the idea of a defined national territory, ethnic segregation and a mono-ethnic government. It was assisted in all things by the Zagreb government, and offered a response to the Serb concept of territorial and ethnic partition. It arose response to the need to protect Croats, particularly from the Serbian aggression, in which they were slaughtered. This last factor was cited as an excuse for Herceg-Bosna´s existence. Judging by everything, Herceg-Bosna was kept in reserve, to be brought out when the concept of ethnic division of Bosnia seemed finally triumphant.

---

[55] Creation of the "Croatian Community of Herceg-Bosna" (HZ-HB – *Hrvatska zajednice Herceg-Bosna*) was announced by Mate Boban on November 17, 1991. It drew relatively little attention as long as it masqueraded as a cultural community of Croats, but in July 1992 its Presidency announced a series of Constitution-like measures which made clear that HZ-HB was a separatist territorial parastate that claimed sovereign powers and aspired to be annexed to the Republic of Croatia.

One can best understand Herceg-Bosna's significance by assuming that the Karađorđevo agreement between Milošević and Tuđman was being implemented. Given this premise, we can conclude the Karađorđevo agreement precipitated creation of the Republika Srpska and the withdrawal of Serb delegates from the Bosnian Parliament. It also underlay the development of Herceg-Bosna and the resignation of the Croat representatives from the joint organs of the state. These episodes illustrate how the concept of the ethnic division of Bosnia, and the ethnic definition of territories within this division, were realized. Steady consolidation of territory progressed to demands for secession.

In July 1992 Herceg-Bosna arrived on the Presidency´ agenda. The discussion centered on prior rulings by the Bosnian Constitutional Court, according to which the para-states of the Republika Srpska and the Republic of Herceg-Bosna, claimed as states by their founders (the RS by the SDS and Herceg-Bosna by the HDZ), were judged unconstitutional. The Presidency endorsed this position, but it had neither the strength nor the influence to halt their progress on the ground.

There were three phases in the life of Herceg-Bosna. In the first phase, Herceg-Bosna and the HDZ were allied politically with the SDA. The second phase, which began in 1993, saw Herceg-Bosna and the SDA go to war. In the third and final phase, Herceg-Bosna became a part of the Muslim-Croat Federation created by the Washington Agreement of March 1994.

This first phase can be described as lasting from the outbreak of war until April 1993, when conflict flared up between the Bosnian Army and the HVO. During this time the HVO was considered a constituent part of the armed forces of Bosnia. Initially the total structure of the HDZ, the HVO and the infrastructure of Herceg-Bosna (then consisting of elements of a state-type organization in Croat-majority regions), were in political alliance with the SDA as the HDZ's partner in power, and allied militarily with the ABH against Karadžić's aggression. During this time there was a high level of cooperation between the personnel of the state organs in Sarajevo, including the Presidency, the cabinet, the Ministry of Defense, and other institutions. In the time of this alliance the joint actions of the HVO and the Bosnian Army were successful, and a large amount of territory lay under their control: they even undertook a few joint offensives. They also advanced on Sarajevo in hopes of breaking the siege, although this particular offensive failed, as already told, for lack of coordination with the forces inside the city. Nevertheless, such cooperation was of great significance for the total growth of Bosnia's power to defend the ideas of multiethnicity and unity. But because Sarajevo was under siege, nobody, including the members of the Presidency, had any access to real knowledge concerning the extent of Herceg-Bosna's activities, as a para-state organization encompassing the Croats of West Herzegovina, West Mostar and the Neretva valley.

This state of affairs lasted until the armed aggression between the ABH and the HVO led to the second phase of the war and the existence of Herceg-Bosna. The HVO-ABH conflict could be called the worst part of the Bosnian war, for it carried the threat of wholesale civil violence and the mutual destruction of all nations. The conflict was primarily the consequence of the peace plan proposed at Geneva in 1993, which advocated for a Bosnia consisting of three territorial ethnic units, with Sarajevo as the capital. The ethnic units were to be formed in accordance with the national majorities supposed to live in each unit.

At that time, it should be noted, Herceg-Bosna was under the government of Mate Boban. On my return from the peace negotiations in Geneva, I spent a short time in Split, and that evening I watched a program broadcast from the Split studio of Croatian Television. Mate Boban, along with several other officials of Herceg-Bosna, was in the studio. I noticed Mile Akmadžić, then the Prime Minister of the Bosnian government, among the others. Mate Boban's theme was that the Bosnian Croat nation had achieved, through this peace plan, international recognition of its identity and international acknowledgement of its institutions. Therefore, if no consensus could be achieved on this peace plan, the Croat nation would resolve the situation by military means. Shortly after this broadcast, military action started, most intensively in the Neretva valley, Prozor and Gornji Vakuf.

This whole episode deserves further investigation. However, what seems clear is that the leadership of Herceg-Bosna, with Mate Boban at its head, seized on the Geneva proposal of three ethnic units and decided that its historic moment had come - believing that contemporary international circumstances would support ethnic partition and homogenization of Croat territories. Theirs was a project identical to that already embarked upon by the SDS under Karadžić. Ethnic cleansing was launched throughout Herzegovina, principally in the towns of Stolac, Čapljina, Prozor, and West Mostar, where earlier the joint forces of the Bosniaks and Croats had ethnically cleansed the Serb population.

Thus the second phase in the life of Herceg-Bosna led to Bosniaks being herded into concentration camps, such as the infamous Dretelj and Heliodrom camps.[56] This kind of step could not have been taken without assistance from Zagreb, that is, from the HDZ-dominated state structures of the Republic of Croatia, and more concretely from the Herzegovina lobby, which was powerful within both the HDZ and the Croatian army. The decision to enter into military conflict was disastrous for the Bosnian Croats as well as the Bosniaks, and for the country as a whole. While the HVO forces in Herzegovina and Mostar, backed by units from Croatia, produced decisive Croat victories in this area, this meant trouble for the Croats in central Bosnia where the ABH was more powerful. Central Bosnian Croats, under the influence of the HDZ, the HVO, and the leadership of Dario Kordić, marked out ethnic territories in which to consolidate HDZ rule. Their attempt was followed by severe reprisals from the Bosnian Army. The Army's actions could be seen as self-defense, or as something more: its furious response to Croat crimes such as the massacre in the village of Ahmići near Vitez led to the killing of Croat civilians in the Neretva valleys and several other places. Moreover, it led to a Croat exodus from central Bosnia.

This struck right at the heart of all that was most vulnerable in the Croat ethnic body, for one of the most significant elements of Bosnian Croat history is their traditional common life with the Bosniaks of central Bosnia. This area was very different from Herzegovina, especially West Herzegovina, where Croats formed a solid ethnic majority and mingled less, shared less of their life and culture with Bosniaks, were always more oriented toward Dalmatia and Croatia.

---

[56] The HVO imprisoned Bosniaks in the hangars of the former JNA helicopter base just Mostar. This camp became known by the name of the military base, Heliodrom.

The unease spread to the cities of Sarajevo and Tuzla, where Croat soldiers were mainly in HVO units under joint command within the Bosnian Army. Croats were also distributed individually in various units of the Bosnian Army and were dedicated to defense of the idea of a multiethnic Bosnia. If they had not been, they would certainly never have stayed in these cities and towns of Central Bosnia and Northeastern Bosnia: Živinice, Lukavac, Tuzla, Gradačac, Srebrenik, and others. Now, however, drawn into conflict with both the rest of the HVO and the ABH, the Croat nation found its future in Bosnia in jeopardy.

One of the worst episodes of the war was the battle between Croats and Bosniaks that ravaged the city of Mostar. The HVO deliberately destroyed the famous Mostar bridge, built in the time of the Ottoman Empire, and subjected East Mostar to ruthless destruction and slaughter. It was not easy, in those days, to be a Croat in Sarajevo. Tensions could be felt at every step and round every corner. I met during that period with many people of the Bosnian Croat nation, including Don Luka Brković of the Marjindvor church. He was a priest who showed profound commitment in caring for his parish, and the relationships of his parishioners with their Bosniak, Serb and other neighbors. As distrust mounted, I gave several public statements on the need to seek for ties between us that could reconcile us, to search for whatever could lead to agreement and hopes of peace. Don Luka asked me to make such statements more often, for tensions fell noticeably whenever one was published in the media. I understood, and began going more often to church and to other institutions of the Croat nation, and talking with people who were giving themselves and whatever they had to preserve our life together in Sarajevo. In those hard days, I helped them see who their friends were. I had various dialogues with Bosniaks too, urging them not to let tensions rise nor seek conflicts, nor allow the mistreatment of Croat civilians in Sarajevo.

But fear was spreading everywhere, as I saw in the Church of Saint Ante at Bistrik when a Mass was held for Fra Miličević, a priest killed in Fojnica. Kljuić and I attended this together. We were the only officials present, but the church was full of people, especially older men and women. The women got up from the pews and clasped our hands, whispering, "Save us, do all you can to save us." Those were hard times for Croat patriots in Sarajevo. It should be stressed that all who stayed in the city, suffered its tragedy, and fought for its defense, stood right in the front line of the fight for a multiethnic Bosnia.

As I found during the war, the Catholic Church played an important role in preserving cooperation and trust between the Croat and Bosniak nations. The church helped call a halt to the Croat-Bosniak conflict, supported the Washington Agreement brokered by the US, and encouraged the unity of Bosnia, the equality of its nations, and the right of each nation to differences of national, cultural and religious identity. Strong leadership was provided by the head of the Bosnian Catholic Church, Archbishop Vinko Puljić (who was made a Cardinal during the war) and Fra Petar Anđelovic, head of the Bosna Srebrene Franciscan Order. These two acted with the force of moral integrity and influence, not only on Catholic believers but generally, in creating a better climate for the preservation of trust and the tradition of common life. Even before the war, they had called on members of the Croat nation to vote for a united, sovereign and independent Bosnia, a civil state of three equal nations, in the referendum held on February 29 and March 1, 1992. Thus they undertook historic responsibility for the destiny of the Bosnian Croats in favor of common life and common growth with the Bosniak and Serb nations.

Throughout the war they carefully fostered interethnic relations, giving statements that helped shape public opinion. They reconciled and united people, and opened up new perspectives. In the desperate years of 1992 and 1993, they were deeply concerned not only for the survival of Catholics but also for that of Bosniaks and Serbs living in the cities. It should also be recorded that the charities *Caritas* and *Napredak* through their soup kitchens and humanitarian activities helped tens of thousands of people of all nations.[57] In places like Bugojno and Travnik, Bosnian Serbs would have barely survived the dire hunger and poverty, had it not been for the generosity of Caritas. The same could be said for Sarajevo and Tuzla. This fact should go into history as an example of interethnic solidarity in the worst of wartime.

---

[57] *Caritas* is a Catholic relief agency; *Napredak* is a Croatian Cultural Society. *Caritas* provided a large amount of the relief supplies that ultimately reached Sarajevo. *Napredak* actively sponsored numerous cultural activities as well.

Archbishop Puljić and Fra Petar Anđelović put brick on brick in their diligent efforts to build peace and preserve trust. In all crises, I found Archbishop Vinko Puljić's door always open to me, ready for the exchange of thoughts: information about new problems, new ideas for solutions. The Cardinal stayed firm in his view that all Bosnians should join in a common destiny, work for the rights of all people as God's beings, and secure their rights to home and identity, to equality, and to diversity. We always had his support for the protection of national, cultural and religious identity, for we Serbs were now the numerically smallest ethnic group in the area controlled by the HVO and ABH, but one which, with others who were like-minded, formed a significant nucleus for the preservation of a multiethnic Bosnia. We had his support for our ideas and actions and our efforts to hold on through the most difficult times of the war, helping us to keep hoping for the light at the end of the tunnel.

Fra Anđelić provided encouragement at crucial times. The departure of Lasić, Boras and Akmadžić from the central central organs of state, at the direction of the HDZ, had jeopardized the trust between the nations and weakened the prospects for joint management of decisions and events. Fra Anđelovic hosted a meeting to which he invited Ivo Komšić, Stjepan Kljuić and myself. He argued strongly for the inclusion of Croats in the Presidency and Government. His persistence encouraged us, and the initiative later bore fruit.

During the dramatic period of conflict between the Bosnian Army and the HVO (April 1993 – February 1994), the lives and safety of the Croats in Central Bosnia were at risk, as were the lives of the Franciscans. Fra Nikica Miličević was killed in the Franciscan monastery at Fojnica, several buildings of the Catholic Church were attacked, and the tensions everywhere rose to extreme heights. Archbishop Vinko Puljić, and Fra Petar Anđelovic sought a meeting with the Chairman and members of the Presidency. This was held in the salon customarily used to receive delegations, and for me it was one of the most difficult meetings of the war. Archbishop Puljić and Fra Petar Anđelovic demanded we act immediately to stop the catastrophic train of events throughout central Bosnia. They feared that the Bosniak-Croat conflict could lead not only to the displacement of Bosnian Croats but also to destruction of the substance of which Bosnia was made, the centuries of interethnic tolerance in these regions. But the meeting ended without any promises from the Presidency, for it would have been impossible to keep them – something I found very uncomfortable.

Together, we also faced the situation in Gornji Vakuf, which was, like Mostar, the scene of fierce military action between the ABH and the HVO. We found ourselves in the position of all wanting the same thing but being unable to achieve it. It was more than clear that the members of the Presidency, and the Presidency itself, could not essentially change the situation, and that the intervention of the church dignitaries would not have the outcome that it should. The conflict spread, gaining its own internal logic.

Fortunately the Bosniak-Croat war abated in early 1994. The international community's support, particularly the Washington Agreement, helped to end the hostilities. This agreement was the first to have the historic role of saving the concept of a multiethnic Bosnia, and became the foundation for later changes in relations among the military forces. It also served as the basis for the Dayton Peace Agreement of 1995.

An assembly of Bosnian Croats initiated the search for a solution that would end the conflict and restore the common life of Croats and Bosniaks in a unified state. The Croat National Council (HNV – *Hrvatsko narodno vijeće*) was formed in February 1994 with the support of Professor Ivo Komšić, the President of the Croat Peasant Party and a member of the Presidency. Later he became president of the HNV itself. This was a saving idea for Croats in Bosnia. It enabled the Croat nation to accept, with international support, the concept embraced by those Bosnian Croats who, by voting for the referendum on Bosnia's future, and enduring the aggression of Karadžić's forces, had chosen to live with Bosniaks and Serbs, and stayed to fight the battle for a multiethnic Bosnia, albeit at a heavy cost to themselves. The concept gained international support, and it eventually took the form of the Washington Agreement of March 1994.

In March 1994 the Bosnian Parliament was summoned to sit as a Constituent Assembly to ratify the Washington Agreement and to constitute the Federation. This assembly was held at the Holiday Inn in Sarajevo and attended by delegates of the HDZ and Herceg-Bosna officials from Mostar, including Jadranko Prlić. This was Prlić's first visit to Sarajevo since the start of the Croat-Bosniak conflict. The Bosniak delegates, those from East Mostar in particular, openly showed their disgust and impatience and pressured the chairman, Miro Lazović, to announce that certain people could not remain present during the session. This, of course, was aimed chiefly at Jadranko Prlić, who was sitting in the chamber. A highly awkward situation resulted, fuelling the disagreements and distrust. The danger loomed that the Assembly would collapse and the Croat delegates would stage a walk-out. A break was called for, and during this break Fra Petar Anđelovic came to me, very worried, and said, "Mirko, do what you can and do as much as you can. Talk to Lazović, ask him to calm things down, and stop them getting out of hand. You know just how much we have gone through to get to this moment, and to see this agreement made."

I spoke with Lazović, and we agreed that the further conduct of the Assembly must take on a different tone, to save not only the Assembly session and the passing of the Constitution, but also the Washington Agreement, from failure. Lazović, although under pressure from so many sides, acted decisively, and when the session continued contributed significantly to reducing tensions and finding the best solutions.

After this assembly I was able to travel through the areas of Bosnia controlled by the Bosnian Army, and those under the HVO. I saw how ordinary people were thankful that the conflict had stopped and the suffering was over. The entire Tuzla region had been without food for nearly a year due to the communications blockade from the direction of Croatia. I know that for many families, including that of my brother, who lived in Tuzla, the long period of conflict and the blockage of the main roads had meant severe hardship. Yet people like Archbishop Vinko Puljić and Fra Peter Anđelovic, as part of their pastoral mission, kept watch over these peoples´ lives. They supported the peace agreement, encouraged tolerance and respect between the nations of Bosnia, and spoke out in favor of the Federation.

Although I am not fully acquainted with all the findings regarding the Karađorđevo agreement, I have direct knowledge of its impact in Bosnia.[58] Let us take the fate of the Croat people in

---

[58] In March 1991 Presidents Tuđman of Croatia and Milošević of Serbia met at the former royal hunting estate of Karađorđevo. The precise details of their

Posavina following the successful JNA-assisted campaign of the Bosnian Serb forces to conquer that area. Long after the Dayton Peace Accords, Croats from Posavina still have not found justice. They were expelled from their homes and property, and this fact should never be forgotten, regardless of any compromise that may ultimately be reached. The legacy of Karađorđevo lingers beyond the Dayton Accords, as manifested by the fate of the people of Drvar. Drvar and Grahovo were places with an absolute Serb majority, and were taken without a battle: bag in hand, the people left the hearths where they had lived for centuries.[59] When we probe deeper into strategic, tactical and other trends, and the question of national interests, it is clear that their fate is the mirror image of the fate of the people of Posavina. The Croats were expelled from Posavina, never to return. The Serbs expelled from Drvar were forced to occupy Posavina, and Drvar became a zone for Croat resettlement.

I talked with one Croat family about their experiences. They were refugees from Dobrinja, the Sarajevo settlement taken by the Serb army in spring 1992. This family was invited, after the Dayton Agreement, to go to Drvar or be left homeless in Sarajevo. They chose to remain in Sarajevo, unwilling to accept the offer at any price, even the cost of being forced to leave Bosnia for a third country. This is just an illustration of how far-reaching was the legacy of Karađorđevo.

In the process of building up the Federation, and under pressure from the Federation's political sponsors, above all the US, Herceg-Bosna proved a hard nut to crack, a resilient structure that would not easily integrate into the joint institutions of the Federation. There

---

talks remain unknown, since only the two of them were present for the sbstantive discussions, but their aides and associates reported that they discussed and agreed in principle on a plan to divide Bosnia between Serbia and Croatia. They failed to reach agreement on a concrete plan of division, but they established a joint commission to work out a map. The commission likewise was unable to reach an agreement on specifics. Despite the absense of specifics, the meeting seemed to encourage each of them to pursue the division of Bosnia by supporting separatist elements among the Serbs and Croats.

[59] Early in the war Drvar and Grahovo were conquered by the HVO. Serbian residents were driven from both towns and their homes were made available to Croat refugees.

are several reasons. For one, Herceg-Bosna grew during the war into an economic giant. Its wealth had twin foundations – one, the aid from Croatia, from diasporas of the Croat nation living abroad, and income from taxes and other levies at the border crossings. The second foundation was the stimulation of private enterprises under Jadranko Prlić as Herceg-Bosna's Prime Minister. Prlić said in one interview that the economic success of Herceg-Bosna was its biggest living achievement. Prlić is a famous economic strategist and practitioner, with both knowledge and experience, and he boosted the Herceg-Bosna economy to enviable levels. Even under the socialist system he had excelled in the management of economic affairs.

But the main reason why it was hard to crush Herceg-Bosna was the lack of any final resolution of the Bosnian question. Would this take the form of ethnic partition, temporary division, or the permanent secession of the Serb and Croat territories? The fate of Herceg-Bosna is to stay forever in step with the Serbian entity and mimic its regime. It embodies the fear felt by the Croat nation, or by a major part of the Croat nation, especially the population now living on the border with Croatia. This nation is a demographic minority among the national groups in Bosnia, and its members fear that they will become, in time, vulnerable to assimilation, forced to struggle to preserve their national, cultural and religious identity. Part of this fear is the awareness of all that the Croats of West Herzegovina suffered after the Second World War, in the time of communist rule, from revanchism and sectarianism. This fear is especially deep-rooted wherever Bosnian Croats live in a de facto enclave encircled by a different nationality.

Insufficient account is taken of these fears. In 1997 Izetbegović received the Award of the American Institute for Democracy in Washington, and in his speech of thanks he did mention the importance of resolving relations between majorities and minorities as vital for the development of democracy. The Croats in Bosnia and Herzegovina had the right to seek a solution, as an equal, constituent nation, but demographically the least numerous. They therefore had the right to ask how their ethnic groups in the municipalities and cantons would be enabled to build separate cultural, educational and religious institutions, to preserve the ethic uniqueness of the Croat people in the areas of language, faith, and information. The feeling of insecurity will further force the Croat nation to seek a radical solution, although it is unclear what the winning concept will be. Some hard-liners in the HDZ favor advancing the idea of Herceg-Bosna, while others share the hopes of the central Bosnian Croats, the refugees from Posavina, the Tuzla Croats, the Catholic Church, and the Croat Cultural Society *Napredak*. These hopes are of fostering and preserving their identity while upholding their differences, and at the same time fully respecting all the values of common life.

In a wartime interview with the Croatian daily *Slobodna Dalmacija*, I noted that *Napredak* sponsored the highest number of cultural exhibitions, displays, and demonstrations in Sarajevo of any of the national cultural societies during the war. If this factor alone were used in making an assessment, it could be said that the Croats were the majority nation in Sarajevo. Thus, numbers are not directly the problem. The issue is more one of attitude - for example whether institutions can become tolerant enough to uphold differences while ensuring mutual respect. The Croat nation wants Catholic schools, where special care would be taken regarding use of the Croat language and the preservation of Croat national identity. This should not be forbidden, either in mono-national or in mixed areas. Let us take the example of the Catholic school center in Sarajevo. This institution has in no way jeopardized the state school system, nor the education and upbringing of young people generally. On the contrary, many people of Bosniak and Serb nationality have chosen to educate their children in this school. *Napredak* and other cultural institutions, along with the media, have protected the language and linguistic culture generally and fostered the identity of the nation. Given that this nation is demographically the smallest in relation to the other two peoples of Bosnia, such activity should be encouraged and protected by the whole society.

It is not only the Croat ethnic community in Bosnia that faces this challenge. The protection and development of Croat cultural identity in Bosnia will test the strength of tolerance in this country, the equality of the peoples and their potential for coexistence and cooperation. Finally, modern democracy requires of Bosnia a model for protecting and developing minority rights, demonstrated by the state's attitudes towards Jews, Roma, and other nationalities living in Bosnia.

In spring and summer 1995 I stayed in Mostar, where I visited Mr. Koschnik and his colleagues at the European Union office in West Mostar.[60] I also visited the headquarters of Herceg-Bosna. Here I talked with Krešimir Zubak, then chairman of the Herceg-Bosna Council - my first meeting with the officials of Herceg-Bosna. Zubak and I were together for half an hour, discussing the basics of achieving peace in Bosnia, for at this point the Dayton peace proposal was nearing acceptance. The balance of military power in Bosnia had changed, and the Contact Group Plan was circulating. Zubak expressed support for the efforts of those Serbs who remained to live in the Federation to find a peaceful political solution that would enable the prosperity of all nations and peoples. We discussed the possibility of activating the Serb Civil Council on the territory of Herceg-Bosna. Zubak suggested that a letter, sent to the government of Herceg-Bosna, containing our request together with the basic programs and status of the Council would receive a positive response – which it did. But, beyond the formation of small founding committees, we could not succeed in developing the activities of the SGV in Herceg-Bosna territory. I talked to some people I knew in West Mostar who wanted to work for the SGV: but when the time came to act publicly, they gave up the attempt, for everybody feared to attract public attention. There was no development of the democratic process and no effort to create an atmosphere in which people could speak and act freely, regardless of nationality, without fear of threats or persecution.

I had many more talks with Zubak, including later when he became President of the Federation and member of the post-Dayton three-man Bosnian Presidency. Zubak was a man always ready to hear other opinions. Arguments could be exchanged with him on the basis of tolerance and equality. In my view he has the qualities of a born Bosnian: a feeling for both the different and the common elements in the interests of all three nations. He was born in a typically Bosnian area, in Doboj, and rose to leadership not only by virtue of his HDZ membership but also as a consequence of his

---

[60] After the Washington Agreements of March 1994 the administration of Mostar, which had been the scene of bitter fighting between the HVO and ABH, was turned over to the European Union. Hans Koschnik, former Mayor of Bremen, Germany, was made the chief administrator, a position he held until 1997.

own soldiership. He is a genuinely Bosnian leader as well as a leader of the Bosnian Croats. Carrying his own experience into his political activities, Zubak diligently protected and promoted the interests and identity of his nation, showing a well-developed feeling for the preservation and growth of common life among the peoples of Bosnia. He also showed a strong sense of commitment to building consensus between the nations that live in this land together and should share a common destiny.

## XI. THE FATE OF SERBS IN THE CITIES

The cities of Bosnia, especially the larger centers such as Sarajevo, Tuzla, Mostar, and Zenica, had substantial Serb populations before the war. In Sarajevo, according to the 1991 census, lived around 150,000 Serbs, and several dozens of thousands who called themselves Yugoslavs but had ethnic Serb origins – the largest single population of Serbs outside Serbia.[61] In Tuzla, Mostar and Zenica were between 20,000 and 30,000 Serbs.[62] Other towns also had Serbs populations in the thousands – take Bugojno, which had almost 9,000.[63] This part of the Serb nation in Bosnia was, due to its educational and social structure, strong in academic and technical qualifications. Many had high school and university degrees in engineering and technology, and a good number held advanced academic degrees.

Apart from the towns of Banja Luka, Trebinje, Bijeljina, Prijedor and Zvornik, now in the Serb entity, the majority of the Serb intelligentsia were located in the major industrial centers: Sarajevo,

---

[61] Of Sarajevo's 527,049 residents, 157,143 (29.8%) declared themselves Serbs in the 1991 census. Another 56,470 (10.7%) declared themselves "Yugoslavs." *Stanovništvo Bosne i Hercegovine* (Zagreb: Državni zavod za statistiku, 1995), p. 15.

[62] In Tuzla, 20,271 (15.4%) of respondents declared themselves Serbs in 1991 and 21,995 (16.7%) declared themselves Yugoslavs. In Mostar, 23,846 (18.8%) declared themselves Serbs and 12,768 (10.1%) declared themselves Yugoslavs. In Zenica, 22,433 (15.4%) declared themselves Serbs and 15,654 (10.8%) declared themselves Yugoslavs. *Ibid.*, pp. 20, 22, and 23.

[63] Bugojno's population of 46,889 in 1991 included 8,673 (18.5%) Serbs and 1,561 (3.3%) Yugoslavs. *Ibid.*, p. 17.

Mostar, Zenica, Tuzla, Travnik, Konjic, Bugojno. In the 1990 multiparty elections, these Bosnian Serbs voted overwhelmingly for the civil democratic parties: the coalition of the SDP and the DSS, the Reformists, and the Liberals, as shown by an analysis of the voting in urban centers. For example, in Brčko, Mostar, Zenica and Sarajevo, a high percentage of democratic civic coalitions stood in the elections. In Tuzla in 1990, the local government was taken over by such a bloc. This part of the Serb ethnic body was not nationalist: national ideologies did not prevail in the group consciousness, nor was national homogenization favored. This fact became evident in the first days of the aggression against Bosnia, especially when the shelling of Sarajevo began. Most Serbs stayed in the city, despite calls from the SDS to leave, summons sent first to its own members and then to all Serb citizens.

Nor did Serbs leave the cities in large numbers in the first months of the war. At the end of April and beginning of May 1992, my neighbors and I often talked about the troubling situation, for Sarajevo was already under bombardment. Rizo Selmanagić, an antifascist from the Second World War, said, "You know, the real beginning of Karadžić's political defeat lies in the fact that all Serbs did not leave the city in a body, the moment the attack started. Karadžić counted on their leaving Sarajevo. But while we are still living together with Serbs, we will be able to cope psychologically with all pressures, all the suffering, all the attacks." At the time I did not see any special significance in what he said, but as the war drew on, this theory from an old antifascist was confirmed over and over, until the moment came for resolving the status of Sarajevo, at the Dayton peace talks in November 1995.

After the peace agreement was signed, and Sarajevo's unity and integrity was assured, Karadžić did everything he could to persuade the Serbs living in the suburbs to migrate from the region at the start of 1996.[64] This stemmed from his refusal to acknowledge

---

[64] In the days before several BSA-occupied Sarajevo suburbs were to be turned over to Federation control, Serb gangs terrorized its Serb residents and burned many buildings in a drive to force all Serbs to leave these neighborhoods. The gang terror proceeded unimpeded by NATO troops of the international peacekeeping Implementation Force (IFOR), who were ordered not to interfere. US Ambassador Richard Holbrooke has called this episode his "worst moment" in the post-war history of Bosnia.

the defeat of his policy of ethnic separatism, and the creation of ethnically pure territories. He had launched this policy by seeking to destroy major cities, with the heavy artillery donated by the JNA. This policy hideously violated all possible human rights, and took a heavy toll of human lives, especially in those cities that were exposed to constant shelling. Sarajevo, which was continuously besieged and bombarded, takes the first place, followed by Mostar, Gradačac, Olovo, Konjic and other towns.

What the Serbs underwent in those days and places is hard to compare with any previously recorded experience. In spite of the attacks on the cities, many Serbs decided of their own accord, and as Bosnian citizens, to continue living together with Bosniaks and Croats, accepting the idea of a unified and internationally acknowledged state. They stayed to live through the worst of wartime conditions, exposed to all the horrors that the Bosniaks and Croats were facing. But the BSA´s destruction of the towns and slaughter of the residents placed the Serbs in an especially harsh position. First, all people who lived in cities such as Sarajevo, regardless of their nationality, suffered *en masse* as they endured bombardment and siege. Life was endangered at every step, and the basic necessities - water, electricity, gas, and food - were cut off by the siege. But along with the deprivations suffered by all civilians, the Serbs had to live with an extra fear. This was the growing distrust of Serbs among certain other elements of the population, arising from the general terror and revulsion against the acts of the besieging Serb artillery and army.

Serb citizens found themselves exposed to a kind of elemental force in the early months of the aggression against Bosnia. This was the time when local units of military police and military defense were forming independently and autonomously. Due to the lack of communication and the constant attacks, there was no proper coordination by any command structure. Thus local units in the cities of Sarajevo, Mostar, Konjic, Travnik, Zenica, and elsewhere took it on themselves to decide independently what course to pursue with local Serbs.

This first became manifest during the searches for possession of arms. Such checks were a military necessity for planning and organizing defense from quarter to quarter, and preventing internal support for the military campaign launched from the surrounding hills and fortresses. In other words, the aim was to prevent the military strength of Karadžić's army from receiving the help of sympathizers within the city. But the weapons checks were an opportunity for Bosniak and Croat extremists to do their worst. People who were for the most part entirely innocent, civilians and patriots of Bosnia, were subjected to hostile investigations, and many were beaten. Ordinary people owning nothing but hunting weapons had these confiscated, partly due to the general paranoia, and partly due to the military units' need for weapons. During these checks, people who possessed weapons but were unable to give satisfactory information about their origins were immediately suspected of supporting the SDS. They were consequently liable to interrogation and temporary detention in the local prisons. Hundreds paid with their lives in Sarajevo, Stolac, Konjic, Čapljina, Bugojno, Mostar and other cities. These crimes should figure one day as part of an investigation into the criminal and moral responsibility for the deaths of civilians in Bosnia.

Conditions were especially harsh in Sarajevo. In April, May, and June 1992 until the end of the summer, the pressures intensified, and the checking, the questioning, and the uncertainty grew. It lessened as time passed, and the restructuring and consolidation of the Bosnian Army and Ministry of the Interior enabled a stable and organized armed force to be built. (See Chapter VIII) But before I joined the Presidency, in the raw atmosphere of suspicion created by the destruction and aggression, an organized search of the apartments of all Sarajevo Serbs was carried out. Special attention was paid to possession of arms, regardless of caliber, and whether they were short or long barreled. The problem was that many Serbs had a large collection of arms from before the war, especially pistols and hunting weapons. Some Serbs who were sympathizers or members of the SDS had received such weapons from the party in February and March 1992, and kept them in their homes. This practice was particularly widespread in the suburban areas. SDS activists distributed the arms, claiming they were needed for defense since mass slaughter of Serbs was about to begin. Whether voluntarily or under pressure, many people had taken the weapons.

When the shelling of Sarajevo began, several quarters of Sarajevo were reduced to rubble, especially Marjindvor, and the destruction put added pressure on the newly formed Territorial Defense units.

These had to decide what to do about people who had large numbers of weapons. It is hard to say how professionally they acted in these searches, made with the aim of establishing the numbers of these weapons, confiscating them, and of course prosecuting any crime the possession of arms might be supposed to signify. People were taken away for interrogation to the local prisons, and never came back. Such cases, of which there were hundreds, are a stain on Sarajevo. Of the extent to which arms were possessed, we have the testimony of the numerous statements made in interviews and articles by the local and city-level commanders. Kerim Lučarević, better known from the war by his pseudonym of "Doctor," commander of the special unit of the military police, gave an interview to *Oslobođenje* on the first of April 1997 in which he claimed that around 20,000 weapons were found, and around 6,000 criminal charges were filed against those possessing them.

I myself had my apartment in Breka searched in a general weapons check. I possessed two pistols, one belonging to my wife Spomenka, and the other registered in my own name. I handed over the registration documents, all of which were in order. The weapons were taken and returned after confirmation. Teams of the newly recruited military police carried out the verification of registration documents. Weapons checks were much briefer in Bosniak homes, and carried out with less rummaging and less suspicion. Such discrimination was part of the general atmosphere. In April, May and June 1992, while the chaos persisted, and prior to consolidation of the Territorial Defense Forces, units of the Ministry of the Interior continued the search for the guilty, for members of the SDS, for people who possessed arms, for those who were seen as having behaved "provocatively" in some way. Suspects were arrested indiscriminately and taken away for so-called "informative talks," especially eminent Serbs with public influence.

On one occasion during the war, a man spent a long time begging me to see him, in order to confess his part in an action undertaken in the first month of the war for my own forcible removal. As both a Serb and a public functionary, I was myself a target, in this dark time of universal distrust. When this man was about to lead his fellows on their mission, one of my neighbors, a Bosniak, stopped them. My neighbor told them not to make the attempt, warning that to do so would be a grave error, and might arouse the neighborhood against them. The affair was given up, but this man now felt the bite of his conscience and wanted to confess. He begged me to give him "halal" (absolution). I forgave him, but this episode is yet another to place in the context of the events from that time, and their consequences.

In one particularly dramatic episode, already referred to, Zoran Cegar, a member of the police Special Unit, decided with his colleagues to use their powers to march a group of Serbs to the Koševo stadium and hold them there. Cegar, attempting by this gesture to prevent the arrest and murder of his relatives in Grbavica suburb, by Karadžić's forces, aroused a general panic that could have led total chaos. Had he not been stopped by an action involving Izetbegović himself, it would have meant the end of Serb life in Sarajevo, and the end of any possibility of preserving coexistence and trust.

I myself was in the Presidency at the time, together with Kecmanović, and I asked Interior Minister Jusuf Pušina to act immediately. We organised a meeting in my office with a number of well-known Serbs. President Izetbegović himself attended, at our request. Several former soldiers from the Second World War were present: Braco Kosovac, Veljo Droca, Savo Čečur, and others. It was a difficult meeting for all of us, especially for Izetbegović as President of the Presidency. The meeting resulted in decisive measures to halt the action taken by Čegar, and to ensure that nothing of the kind would ever be repeated. Pušina and President Izetbegović played a considerable part in this effort, and Čegar was stopped. However this example showed the lawlessness of the individuals in the police or military and how readily this suspicion could develop into revanchism, the persecution of ordinary people, and the annihilation of their trust in the legal government.

Čegar claimed that all the Serbs arrested in his action were officially listed as suspects, that they possessed weapons and were members of the SDS, or that members of their families were Karadžić supporters and therefore fifth columnists. His claim could perhaps be proven by documentation, but it is well known that the lists drawn up at the time were lists of all Serbs, and that the arms checks and apartment searches were measures carried out against all Serbs. If there was a list, then all Serbs were potentially on it. But people like those who took part in the meeting at the Presidency were certainly not fifth columnists. They could not in any way be suspected of having concealed arms nor of having received them from the SDS. Zoran Čegar's claim, therefore, is in itself evidence that this was a time of chaos and paranoia in which more or less every Serb was seen as a potential traitor. This was one of the worst of times, not only for Serbs but also for the city of Sarajevo, and the future of Bosnia.

Dr. Zlatko Vuković from Mostar was a well-known specialist doctor in the University Clinical Center in Sarajevo. He was of mixed parentage: his father was a Bosniak and his mother a Croat. He has described how he was jailed, searched and interrogated at length, until it became clear there was nothing at all that could serve as evidence for an accusation against him. One of his interrogators then demanded, "Well, why didn't you say you weren't a Serb?" Zlatko answered, "You know, you never told me you were jailing me just because you thought I was a Serb."

Once we joined the Presidency, in June 1992, Kecmanović and I had to open our doors several times a day to family members and group representatives from various suburbs, who came to seek interviews and, usually, help. They used to wait patiently for hours for us to finish work or meetings, until finally, late in the evening, we were free. This was during one of the darkest periods of the war. Many people died daily from shells and sniping, while others were dragged away to the local prisons. Families came in terror to seek help and information, which we did not possess. We did what we could, but we realized that trying to intervene day after day in individual cases meant running in a closed circle without hope. We sought information at the sessions of the Presidency, from the staff of the Territorial Defense, and from the police. Hardly a day was free from the bitterness of the troubles we had to listen to, investigate, and become involved in.

A supreme example is the fate of the family of Dr. Trifko Guzina, the distinguished urologist from the University Clinical Center in Sarajevo, who helped many people of Sarajevo and from all over Bosnia. One day his wife, from Dalmatia by origin and an intelligent and determined woman, came to our office and refused to leave until she knew what had happened to her husband, who had been arrested at their home in Ciglane. She was prepared to spend the night in our office if necessary, just to get news of him. We did what we could to find where Dr. Guzina was, and what had become of him. Some time before dawn the next day, Ismet Bajramović Ćelo, already mentioned as a commander of the military police, who always gave his wholehearted help whenever Kecmanovic and I sought it, brought Dr. Guzina to my office. Dr. Guzina was exhausted, lost and confused. He told us he had spent a hideous night in prison at the Hotel Zagreb, where he and others had been tortured, and had been forced to listen to traditional Ustasha songs, then sing the songs for their tormentors.

Kecmanović and I began asking what the purpose of this prison was and who controlled it. The prison soon vanished, purely because we had started asking these questions. According to those who could have answered, this prison was managed by the Croatian Defense League (HOS - *Hrvatske obranbene snage*).[65] It was intended for notable Serb intellectuals, particularly those in any way connected to the SDS. Guzina himself had been on the SDS advisory board, but he was capable of objectively criticizing his party. He subsequently took part in founding the Forum of Citizens of Serb Nationality in Sarajevo, in June 1992.

Dr. Guzina, on his release from prison, tried to continue his work at the clinic and his activities in the Forum. One afternoon, however, his wife came again to beg my help. She said that Dr. Guzina was wracked by fears, whether at the clinic or at home, and simply did not know any more what to do. She asked if he could be helped to leave Sarajevo, for, in her opinion, he had lost all trust in himself and others. When I talked with her husband I tried to convince him to stay. However, his fear was stronger than any persuasion. He openly told me, in my office, that he feared to be killed and that he had in some way been forewarned. Neither I nor anybody else could free him of this fear, and he left.

Another time, I was approached by Professor Vojo Magazinović, Pro-Rector of the University of Sarajevo in my student days, and a

---

[65] HOS was a paramilitary force of the Croatian Party of Right headed by Dobroslav Paraga. It operated both in Croatia and in Bosnia. In August 1992, after the events described here, HOS Chief of Staff Ante Brkaćin agreed with Mate Boban formally to disband HOS units and integrate some of them into the ranks of the HVO. James Gow, "One Year of War in Bosnia and Herzegovina," *RFE/RL Research Report*, Vol. 2, no. 23 (4 June 1993), p. 3.

well-regarded member of the Veterinary Faculty. Of him it could reliably be said that he was not an SDS sympathizer and had never engaged in any of its activities. He now came to me, furious and visibly distraught, to demand that I help him visit his son in law, Bobar, in prison at the Viktor Bubanj barracks. With the Professor present, I tried to arrange this, but immediately ran into difficulties. Professor Magazinović noticed, and asked contemptuously, "What kind of government is this, if it doesn't even have the power to allow those who are thrown into jail under any kind of suspicion, to receive visits, packages, blankets, or letters from their families? Even the infamous Ustasha government in the last war, which I can still remember, provided that service." Not guilty myself, I had to endure the Professor's anger and his comparisons, which I found difficult to take. Nevertheless, because of my presidential office, he had the right to demand answers from me. I finally succeeded in ensuring his request was met, but this was for me a depressing encounter.

Not all the people who wished for or needed our help came to us. Some could not come at all. Those who did come received our aid, and after Kecmanović left Sarajevo they still had mine. For me there were plenty of hard moments, full of bitterness. I lost count of the number of times I tried to raise these problems in the Presidency, with the security organizations, and the various bodies of the Territorial Defense, and, later, with the Army. But apart from solving cases by individual intervention, there was no overall solution for these issues, and no kind of system to address them. The problems abated only after the Presidency established a system for military prosecution, a system of organized command within the military and the police, legislation to regulate criminal prosecution, and criminal legislation for wartime. These efforts gradually created a more satisfactory situation for all people, regardless of nationality, but for Serbs in particular.

I was deeply preoccupied by the need for a security system to protect people as citizens, regardless of nationality, so that the principles of the rule of law and respect for human rights could be equally applied. We struggled hard to put an end to the distrust aroused against Serbs by the daily shelling of Sarajevo. Serbs from the hills around were busy slaughtering their fellow Serbs along with the rest of the citizens: of the 12 500 civilians killed in Sarajevo, a high percentage were Serbs.

Early one morning I heard how the murdered body of Professor Milutin Najdanović had been found. I tried to gather all possible information that same day, but could only establish that he had been shot. I was unable to learn exactly what had happened, or who the killer was. Professor Najdanović had been a member of the SDS and a delegate in the Bosnian Parliament, but he was also a well known professor and doctor in the University Clinical Center. He had chosen to stay in Sarajevo, in spite of his party's call for the departure of all Serb citizens, SDS members and sympathizers above all. He had never consented to the use of force to resolve relations between the nations of Bosnia. To this day, nothing further about his murder has ever come to light. His rejection of the SDS, of which he had so recently been a member, inspired me to announce publicly both the fact of his murder and my condemnation of it, in the name of the Presidency. I appealed for an end to all such acts, warning that they endangered the fragile thread of interethnic trust between the city's Serbs, Bosniaks and Croats.

Several days later, a man came to tell me, confidentially, that my condemnation of Najdanović's killing had aroused negative reactions among part of the population of Sarajevo, in particular those originally from Eastern Bosnia, whose relatives there had been expelled or slaughtered.[66] This was not unknown to me. However, another man, a Partisan and antifascist from the Second World War, of Serb nationality, also urged me to think very carefully about my reaction to such events. But I still felt that we needed not only to prevent this kind of occurrence, but also gradually to rebuild trust among the remaining Serbs, the Bosniaks, and the Croats – especially while the Serb forces surrounding us were killing a dozen or more people every day, and spared no one. Of course, I thought hard about this well-intentioned suggestion, and worked more on building security establishments inside the police and army. The warning that I had received did not become the dominant influence on my actions, although it did remind me that sudden death could happen to me also. But I could not be afraid, since I passed through shelling every

---

[66] Large numbers of Bosniaks, driven from their homes in Eastern Bosnia by paramilitary forces loyal to the SDS, fled as refugees to Sarajevo and other cities under the control of the ABH. Some estimates place the number of such refugees in Sarajevo alone at around 100,000 persons.

day, and the boundary between life and death was thin. I remained convinced that none of the Serbs who now remained in Sarajevo and participated in public life and in government could solve these problems, or change the state of distrust, by politicizing the situation.

There was criticism of the method we chose. Sometimes these criticisms, implicit in the Sarajevo media, but open in the media of Pale, reached the point of saying that we Serbs who held office were passing over the killing of fellow Serbs in silence, while failing to take sufficient measures to prevent their murder. But it cannot be said that the legal government deliberately allowed this to happen. On the contrary, step by step, the government was consolidating the much-needed security establishment within the military.

Gradually, Serbs regained some confidence in the government. Matters were aggravated, however, by events in the battlefields of Eastern Bosnia. Whenever offensives were launched against Goražde or Žepa, tensions rose in Sarajevo.[67] Echoes of the onslaught could be heard among people of Žepa living in Sarajevo, who muttered that if the worst happened to their families in Žepa, they would retaliate in Sarajevo. They made no effort to conceal either their fears or their threats. One evening in autumn 1992 I returned home late to my Breka apartment. There was no electricity, and I was sleepy. I was roused by security colleagues, who told me I must immediately receive a delegation from the Citizens of Žepa Association, as a matter of urgency. I let the Association's representatives into my apartment, and we talked by candlelight. The interview was conducted in a reasonably civil and tolerant spirit. They asked me to do something to turn aside the danger now threatening the people of Žepa: I told them that the possibilities were few, but I promised an attempt would be made.

This attempt consisted of a joint letter from Miodrag Simović and myself to the President of Yugoslavia, Dobrica Ćosić. We begged him to prevent the ultimate disaster and halt the offensive against

---

[67] The Eastern Bosnian towns of Goražde and Žepa were surrounded early in the war by BSA forces and remained under siege for over three years. Their populations of Bosniaks were swelled by other Bosniaks who fled as refugees from nearby villages and towns, and both were the targeted for regular shelling and occasional ground probes by the BSA. Žepa was taken by the BSA in July 1995 a few days after Srebrenica; Goražde was never conquered.

Žepa, warning that this could result in serious consequences for Serbs in Sarajevo. How much psychological effect this letter had in calming down the leaders of the Citizens of Žepa Association, I don't know. They were under extreme pressure from the men from Žepa, who had joined army units in Sarajevo, and were now tormented by fear for their relatives in their home town. But our approach was sharply criticized by several Sarajevo Serbs, who felt that we had only increased the tensions. Overall, this episode is a good indicator of the atmosphere of the time, and the mounting fear that the Bosniaks were feeling for their own security.

Some days after my nighttime session with the people of Žepa, I was told they had originally contacted Sefer Halilović and Izetbegović before approaching me, and had told Halilović, "If the people of Žepa suffer, we will make the Serbs in Sarajevo pay, starting with Pejanović." Sefer told them categorically that they neither could nor should even contemplate such an option, and criticized them severely for having allowed themselves to even talk in such a way. He thus succeeded in preventing them from spreading this mood through the army. But some people in the žepa Association later tried this kind of argument again - that any action by the Serb forces in Žepa would produce a reaction against Serbs in Sarajevo. We were thus perpetually on the verge of some new outbreak or fresh tragedy.

Something of this kind may have been hanging over our heads during the harsh offensives of the BSA against Goražde in 1993 and 1994. A big rally was held on behalf of Goražde in Tito Street, at the Eternal Flame. Among the many who spoke was Radoslav Marjanović, Secretary of the Serb Civic Council, who expressed sympathy with the people of Goražde and support for their heroic efforts to defend their families, their city, and their country. Then, in response to an appeal I had made earlier, President Izetbegović made a statement that proved decisive in reducing the hostility toward Sarajevo Serbs, who by then were living in fear, often staying away from their own homes in the evening hours. He said, "Those Serbs who live with us and fight alongside us are our fellow soldiers. They too seek to protect us from the monster which kills civilians and is destroying all that lies before it."

The early months of the war brought chaos to Sarajevo, and devastated individual lives. One day I received a call from Fatima

Bambur, who worked in the field of humanitarian action and information. She had a message from Marko Pržulj, who had been imprisoned with his young son in the Kruskin jail in Ali Pasina Polje. I knew them from before the war: Marko owned the "Holiday Inn" restaurant in Džemal Bijedić Street. I did everything in my power to get Marko and his boy released. When they were freed, two days later, I went to his house with some colleagues. Numerous Bosniak neighbors had gathered in the house to welcome him back to the neighborhood. But Marko's family was clearly traumatized. The house had been looted and the flooring taken up in a search for either money or weapons - an ugly sight. Marko told me that while he was in jail, undergoing an agony of fear and uncertainty on behalf of the child who was with him, a foreign journalist had visited the prison with Fatima Bambur. Fatima asked Marko whom she could call on his behalf, to get help, and he told her to call Mirko Pejanović in the Presidency.

After this experience, Marko lost all desire to live in Sarajevo. He soon left, but not to join those of his fellow-nationals who were destroying Sarajevo and killing his neighbors. Instead he went to Germany, where he continued in his profession as a restaurateur.

Even after those first months of chaos, and after the maverick campaigns of local commanders had been restricted by the imposition of a regulated command structure, a number remained arrogant and overbearing as a result of their earlier independence, heedless of the principles of military discipline. The best known of these commanders was Mušan Topalović Caco, who led the Old Town army units. There was too much of a tendency to compromise with these men, too much fear that bloodshed and chaos would result from any organized action against them. President Izetbegović in particular seemed to feel this fear, and in my view he was responsible for the policy of compromise and waiting. All attempts to solve the problem were nothing but one step forward, two steps back. I used the pressure placed on me by the civic opposition parties and the people themselves to take a public position on this issue in the Committee for the Protection of the Constitutional Order. This helped create a climate less conducive to compromise with the outlaw commanders.

At last an action was decided on and executed in October 1993. Caco was removed from the scene and Ramiz Delalić and others brought to justice.[68] All citizens of Sarajevo breathed a sigh of relief, especially the Serbs, who dreaded even their own shadows in the general terror of Caco's heyday.

Viewed objectively and with the benefit of hindsight, the lawless abuse of individuals by Caco and his cronies did great damage to Sarajevo's internal defense. In particular, these abuses increased Serb motives for departure and lowered their ability to endure the hell that Sarajevo had become. Many Serbs fled solely from fear of Caco's persecution. The local prisons, initially under the authority of the local commanders, were scattered about the city, but arrests and beatings were particularly frequent in the area run by Caco's Tenth Hill Brigade. There are different estimates of the numbers killed by this unit, whose commander was finally arrested during the process of consolidating the Bosnian Army and - according to the official version - killed while attempting to escape.

Just how many Serbs were murdered by these renegade local commanders, backed up by equally renegade local authorities, who took it on themselves to deal out their own particular brand of justice? The number of deaths can only be roughly estimated, and estimates vary. From the available data, it appears that a larger number of Serbs were killed than the government will admit. The number of Serbs who died from all causes in Sarajevo has never yet been verified by research, and so all state and international organizations responsible for investigating the numbers of civil victims in Bosnia remain obliged to finally establish the figure. No one made or kept a complete database. In the first months of the siege and bombardment, shells and snipers killed civilians of all nationalities, including a significant number of Serbs. More were killed trying to escape the city; others died from torture and abuse in the infamous local prisons. A number of the killed were registered simply as missing. Many of those who were illegally arrested and compelled to dig trenches also perished, and many more died as the consequence of Karadžić's mass slaughter of Sarajevo's civilians. The findings of the official state investigation into war crimes in Kazani - suspended for reasons unexplained to this day – simply offer further illustration of the suffering of Serbs in Sarajevo.

---

[68] Topalović was killed in this raid. Delalić, who had acquired notoriety as a criminal apparently immune from prosecution, was arrested and later released.

The many statements and appeals made by family members of the killed confirm that such murders took place in several parts of the city. These appeals started coming in after the first long ceasefire in 1994 and multiplied after the announcement of the Dayton Peace Agreement in late 1995. Families came to beg my help, for in wartime it had not been possible to carry out post-mortem exhumations of their loved ones. Most had been victims of Caco's and Juka's banditry. All their families knew was the little they had heard or been told during the war. Their appeals proved slow to process, with many still remaining to be solved.

During the war we did not publicize this issue in the ways that some Sarajevo Serbs expected of us, especially those who were more nationalist in feeling. We did, however, warn the Envoy for Human Rights to the UN Secretary General, Tadeusz Mazowiecki, and his colleagues, by way of a delegation sent in 1994. But the final responsibility for these deaths has yet to be established. During the trial held after the actions launched against Caco and Delalić, there was deliberate avoidance of giving any legal qualification to these crimes against civilians that would enable them to be classified as war crimes.

While we were debating how to react, the Bosniaks were suffering mass slaughter in Žepa, Goražde, and Srebrenica. Politicizing the Sarajevo murders during this time would have been counterproductive, and damaging to the Serbs of Sarajevo. I myself, and all of us who represented the civic opposition in public and social life, followed the policy of focusing primarily on the principal cause of evil, the destruction of Sarajevo and other communities by Karadžić's army. Our actions were dominated by our view that creation of a firm government and proper defense and judiciary systems would ensure the equal rights of all citizens to protection. Our policy ensured that direct help would be offered to all people whose civil rights were in any way violated. We tried to encourage all subjects of the state to prevent the violation of citizens' rights. We made it our priority to prevent the primary cause – the shelling of Sarajevo – from resulting in a double danger, both from the hilltops, and from inside the city. This was a policy of patient drudgery, of refusing to pour oil on fire, a policy based on trust in the idea of common life and the return of interethnic confidence.

Our refusal to radicalize this issue drew plenty of protests, often made to me personally. We were asked why we did not act as HDZ leader Miro Lasić did when Josip Gogalo was murdered in Sarajevo. I do not dispute Miro Lasić's action, but he was merely visiting Sarajevo as a political tourist in wartime, to spend a few months in the Presidency before leaving to take up high diplomatic office in the Republic of Croatia. His Zagreb life was secure: Sarajevo was for him a hastily turned page. The failure of leading Croats (Komšić and Kljuić being the exceptions) to take political responsibility and participate in the highest organs of the state government must be examined in the context of the vital need to establish and preserve trust between the Croats and other nations. We Serbs who remained in the wartime government believed, and still believe, that those who wanted to preserve the values of life together must endure trouble together and together build a civilized foundation for normal life. This belief and practice played a significant role in the preservation of a multiethnic Sarajevo, and in achieving a peaceful solution for Bosnia.

I am not excluding the possibility of further criticism. Wartimes are hard times, in which mistakes once made cannot be mended. History will decide whether more could have been done, and done better. But we tried as hard as we could to act responsibly for the human rights of Serbs as citizens, and did what we could to build an establishment that would enable the security and protection of all people, regardless of nation and faith.

Of course, all these questions were the topic of propaganda. The Pale propaganda machine claimed in the war that Bosniaks killed 20,000 Serbs during preliminary "ground-clearance" at the start of the war. This fantastically high figure betrays itself, but it was used to manipulate the public and distract attention from the crimes already committed by the Serb forces in other parts of Bosnia.

The reckless campaigns of local commanders, the shelling, the hunger and cold all added to the strong pressures to leave Sarajevo. Convoys of departees were organized three times during the war. Many invalids left in hopes of joining their families, and were accompanied by a number of people who just wanted to put an end to their sufferings in Sarajevo. A smaller number made deliberate use of certificates of illness in order to leave the city and join the nationalists then so enthusiastically engaged in bringing about national homogenization. I myself took part in organizing convoys but from exclusively humanitarian motives, to help people survive, to go where they could find more tolerable conditions. A number of Sarajevo Serbs left in the convoys, and thus the total number of Serbs in the capital was diminished. But their departure was the work of war. The majority of those Serbs who left in the convoys supported the concept of common life. When peace came, many returned to knock on the government's doors, to ask for the return of their residential rights, and to continue their lives in the city.

When Ejup Ganić declared that Serbs were "collectively guilty" for the war against Bosnia, with all its tragic consequences, his statement was, in my opinion, careless rather than deliberate. But it automatically increased Serb fears of yet another load to bear. This added to the suspicion and paranoia already aroused by Karadžić's forces and stirred up the public mood. Tanja Ljujić-Mijatović, the second Serb member of the Presidency, and I, issued a joint statement the day after Ganić's proclamation, in hopes of calming the situation. We focused on the issue of responsibility and stressed that there is always an individual, party, group or movement responsible for a crime, but never a whole nation.

We affirmed our position that the condemnation of crimes committed by the Serb nation was, above all, a moral issue. In our view, crime always has its specific birthplace, a name and surname, a perpetrator. But to turn criminal responsibility into a collective category, on the level of an entire nation, would have provoked displays of intolerance toward Serbs who had remained to live in community with the other nations, in common suffering and hardship. It would have meant an end to common life in Bosnia. It would also have enabled those directly responsible for war crimes to shelter behind the formula of collective guilt, while individual responsibility for crime would have disappeared. We affirmed that these same principles should apply to crimes committed by members of the other nationalities of Bosnia.

Ganić took our statement badly, but he made no public reaction. This helped prevent the theory of collective guilt from spreading too widely, although it found a voice from time to time in the pro-Bosniak publication *Ljiljan* and in various public gatherings.

The situation of Serbs in the cities, and their fate, deserves special attention, since considerable numbers of Serbs remained in the cities from the outbreak of war until mid-1993, refusing to accept the SDS policy of destroying urban centers. During the hardest times, therefore, they stood for the historic traditions in Bosnia of mutual respect and common life. Serbs and their Bosniak and Croat neighbors have endured and created much together – as witnessed by this country's significant percentage of nationally mixed marriages, 30% in Sarajevo, and nearly as high in Tuzla, Mostar, and elsewhere.

But what is known must be told. Serbs suffered severely in Mostar, Čapljina and the Neretva valley, including Konjic, as did their material goods, cultural monuments, and religious buildings. This persecution followed the JNA attack on these towns. The JNA shelling of Mostar and Konjic evoked an outpouring of nationalism among certain forces within the Croat nation. In the Neretva valley churches and monasteries were sacked and destroyed, including the Orthodox monastery at Žitomislići and the great Orthodox church of Mostar. Assault squads of HOS and HVO extremists, initially mixed forces of Croats and Bosniaks, were active in destroying and burning Serb houses, persecuting civilians, and maintaining various detention camps. The time will come when these atrocities, too, are made public. I myself learned of the scale of the persecution only in 1993, when I was once more able to visit these regions.

There were other towns in Bosnia, such as Travnik, Bugojno, and Livno, where Serbs formerly made up a large proportion of the population. In Bugojno district, at the beginning of the war, the whole Serb village of Čipurići, between 4000 and 5000 inhabitants, was razed to its foundations, and many of its people murdered. Very few Serbs remain in Bugojno itself. Similar events took place in Stolac, Čapljina, Konjic, Lukavac, and Živinice. Following the arrival in Kladanj of refugees from Vlasenica, a state of general paranoia resulted, and the Kladanj Serbs left their own villages for Vlasenica and Zvornik. There were no murders, however, except in one village. Serbs were similarly displaced from Travnik and Tešanj. Widespread migrations occurred at the end of 1992 and in the winter of 1993, brought about by the endless shelling, the Serb media's incessant flow of propaganda, and the increasingly difficult position of all remaining Serbs. Refugees from the Bosnian Krajina who had suffered expulsion and torture flocked into the cities, while the local authorities, under the influence of the SDA, silently accepted the exodus of the Serb inhabitants[69] - this was the case in

---

[69] Bosniaks and Croats, driven out of cities and towns in the Bosnian Krajina in northwestern Bosnia, often fled to cities under control of the ABH and HVO as their first stop. These refugee flows placed added strain on cities already struggling with privation and the other consequences of war.

Zenica, for example. By 1993 the cities were largely emptied of Serbs, many of whom left to seek new homes in the Republika Srpska. The majority, however, went on to Serbia and Montenegro, and subsequently to Europe and overseas - especially the young.

This silent exodus of Serbs from the areas controlled by the ABH and the HVO meant, in effect, the departure of the most vital part of the Bosnian Serb population: educated people with specific professions, technical experts, economists, professors, and successful businessmen. According to estimates by international organizations, approximately 400,000 Serbs chose to leave Bosnia during the war, often going first to Serbia and Montenegro and then to Europe or across the seas.

According to the 1991 census, there were around 1,300,000 Serbs in Bosnia. By the end of the war, around 80,000 to 100,000 were left in the Federation, while, as we have seen, some 400,000 had left the country altogether. The remainder lives in the territory of the Republika Srpska. After the Operations "Lighting" and Storm" launched by the Croatian Army in 1995, a considerable but unknown number of Croatian Serbs fled to the RS, swelling its population.

There is no question that the SDS was by far the most extreme in implementing radical methods, and pushing its sympathizers into war crimes in order to achieve the goal of an ethnically pure territory. The party wanted absolute ethnic homogenization and government on an ethnic basis, one nation with one leader, one party, one television, and one truth. The SDS, in carrying out this project, counted on the fact that this would provoke the other nationalities to use identical methods, manifest in retaliatory outbreaks against the Serb people, forcing the Serb nation as a whole to move. The counterpart armed forces, Croat and Bosniak, responded as predicted. They conducted ethnic cleansing, destroyed religious monuments and the heritage of cultural tradition, and destroyed or looted the goods of their neighbors. They used the resulting vacuum to build up their own cultural and religious institutions, joining the SDS in the vicious circle of territorialization and ethnic division.

The behavior of the urban communities in wartime followed a very specific pattern. At the beginning of the war, aggression by the Serb army unloosed a flood of distrust against Serbs generally, followed by wholesale dismissal of Serb personnel from vital positions in the economy and public services. This was particularly widespread in Sarajevo, Zenica, Travnik, Bugojno, Tešanj, and also took place to a considerable extent in Tuzla and many other towns. This phenomenon peaked with the onset of war and remained constant as the war unfolded. It survives in milder forms to the present day. In education, culture, science, information, social activities, the economy, and in regional and local government, Serbs have lost their former position. For example, in the University of Sarajevo, none of the deans of faculties is a Serb. Serbs occupying leading posts in business were dismissed, pressured into leaving, or driven to resign upon finding that the prevailing mood left them unable to continue their work.

Predrag Lukac, director of the Sarajevo water utility company, provides a classic example of these trends. He was a popular and successful director, and was elected in November 1990 as a Reformist delegate to the Bosnian Parliament. Predrag remained in the city after war broke out, but encountered numerous obstacles to his work. The water company was a public enterprise tasked with supplying water daily to the citizens in the worst conditions of wartime. The installations and systems of the water company were exposed constantly to shelling and other types of damage, and in this situation it was very difficult to ensure the functioning of all parts of the system. The main water source was in Ilidža, under control of the RS Army. These factors jeopardized the operation of the water company, and public pressure on Lukac grew. On top of all this was the ill-will of individuals in the company, who showed open distrust of anyone of Serb nationality. Lukac several times faced displays of hostility.

He came once to my office, and another time to my flat in Breka, deeply perturbed. There were threats against him, and simply doing his job was growing daily more impossible. Every time shelling caused a leak in the water system, there was a public outcry against the Chetniks, accompanied by statements like "Well, our director is a Serb, too, so he must be a Chetnik." These criticisms created a hopelessly hostile climate. In our second talk, although I understood his position fully, I begged him to meet once more with the Mayor of Sarajevo, Muhamed Kreševljaković. When arranging the meeting, I was told by Kreševljaković that in spite of the unconducive circumstances, he had fought for Predrag Lukac to continue as head of the water company. Predrag was an experienced specialist and since the city authorities nominated people for this post, it was possible for the city to extend his term as director.

The next time we talked, Lukac himself finally decided the matter. He said that conditions for carrying out such responsible work had deteriorated to an impossible extent. The atmosphere was so poisoned that he could achieve nothing, and the whole burden of responsibility was thrown upon him personally and on his nationality. He had therefore come to tell me of his choice to withdraw his candidacy for renewal of his directorship. He subsequently left the city on account of some business he had undertaken as member of Parliament and joined his family, with whom he spent the second half of the war. Today he and his family live in Vienna.

There developed a hierarchy of trust. The top level of official trust was in members of the SDA, the second level of trust was in Bosniaks generally, and in the third place, if there was one, were members of other nations, particularly Serbs. Proof of this is furnished by the incident of the Economic Bank director's mandate. Sarajevans knew Đorđe Zarić as a successful economist and a social and sports activist, but most of all as a distinguished banker. I myself knew Zarić personally, and worked with him: he was one of the founders of the Serb Civic Council. Over a long period he had managed affairs at the Sarajevo branch of the Economic Bank, becoming director at the start of the war. There were various accusations against him and some doubts about his work, but all had been refuted. The campaign now launched against him was conducted according to the now fully-established system. First came a hostile article in the press, creating a climate in which it was easy to discover that he was unfit for his job. Criminal accusations were even spread about, but these were initially dismissed as untrue.

In 1994 public clamor arose for him to be demoted. Zarić came to me first, and I passed the message on to fellow Presidency members Miro Lazović and Tanja Ljujić-Mijatović. We informed Izetbegović and all other members of the Presidency, and we wrote letters on behalf of Zarić that ran to several pages. It could not be said that we did not follow the principles for which we fought; but there was a lack of will to change the course of events. President Izetbegović was insufficiently ready to intervene. Somehow the issue was suppressed, and no positive step was ever taken. The decision on the renewal of his term was deferred to allow time to find a satisfactory solution. After a long delay, Zarić decided that in the absence of sufficient trust, he could no longer act as director. He withdrew his candidacy, and Fatima Leho from Mostar took his place. Zarić continued, however, to act as deputy, and so his professional experience and knowledge remained in use. But the whole episode shows how such a climate and attitude could be created, step by step, and how citizens of Serb nationality, regardless of their patriotism and their shared endurance with Bosniaks and Croats of the troubles common to all, came to lose their positions as managers and leaders.

This process was carried to its logical conclusion in Sarajevo, Zenica, and West Mostar. Tuzla preserved its former structure better, but not well enough. Nevertheless there are a few places that can be taken as a model. In these towns, people not only shared a common life and a common fate, but also chose to uphold civic values and to endure all troubles in mutual trust. In East Mostar, Serbs went on holding leading posts in wartime, including those they had held right at the start of the war. The most convincing example is that of Obren Lozo, economist and businessman in the Mostar tobacco factory, who kept his pre-war position throughout the war. A similar case could be made for Kladanj, where those who held managerial posts kept them during and after the war.

The positive examples show what the legal government could do when it wanted to. In Gračanica and Živinice, the government and army deployed Serbs mostly in logistic and civil protection units. They did not send them to the front line or even make them undergo compulsory mobilization. The Bosniaks of Gračanica told me they had in mind the fact that every second inhabitant of their city had a close relative on one of the battle lines, and that the time would come to stop fighting, live together once more, and return to a state of trust. They told me they regularly received messages and signals from the Serb forces warning them to lie low on the days when the so-called weekend brigades, soldiers from other regions, held the front. Somehow a mutual concern for confidence between the nations was fostered, in the hope that trust would sometime prevail as the foundation for peace.

These exceptions underscore the general failure, which did great damage to the defense and preservation of a democratic, secular and multinational Bosnia. The responsibility belongs chiefly to the ruling parties, who in this respect were at their most unchecked in West Mostar, Livno, Čapljina, Bugojno, Zenica, Sarajevo and Travnik. If we look at Serbs in leading positions in the police and education services, from 1993 onwards a dramatic drop in their numbers takes place.

Taken altogether, the radical principle enacted by the ruling parties had a negative impact on both Serbs and Croats living in cities ruled by the SDA. The members of the Jewish nation did not fare much better, nor did Bosniaks who were not active in the SDA. The well-known economist Muhamed Cico, director of Energoinvest but not a member of the SDA, was dismissed in a hurry. He was officially informed that he must go, and the Deputy Prime Minister of the Bosnian government, Edib Bukvić, a noted party activist, promptly took his place. (For an account of Bukvić's abortive quest to become Prime Minister, see Chapter XII.) The latter's aptitude for the post proceeded above all from his party membership. Expert ability and all else took second place. A similar phenomenon can be seen at work in the election of the director of the Zenica Steelworks, Hamdija Kulović. The struggle lasted long: the managing board recommended he should be chosen, but he did not suit the SDA. Kulović maneuvered himself closer to the party and was immediately elected.

Many people that I knew myself from before the war retained leading posts in their professions only by becoming members of the SDA. The same process, in a more extreme form, operated wherever the HDZ held power. This impoverished and stripped all personnel structures, contributing to general loss of confidence, and the departure of many professionals. The personnel of TV Bosnia and Herzegovina, for example, were exposed to particularly marked forms of extremism. Top quality journalists and media professionals left one by one, due to unfavorable working relations, insufficient trust, and lack of support. These journalists included Mile Đurđević, Kosta Jovanović, and Budo Vukobrat. Jovanović returned to Bosnia at the beginning of 1995, first to Tuzla, then to Sarajevo. It is to be hoped that others will start to return as well.

## XII. HARIS SILAJDŽIĆ RESIGNS

Under the Constitution, the Presidency had the task of naming the members of the government. Additionally, in its wartime role as substituting for the Parliament, it had to confirm all such nominations. In this capacity the Presidency also reviewed and approved the proposed general policies of the government and its various ministers.

There were several different governments during the war, covering the period from May 1992 until the Peace Agreement of 1995. The Prime Minister of the first government was Jure Pelivan. Formed in June 1992 on a broad patriotic base, this was a government united in defense of the idea of Bosnia. Haris Silajdžić was Foreign Minister and Jusuf Pušina was Minister of the Interior. This was a government of experts: its members were highly regarded by the public and were people of moral integrity.

Working with the Presidency, this first wartime government did much to organize defense, build up the armed forces, and manage the diplomatic and political aspects of international negotiations on behalf of a multiethnic Bosnia. The government prepared for the first talks on solving the Bosnian question, held at the London Conference.[70]

---

[70] The London Conference of August 1992 was the first major international gathering to deal principally with the Bosnian war. It established the International Conference on the former Yugoslavia, whose co-chairs Lord David Owen and Cyrus Vance were tasked with negotiating a peace agreement. For a succinct summary of the various peace initiatives and plans to end the Bosnian war, see David Campbell, *National Deconstruction; Violence, Identity, and Justice in Bosnia* (Minneapolis: University of Minnesota Press, 1998), pp. 125-155. Campbell notes that during the first phase (June 1991 – February 1994) proposals were initiated primarilz by the European Union (before January 1, 1993, the European Council) and the UN, in the second phase (February 1994 – November 1995) by the US, Russia, and other leading players.

Silajdžić, as Foreign Minister, was often more out of than in the country; in fact, he was virtually never at home. He worked intensively to gain international support for the idea of a multiethnic Bosnia. This government fell after the conflict broke out in 1993 between the Croats and Bosniaks. Its demise began with the blow inflicted by the HDZ, then led by Mate Boban, of forcing Stjepan Kljuić to resign from the Presidency and Jure Pelivan to resign as Prime Minister. Their departure meant that a new government had to be formed. As a result of lobbying by the HDZ, Mile Akmadžić became the new Prime Minister.

The Akmadžić government was short-lived and made no significant impact. Akmadžić, together with Presidency members Franjo Boras and Miro Lasić, was shortly to leave Sarajevo and withdraw completely from the common institutions of the Bosnian state. This was a crisis period for the central state bodies. It was also a blow to those Croats living in Sarajevo, Tuzla, Zenica and other cities, who did not want Bosnia to be ethnically divided, and therefore did not support the withdrawal of Croat representatives from the state organs.

The residual government was presided over by Deputy Prime Minister Hadžo Efendić. This was a period in which the government had little strength and made no significant progress, particularly in foreign affairs. The idea arose of forming a new government with greater influence on economic, political and social matters, to further the defense of Bosnia. This proposal was linked with the necessity of ending the Bosniak-Croat conflict by adopting the Washington Agreement and the proposed Constitution of the Federation. The SDA initially proposed Edib Bukvić as Prime Minister, a man who until then had worked in the Social Accounting Service. The SDA went ahead and made their proposal public without any prior consultation either with other parties or with the Presidency, the body responsible for appointing members of the government. Bukvić even promoted his political platform in the daily press. His candidacy led to a degree of polarization about the appointment that the public was not accustomed to. There were other options for the position of Prime Minister: I personally suggested Mehmed Drino, a businessman and director of the Sarajevo water company. Drino was a Sarajevan, a Bosnian patriot who was thoroughly Bosniak, yet a man who knew how to build respect and tolerance between members of all nations. Izetbegović did talk to him about standing, but Drino refused, since he was trying to save the water company.

After his interview with Izetbegović, Drino came to my office that same evening to suggest that Haris Silajdžić should become Prime Minister. Drino did not question Edib Bukvić's integrity, commitment to the job, nor any other aspect of his personality, but he felt it was vital for wartime Bosnia to have a leader of international reputation, who could find concrete assistance for Bosnia in countries abroad. For Drino, that meant Haris Silajdžić, and he made the same suggestion to President Izetbegović. I agreed with Drino's proposal, and he asked me to take the lead in promoting the idea. I first consulted with Miro Lazović, Speaker of the Parliament, and Tanja Ljujić-Mijatović, my colleague in the Presidency. Both agreed. We broadened our consultations to include our Presidency colleagues Nijaz Duraković, Ivo Komšić, and Stjepan Kljuić, and decided together on a course of action.

The following day I met with Silajdžić, who happened to be in Sarajevo at the time. Sarajevo was then undergoing severe privation from lack of food combined with extreme cold. I presented the proposal to Silajdžić, as the common position of several members of the Presidency. After a short period for reflection he said, "I keep on doing what I have always done, which is to fight for this people and this country, to bring about peace so that this country can move towards prosperity and growth." He thus agreed to stand for Prime Minister.

We next informed President Izetbegović, who was already aware of the idea. He neither accepted nor rejected the notion of Silajdžić's candidacy. We had the impression that he had nothing against it, but he had already committed himself to Bukvić's candidacy, which made it difficult for him to act in the matter. I talked to some members of the Sarajevo City Council about our proposal, and they were enthusiastic, including the Mayor, Muhamed Kupusović, an SDA leader and later Bosnian ambassador to Libya. The broadening support base for Silajdžić's candidacy created a political climate that made it possible to switch candidates and elect Silajdžić rather than Bukvić.

More talks with President Izetbegović followed, in which Miro Lazović, Bogić Bogićević and Gradimir Gojer represented the SDP, while Edhem Bičakčić represented the SDA. There were difficulties at first, due to the problem of withdrawing the various current candidates. At one Presidency session, the parties gave their opinions. Bičakčić claimed that the SDA held the mandate, and that if any change was needed, that party alone should decide. However, the SDP representatives argued insistently and skillfully, and their arguments for setting Bukvić's candidacy aside succeeded. The SDA leaders realized their nominee could not gain full support within the Presidency. Haris Silajdžić's candidacy was accepted, and time mellowed the bitterness. It became clear, however, that what the parties proposed was one thing, but that what the Presidency would agree to was another.

We could then announce the appointment publicly. Silajdžić stated his political program for the government at an open session, broadcast on TV. The public approved wholeheartedly, in hopes that his government would take new steps to revive Bosnia's defense and its representation on the international scene. What followed was a difficult period, but a period of growth and change. In Silajdžić's first year as Prime Minister, relations improved between the Bosniaks and Croats and negotiations, headed by Hasan Muratović, were opened with the Serbs at Sarajevo airport. Many roads were freed from roadblocks, including the important western road to Mostar and Metković. A flood of humanitarian aid arrived, enabling a better response to the crises in many parts of Bosnia. Talks started on rejuvenating the economy and restoring ordinary life. We were finding our way out of the worst of the war and the desperate humanitarian situation. Possibilities of movement for people and goods were slowly opening up. These developments were crucial for building the economic and social infrastructure of the newly created Federation, and for enabling this process to spread to the rest of the Bosnian state.

Later, however, relations soured between Silajdžić and the members of his cabinet - or rather, between Silajdžić and the SDA. The problems peaked at a Parliament session held in Zenica in August 1995, and the debate about Silajdžić's possible removal began shortly after. In the first round, the Presidency, or rather all its members except Izetbegović and Bičakčić – the latter had taken over from Ganić, who was unwell – supported Silajdžić, and wanted his mandate extended. Public satisfaction at this decision was widespread - there was already a considerable list of signatures on a petition for his mandate to continue.

Izetbegović and Silajdžić disagreed sharply over the government's ability to act independently on questions of defense, the revival of the economy, the management of funds including all foreign aid, and several other issues. We in the Presidency succeeded in obtaining a consensus on extending the work of the government, although it took the whole afternoon, and Silajdžić's presence was a strain. Later, however, relations deteriorated still further, and made cooperation impossible. Silajdžić resigned and began forming his own party. There were no further attempts to dissuade him from resigning. Hasan Muratović was elected Prime Minister of what was, in Silajdžić's time and in his own, the government of both the Federation and the Republic of Bosnia and Herzegovina.

Muratović remained Prime Minister until the Dayton Peace agreement was signed. As an experienced economist, he supported various economic projects and started preparing for reconstruction. This process continued on the lines laid down by Silajdžić's government, and was carried on successfully well beyond the signing of the Dayton Peace agreement, until the post-war elections of elections of September 1996.

As for Silajdžić's motives for resigning, Silajdžić himself spoke freely on the subject, as did other highly placed members of the government. According to what he said at the time, the reason was his refusal to let the SDA interfere in the management of the government or to conduct unilateral party rule through propaganda. In one well-publicized incident of the conflict between Haris Silajdžić and TV director Amila Omersoftić, the electricity failed, suspiciously, just before he was supposed to appear on TV to discuss government issues. The SDA leadership then promptly imposed the injunction that Silajdžić could not speak alone about government problems on TV. This was one obvious reason for Silajdžić to resign.

The second issue concerned the Prime Minister's financial authority. This was never publicly debated. I believe, however, that this was one of the factors behind his initial threat to resign. The first time the possibility of his resignation came up, the Presidency put the question back on the agenda and urged Silajdžić and Izetbegović to try to find a solution. However, overall relations did not change. In an interview given at the time, Izetbegović made the well-publicized remark that Silajdžić never listened. The SDA demanded obedience to the party, but it was inappropriate for this relationship. The government, like the Presidency and the Parliament, required its own sphere of responsibility, its independence. The SDA used its Parliament majority to influence the final outcome. Silajdžić was compelled to resign, since many of the powers of the Prime Minister had been taken out of his hands. This episode will one day be investigated, and those who made the crucial decisions will have to testify. My own opinion is that the management of foreign aid was one of the most important motives behind Silajdžić's resignation. His government could not continue to function under such restrictions.

## XII. THE GENEVA PEACE TALKS

The Presidency selected and prepared the delegation that would take part in the Geneva peacetalks. The original Platform on the work of the Presidency in wartime was proposed as the foundation for the delegation's position, augmented by a few suggestions. An expanded session of the Presidency was called, attended by representatives of all parliamentary parties. At this session it was agreed that since this was to be a Bosnian state delegation, its structure should reflect the essential character of Bosnia, and therefore be multiethnic and pluralist. Haris Silajdžić, then a member of the SDA and Foreign Minister, was appointed head of the delegation: he was already abroad at the time. Other delegation members included Professor Muhamed Filipović, Deputy President of the MBO and a Member of Parliament; Miro Lazović, Member of Parliament and representative of the SDP, the largest opposition party; and myself as a member of the Presidency. As for expert members, Constitutional Court judge Kasim Trnka was nominated, along with Professor Dragoljub Stojanov of the Economics Faculty.

Sarajevo was then in a state of total ground siege. Available air transport was provided by the United Nations, chiefly to deliver humanitarian aid, and even that was frequently interrupted. It was finally announced that we would travel in UNPROFOR Armored Personnel Carriers (APCs) to Butmir, Igman and Hadžići, and then make our way by road to Mostar and Split. It was a risky departure, since in those days leaving Sarajevo was virtually impossible. On the morning of 16 September, the delegation set off, traveling in APCs. There was a typical morning mist below Mount Igman. We stopped at the former Institute of Culture, where representatives of the local authorities and the commander of the local unit of the Bosnian Army were expecting us. Here I had the chance to meet several of my friends from before the war, including Zaim Lokvančić. After a warm greeting, and questions about the family, Zaim briefly disappeared, and a selection of fresh-picked plums and apples suddenly arrived on the table. This was a real restorative for us Sarajevans, since the siege deprived us of any fresh supplies.

The local army commander now implored us to think hard about the conditions for traveling over Igman, for the road from Hrasnica to the forested lower slopes of Igman had been shelled twice already, as had the descent from Igman to the village of Lokve. The commander's advice was that we should wait until the situation changed. We all looked at each other, and Professor Filipović asked, "What shall we do?" I answered: "We are going to carry on - even under shelling." Filipović agreed, and we set off once more. When we drew near Lokve, which had no forest cover, our column of two APCs was shelled. Resad Hadrović, a Sarajevo writer and journalist, was in the same vehicle as I. He was leaving the city after considerable suffering, since an operation was needed to save his eyesight. We sat pressed against one another, trying to cope with our fear, as shells started falling close by. One hit the vehicle, but we were saved by the readiness of the French soldiers to keep moving, and none of us panicked.

We had a short rest between Konjic and Jablanica, where, for the first time, we found ourselves in free territory, with no trace of shelling or other military action. We refreshed ourselves with water from a spring, and felt revived. Just then a group of children, ten to twelve years old, came by. Professor Filipović asked, "Hey, kids, where are you from?" They replied they were from Gacko. Refugee families from East Herzegovina had already re-created their lives in the Neretva valley.

When we left the valley, we took the paved road to Široki Brijeg, via Dreznica, and from Široki Brijeg to Split, arriving around nine in the evening. We were tired and dusty. We flew from Split airport to Zagreb, where we took the plane to Geneva. Here the Bosnian representative to the United Nations, Mustafa Bijedić, was waiting for us. As we left the airport for Hotel Eden, where we were booked to stay, our eyes still retained their vision of the empty streets and ruined buildings of our Sarajevo.

The next day we had a meeting with Silajdžić, who had been waiting in Geneva for our arrival. We lunched together in the Hotel

Intercontinental. With us was a Swiss journalist called Laura, who interviewed Lazović and myself in the hotel garden. It was a beautiful September day, and I felt a strong sense of unreality due to the weather, the place and the surroundings: as if I was not really in this country at all, not in the free world of European civilization. The pain that had traveled with me all the way from Sarajevo was still gnawing at me. I was physically in Geneva, but my soul was in Sarajevo.

Gradually I adapted myself to the work that had to be done. Our delegation met several times over the next few days, before we set off together for the UN building where we would meet with Lord David Owen, co-chair of the conference for former Yugoslavia, and his assistant, Mati Ahtisaari. Before we left for the UN, our delegation worked nearly half a day on defining our platform for the talks. Our technical capacity was very limited. The delegation's secretary, Amira Kapetanović, bore the brunt of all our practical problems, while Professor Kasim Trnka assembled the suggestions made during our discussion. We now had our first two meetings with Owen and Ahtisaari, in which we introduced ourselves and presented our concept for a peace agreement for Bosnia.

This derived from the concept underlying the Platform on the work of the Presidency in wartime. It supported, first, a united Bosnia within its internationally recognized borders; second, parliamentary democracy; third, common life and equality for the citizens and all peoples of Bosnia, that is, Serbs, Croats, Bosniaks and other peoples living in the state; fourth: human rights according to international standards; and fifth: an internal structure founded on modern experiences of regional and local self government. This would be a structure based on the constitution of the regions, provinces that had shaped themselves naturally during the historic growth of Bosnia, as geographic, cultural and economic units. We ourselves were convinced that our platform offered a concept on which the political future of Bosnia could be built, the war stopped, and peace and stability re-established. Thus the country would retain its historic unity and its legal identity as a state, jointly constituted of its equal citizens and nations.

But Karadžić's delegation envisaged a very different future for Bosnia. Their concept paper was very short. Only one issue was seen as potentially common to all nations; all others fell within the sole competence of the government of what was described as the Serb territory in Bosnia. This single common issue was joint sources and systems of electric power. There was nothing else. By itself, this fact tells plainly what their starting position was in seeking a solution for Bosnia.

Following the first meeting, a series of talks took place between the delegations and the mediators of the international community. With small breaks, these talks lasted from mid-September until mid-December, and the first plan of the Geneva negotiations, known as the Vance-Owen Peace Plan for Bosnia and Herzegovina, was subsequently drafted. (Vance and Owen presented their peace plan to the public in January 1993. In this plan, three provinces had a Bosniak majority, three had a Croat majority, and three a Serb majority, while the tenth province, Sarajevo, had a mixed government of three national bodies. The plan failed because the RS Assembly rejected it in May 1993.)

At the beginning we spent much time in talks led by Ahtisaari, Owen's deputy. Own also presided occasionally, but he took several breaks, as he had to do much traveling and hold various meetings, prior to preparing the plan. I think Ahtisaari felt much understanding for us, and our views. I found him a deeply interesting man. He did not hide his sympathy for the arguments of the Bosnian state delegation, and for its members as individuals. His main aim was to create a climate for the ending of hostilities and the cessation of war. He did not harp on the theme of "different sides in the conflict," which was the general style of the international community's approach. He was exceptionally well informed about the purposes of the war in Bosnia. He attained this level of understanding because he was fair-minded, just, and systematic. He knew that Karadžić represented a great military force, busy using fascist methods as an iron broom to carry out ethnic cleansing, and inflict violence on civilians. At the end of the year, however, Ahtisaari ran for President of Finland, won the elections, and ceased to be a part of the Geneva conference.

Lazović, Professor Filipović, and I told Ahtisaari about the multiethnic structure of Sarajevo, and he chose his words well when talking about the slaughter of its people. From us he learned the views of the Social Democrats, Socialists, and Liberals on possible solutions to the Bosnian question, in addition to what he had already learned from Silajdžić and Ljubić. There was no essential difference between the views of the opposition component of the delegation, as represented by Filipović, Lazović and myself, and the views expressed by HDZ delegate Mariofil Ljubić, or by Silajdžić as head of the delegation and member of the SDA. Ahtisaari himself acted like a true democrat, a man who promoted modern European democracy or one of its visions - European social democracy. The use of veiled threats and compulsion, through references to "the real situation on the ground," was never part of his approach.

Owen, unlike Ahtisaari, was always official and cold in the typical manner of a powerful Englishman. Nevertheless, he was patient in listening to our arguments, suggestions, and requests. His approach to the Bosnian war and the Bosnian question was founded on two premises. The first was that the various ethnic groups could not tolerate each other, and that this was the chief reason why they were in conflict. His other obsession was evident in his frequent question, "How do we resolve the actual situation on the ground?" – this was the result of pressure from Karadžić, whose forces currently controlled 70% of Bosnia's territory. Owen did not admit it openly, but this consideration governed his entire approach. To begin with, however, he avoided letting ethnic criteria predominate in the plan of ten provinces that he and Vance jointly proposed in December 1992 and which came to be known as the Vance Owen Peace Plan. However, when this plan was rejected at the start of 1993, Owen moved towards ethnic criteria as the foundation for solving the Bosnian question, as can be seen in his 1993 proposal of three ethnic republics, Serb, Croat and Bosniak. When this idea was rejected by the Bosnian parliament, the next proposal took the form of two entities, in the Washington Agreement and the plan of the Contact Group.

During October and November, the Bosnian State delegation never met face to face with that of Karadžić. Talks were carried on in different rooms and different appointments were scheduled with the mediators. I myself personally avoided any situation in which I might encounter Karadžić or other members of his delegation – for obvious reasons. However, one day at the start of October 1992, a UN security guard handed me a letter at the entrance to the UN building. It was from Momčilo Krajišnik and expressed full confidence that all was over, the war finished, and the victor obvious to all. The letter suggested that I should leave the state delegation and that I had a secure future with the nationalist Serbs if I agreed to defect. Such a letter could not surprise me. It was part of their strategy to make the state delegation mono-national, the more easily to impose ethnic criteria for solving the Bosnian question, by partitioning and dividing Bosnia on ethnic lines, as planned by Karadžić. There were no threats in the letter, unlike those that had often reached me previously by various routes, and I did not mention it to anybody. I simply kept it as a personal souvenir of the Geneva negotiations and the war itself.

I knew Krajišnik from before the war. We had enjoyed considerable mutual respect, and as far as I could see, this was the reason why Krajišnik was the first member of the Serb delegation to try and pressure me into leaving the state delegation. Before the war, "Momo" Krajišnik had often invited me to visit him in the Parliament Speaker's office in Marjindvor to discuss many topics, and I had had no problem about dropping in. He used to tell me that he admired my work in the Socialist Alliance of Sarajevo and the Republic of Bosnia. He himself, as he used to say, had been an activist of the Socialist Alliance in Rajlovac, and his own village of Zabrđe. He admired the Alliance's activities in building community infrastructures by way of initiating voluntary communal contributions.

Carefully and skillfully, he had frequently led the conversation to the issue of Bosnia's position in the Yugoslav crisis. He never once questioned the coexistence of the nations of Bosnia. His only objection was, as he expressed it, that "nothing can be agreed with the Muslims." This sentiment, in my opinion, stood for the official position of the SDS: that common life for the nations of Bosnia is impossible. The theory derived its strength from the other ruling parties' political opposition to the SDS program, this program being to promote ethnic division and the annexation of part of Bosnia to the remodeled state of Yugoslavia, or rather to Greater Serbia.

Krajišnik was always bothered by the phrase "a sovereign Bosnia." I used this phrase several times in our dialogues, and it annoyed him every time. I reminded him that under the socialist constitution, which had governed the Parliament in which he himself had been elected Speaker, Bosnia was a sovereign republic inside the Yugoslav federation, with three nations, the Bosniaks, Croats and Serbs, constituting the state community on principles of complete equality. I reminded him that this was adopted as the will of the people at the 1943 session of the ZAVNOBiH in Mrkonjic Grad. Krajišnik realized that we had no common view on this issue, and he let the subject drop.

Efforts to encourage my resignation from the Geneva delegation did not end with Krajišnik's letter. Later in October 1992, a UN security official entered the conference room where the state delegation was just settling down to work, and presented an invitation for me to come immediately into the next room, the main negotiating chamber, where Owen was waiting. When I went in, Owen was sitting nearest me, and with him were Karadžić, Krajišnik, Koljević and Buha, all in dark suits, looking as if they were celebrating. They made no attempt to hide their sense of victory. It was a highly awkward situation. Momčilo Krajišnik approached me first and suggested again that I should leave Sarajevo, telling me I must accept the fact that the war was over.

After Krajišnik's invitation to leave Sarajevo, came questions from Karadžić and the others, who wanted to hear how matters stood in Sarajevo, how many Serbs remained in Sarajevo under the control of the Bosnian Army, how many had been murdered, how many Serbs were in prison. I tried, unhappily, to answer. I said that according to current estimates around 70,000 Serbs remained in Sarajevo. Unwilling to say more on this topic, I said, "I'm not leaving Sarajevo. This is my choice. There is nothing that can persuade or pressure me into changing my mind." Not wanting to talk further, I walked out of the room and returned to my own delegation. To be honest, I felt agitated and shaken, but I succeeded in calming myself down sufficiently for this not to be noticed. It was not until later that I told my friends that pressure had been put on me to leave the delegation.

I knew, and I saw it clearly during my encounter with them, that both Karadžić and Krajišnik were preoccupied with the issue of the Serbs remaining in Sarajevo. In fact I had the impression that those Serbs in Sarajevo constituted a major stumbling block to their strategy, and an insoluble problem. They knew very well that if I resigned from the Presidency and left Sarajevo, it would become much easier to pressure the international community and Owen into accepting ethnic division as final. They knew it would also then be easier to pressure the remaining Serbs into leaving Sarajevo, and thus they themselves would finally be rid of their bugbear. Militarily, the resistance of the citizens and patriotic forces within the city had prevented them from taking the city completely. Politically, they wanted a concept for the ethnic division of the city of Sarajevo, as I had learned during the visit that Kecmanović and I made to Krajišnik in early April 1992.

In the Geneva negotiations Karadžić deftly turned to his advantage my discussion of the multiethnic defense of Sarajevo as a Serb, Croat and Bosniak city. For example, he used to say, "Pejanović mentioned how many Serbs are living in Sarajevo. Why are you mobilizing them in the Muslim army? Why are you sending them to shoot at their fellow Serbs?" He even demanded that there should be no conscription of Serbs whatsoever into the Bosnian Army. Or, taking another tack, he would say, "You can have your Muslim Sarajevo, as long as Grbavica or Ilidža are left for us Serbs. You can have it in exchange for the whole of Eastern Bosnia, the whole of Podrinje." Karadžić openly admitted, "We are sacrificing the Serbs under your Bosniak control, and under Serb control: in Vogošča, Ilijas, Hadzići, Reljevo." He made no attempt to hide the exploitation of ordinary people, in this case Serbs, for the SDS goal of creating ethnically cleansed regions which could join Serbia. My own impression was, however, that Karadžić did feel some discomfort regarding the fate of the Serbs who remained in Sarajevo.

Shells fired from the BSA positions killed people of all nations in Sarajevo. Of 12,500 civilian Sarajevans killed, several thousand were of Serb nationality, or of ethnic Serb origins but born of mixed marriages. In the press conferences that our delegations gave once a week in the UN building in Geneva, appeals for aid to the people of Sarajevo were my constant theme. Silajdžić led these conferences with his usual challenging approach, arousing the interest of world journalists from America to Japan. Professor Filipović used to attack the international institutions and world powers for their failure to stop the fascist implementation of genocide against the Bosniaks. Filipović was always most impassioned, and with good reason, when he spoke of Banja Luka, Ključ, Prijedor and Sanski Most. Ključ was home to a great number of his near relatives, many of whom went missing or were killed at the start of the war. I myself kept to the topic of Sarajevo, regularly asking our *Oslobođenje* reporter, Mehmed Husić, whether there was anything new about

Sarajevo in his report. I was greatly troubled about my city, and so was Filipović, for his entire remaining family were now in Sarajevo. We waited tensely for every evening newscast from Radio Sarajevo, always afraid to hear of yet more shelling, assault and death.

During the first break in the negotiations, in October, Filipović, Amira Kapetanović and I went back for a brief stay in Sarajevo. Lazović went to Dalmatia, where his wife and children were, and Ljubić back to his Hercegovina, to Široki Brijeg. Our suitcases were full of money parcels and medicines for the people of Sarajevo sent by their relatives and friends, together with as much food as we could carry. When I got out of the APC, in front of the Presidency Building, a crowd was waiting, including many of my friends. They were all even more haggard than before; the sight of them was horrifying. It was the beginning of the hardest winter of the war in Sarajevo. There was less and less food and no fuel at all. Between November 1992 and March 1993 there were new hardships to suffer. People started to cut down the trees in the parks for fuel, and many died of cold and hunger. I used to freeze in my flat in Breka, and my grandmother Sofia was saved only by the care of Hasan Kadrić's family in Old Breka. (They heated her house with some of the pre-war stock of coal they had managed to save.) In this atmosphere it was vital to keep on talking to journalists and to go out in front of the cameras and talk to people – as when several associations got together and asked to discuss the Geneva negotiations. It was also essential to visit the soldiers on the front line.

I had the good fortune never to lose my optimism and my faith in the possibility of achieving a peaceful political solution for Bosnia. I always believed that this was possible, although it could not be certain without the decisive commitment of the international community. On the TV program "Wartime," edited and hosted by Vladimir Bilić, Professor Filipović and I spoke positively about the preparation of a peace plan based on the Geneva negotiations. We discussed the concept of a whole and multiethnic Bosnia, as a state built on consensus, with a Council of Nations to protect national equality, and an internal structure consisting of provinces with local self-rule and regional autonomy. To the frozen, hungry Sarajevans, it offered some little consolation that better times might come, and that peace was possible. They hurt me deeply, these people worn out with suffering. At the same time they kept me going, and inspired me to keep on talking about peace, for only the end of the war could stop this anguish.

I was especially moved by meeting with my good friend Živko Babić a former Mayor of Banja Luka, loved by many people in Sarajevo. I first met him as a student, when I was a member of the delegation that visited Banja Luka after the town was hit by an earthquake, in 1969. Later we collaborated when he was working in Sarajevo. Now he had come for my aid. Even to climb the steps of the Presidency Building, he needed help: unbelievably emaciated, he could barely walk. The state to which he had been reduced is just one example of the general suffering in Sarajevo at this time. For me it was an especially bad moment. Following each of my visits home, everything I said when I returned to Geneva, whether in the delegation or in press conferences, was an effort to communicate the truth about Sarajevo.

## XIV. THE VANCE OWEN PEACE PLAN

Toward the end of 1992, in the third month of the Geneva negotiations, we in the Bosnian state delegation submitted our proposal for the constitutional organization and internal structure of the Bosnian state. Our suggestion was based on two ideas. First, the Bosnian state should be a community of citizens and nations with a two-chambered parliament. We envisioned a Council of Nations to protect the vital interests and national equality of the Bosniaks, Croats and Serbs. The second idea was that the state's internal organization should consist of thirteen regions, each with a distinct history and a great degree of autonomy, to be known as provinces. Professor Filipović and I put together our proposal of 13 provinces one weekend in Zurich, with the help of Adil Zulfikarpašić. (Filipović was then Deputy President of Zulfikarpašić's MBO.) Later, in the final draft of the Vance-Owen Peace Plan, ten regions were envisioned: Banja Luka, Tuzla, Mostar, Bihać, Zenica, Bijeljina, Travnik, East Herzegovina, Posavina and Sarajevo. Sarajevo was to have special status. On our return to Sarajevo, when the plan had already taken shape, the Zagreb media broadcast the basic contents of the plan from Geneva and briefly mentioned that the plan derived from the wishes of the population and the proposals of the opposition parties within the Bosnian state delegation.

At the time of the delegation's stay in Geneva, we initiated talks with key people in the principal European countries, the USA, and the UN headquarters in New York. Professor Filipović and Miro Lazović took part in several meetings held in European countries, mostly in Germany, by associations of refugees from Bosnia. Haris Silajdžić as Foreign Minister was meanwhile active in setting up meetings with the foreign ministers of the member countries of the

European Union and the Islamic Conference. Together, as a delegation, we visited Washington and New York in October, and Bonn in November. In New York we met with ambassadors of the countries of the Islamic Conference, and with the UN Secretary General, Bhoutros Ghali. In Washington, we had talks in the State Department, and with General Brendt Scowcroft, security adviser to President Bush. In Bonn there was a celebration in honor of the establishment of diplomatic relations between Germany and Bosnia, presided over by German Foreign Minister Klaus Kinkel.

The meeting with the ambassadors of the Islamic Conference members resulted from Silajdžić's presentation of the situation in Bosnia. The first reports had just arrived of the slaughter of Bosniaks in Kozarac and Prijedor, in camps such as Manjača and Keraterm. Silajdžic took the position that if the international community went on refusing to lift the arms embargo then in force against Bosnia, then it would be obliged to intervene in order to stop the war, and the persecution and slaughter of members of the Bosniak nation. All ambassadors from Islamic countries received his statement favorably. Their predominant belief was that the war could and should be stopped by a peaceful, political solution, which would preserve the international and legal rights of the state of Bosnia. They showed a clear sense of responsibility for the Bosnian tragedy. However, they were realistic in their appraisal of the position of the leading world powers in the Security Council. Almost all ambassadors from the Islamic Conference countries placed the Bosnian question in the context of the relations between the world's leaders. It was well known that the US at this point was not prepared to do anything that went against the wishes of its European allies, especially England.

We used our reception with Bhoutros-Ghali to try to convey the degree of the slaughter of Bosnia's people, and the danger of a humanitarian catastrophe. We presented our proposal for a peace plan, the proposal that subsequently emerged as the Vance-Owen Peace Plan in January 1993. After the talks in the UN headquarters in New York, there was a crowded press conference at which Silajdžić spoke first, followed by Professor Filipović, then Miro Lazović and myself. For journalists and media, our delegation's visit to New York was an appealing story, especially the multicultural nature of our delegation, and what Lazović and I, as Serbs, had to say about Bosnia.

In Washington, our interview with the US President's National Security Advisor, General Brent Scowcroft, seemed the most significant. It was held in the White House, and we had to pass several security checks in order to reach the inner center of US foreign policy, in the basement area of the White House. When we finally arrived, we encountered a pleasant surprise: the Deputy Secretary of State, Laurence Eagleburger, was in the office of the Security Advisor. We had previously been told that we would not be able to meet with Eagleburger due to the ongoing election campaigns.

The meeting turned into a long, exhaustive search for a formula to solve the Bosnian question. The American officials accepted the arguments of our delegation that the war in Bosnia was waged with the involvement of the Belgrade regime. But when we came to the question of whether international forces, including American forces, would intervene, the response was exceedingly restrained. Eagleburger referred to the US public's psychological fear, a syndrome persisting from the Vietnamese war. He added, "The Bosnian mountains are difficult terrain for military action. There is a lot of experience left over from Partisan warfare." This showed at least that they were familiar with the region and its geographic configuration. (During this period, returning via Zagreb to Sarajevo, I found an interview Karadžić gave to the Zagreb paper *Globus*. Asked where the war might lead, Karadžić replied, "The Bosnian mountains are hollow, filled with warehouses of weapons and fuel from Tito's time. We can fight for 50 years: Tito's JNA prepared it all.")

It became clear to us that there would be no classic military intervention on the part of the international community. It was also obvious that there would also be no response to our appeals for lifting the arms embargo. Eagleburger told us, "We have no consensus with our European allies, above all England and France, either for lifting the arms embargo or for eventual military intervention." This was the time of the election campaign, in which George Bush's chances of renewing his presidential mandate looked slim, as was confirmed by Bill Clinton's victory in the 1992 US elections. This meant considerable caution and deliberation over the Bosnian question. However, our talks revealed continuing interest in the Bosnian drama. Both Eagleburger and Scowcroft showed concern for stopping the ethnic persecution of the people, and the torture and killing in the camps.

With Clinton's victory a new phase began in the US approach to Bosnia's war. However, the US spent a long time developing this new approach, which emerged only in 1994 and 1995 as the American peace initiative. This involved using the consensus of the five leading powers of the Contact Group, together with military force, to lift the siege of Sarajevo.[71] It also involved air strikes on key points in the territory under the control of Karadžić's army.

During our stay in the US, the state delegation was very modestly accommodated. We mostly traveled by taxi. Nedzib Saćirbegović, better known in Bosnia as the "older Saćirbegović," was very attentive to our needs.[72] A young man named Adnan Bešlagić from Doboj used his own car to drive Lazović and myself in Washington. He had completed Sarajevo's Faculty of Natural Mathematics and was then teaching at a university in Washington. He was comfortably off, according to the living standards there, but his behavior to us was very humble, and we could see that he was suffering because of what was happening to Bosnia. He wanted to hear more from Lazović and myself, and one evening we managed a long talk. He told us that night, " I am glad to have met you. I am glad to see, for the first time, a Bosnian delegation that does not consist only of Muslims (Bosniaks). I can only believe in Bosnia and its survival, if all three nations are in power, and all are present in all international delegations." We met many such people among the diaspora populations in Europe and overseas. (Sadly, I later received the news that Adnan had been killed in a traffic accident.)

Our delegation's visit to Bonn was linked to the establishment of diplomatic ties between Bosnia and Germany. The first event we attended was the celebration, which was low key, but symbolic. German Foreign Minister Klaus Kinkel and Bosnian Foreign Minister Haris Silajdžić made speeches to a sizeable group of attendees. Various public statements followed, and our delegation then

---

[71] Contact Group member countries were Great Britain, France, Germany, Russia, and the US.

[72] Nedžib Šaćirbegović, a long-time associate of President Alija Izetbegović, is a retired doctor living in Virginia. His son, Muhamed Šaćirbegović, was for some years the Permanent Representative of Bosnia and Hercegovina to the United Nations. Both father and son are known by a shortened version of their name, Šaćirbey, in the US, but as Šaćirbegović in Bosnia.

embarked upon a long interview with Foreign Minister Kinkel. During our meeting, Kinkel showed much interest in the Bosnian situation and a clear desire for Germany to help. At one point he said, "We have received your refugees, and we are doing what we can within the European Union to find a peaceful solution for Bosnia. But we are limited by our Constitution with regard to German Army involvement in international peacekeeping forces, due to constraints resulting from the Second World War. When the question of relations with Bosnia is raised in the European Union, some have their Croats to support, some have their Serbs, but nobody ever has Muslims." Professor Filipović responded with a question: "What can you do to change Tuđman's attitude to Bosnia? We can more easily stop Karadžić if Zagreb isn't working for the ethnic division of Bosnia." Kinkel's reply was positive: "I will do everything I can to make Zagreb cooperate in finding a solution for Bosnia." Kinkel also ordered new actions to relieve the humanitarian situation in Bosnia.

Next followed a press conference. All of us from the delegation took part in answering the journalists' questions. One of these was, whether the Muslims (Bosniaks) were, as a nation, supporters of Islamic fundamentalism. I did not wait for this question to be answered by a Bosniak member of our delegation. I immediately explained that the Muslims (Bosniaks) were an indigenous nation of Bosnia, along with its other two peoples, the Serbs and the Croats. Under Ottoman rule, dating from the fifteenth century, a part of the indigenous Bosnian population converted to the Islamic faith. During the nations' historic development, especially from the 18$^{th}$ century onwards, this part of the Bosnian population, like the other Bosnian peoples, achieved its own national identity. The Bosniak nation differed from that of Bosnia's Serbs and Croats in being based on the Islamic faith.

I said, "You in Germany have one nation, the German nation, but you have plenty of different religions. Some are Catholics, some are Protestants, and others are Evangelicals. Islam, as one of the faiths in Bosnia, has shown for many centuries a high level of tolerance towards the other Bosnian faiths, Catholicism and Orthodoxy. The common life of people who belong to different faiths and nations has been respected. In the past there has never been any political organization of the Bosnian Muslims on the basis of their religion, apart from isolated phenomena like El Hidaje in the Second World War. Thus the Bosnian Muslims (Bosniaks) cannot be equated with Islamic Fundamentalists. Such a hypothesis is contradicted most of all by the fact that 99 percent of the Bosniaks expelled from Bosnia have solved their destiny by entering European countries, the US, Canada, and Australia – all of which, in the religious context, are typically Christian countries. Bosniaks, in their entire way of life, belong to European civilization, as does the country of Bosnia, of which they are an indigenous nation. If it were otherwise, Bosniaks would prefer to seek their destinies in Turkey, Pakistan, Egypt, Iran and other Islamic countries. On the contrary, those who were driven by necessity to Turkey and Pakistan, as refugees from Herzegovina during the Croat-Bosniak conflict, have either arranged to return to Bosnia as soon as possible, or are seeking refugee status in European or transatlantic countries."

For many journalists these facts about Bosniaks were new and fascinating. But fear and prejudice against Islam remains a problem. In all efforts to portray Bosnia's status in global politics, account should always be taken of the European prejudice against Islam. Bosnia's integration into European institutions should be given greater encouragement. Despite all, Bosnia's centuries-old experience of tolerance and the coexistence of different cultures and faiths, points to the greatest role that Bosnia can play in building Europe as a multiethnic community of free nations.

When the Vance-Owen Peace Plan was made public, hopes rose that this would provide a foundation for ending the war and returning refugees to their homes. The first four months of 1993 saw vigorous activity on the part of the international community in pressuring all sides in Bosnia to accept the plan. That part of the country under the control of the ABH, the legal government of the state, agreed to the plan. That part of Bosnia under the control of the HVO also readily accepted the plan, in fact did so while it was still being prepared, and before it was made public. Leaders of the HVO and HDZ also began preparations to define Croat-majority provinces on the basis of the plan.

Obtaining Karadžić's acceptance of the Vance Owen Peace Plan proved the real challenge, however. Pressure from the European community and the European Union, accompanied by pressure from the governments in Belgrade and Athens, produced preliminary results: Karadžić expressed initial acceptance of the plan while visiting Greece. Later, however, the plan was rejected by the Parliament of the Republika Srpska in its session on Jahorina. Attending the session were Milošević, Ćosić, and Micotakis, the Prime Minister of the Greek government, but the majority of the Serb assembly delegates supported General Mladić's demand that the plan should be rejected. Mladić's demand was all the more easily acceded to, since many of these delegates had already dirtied their hands in the ethnic cleansing of Bosniaks and Croats, and some had committed actual crimes in Eastern Bosnia, the Bosnian Krajina, Posavina, and East Herzegovina.

The rejection by the Serbs of the Vance-Owen plan gave rise to a new state of affairs in Bosnia. Meanwhile, the Norwegian diplomat Thorvald Stoltenberg took over as new co-chair of the peace conference in Geneva.[73]

---

[73] Thorvald Stoltenberg replaced the former American Secretary of State, Cyrus Vance, on May 1, 1993. Stoltenberg was a former Norwegian Minister of Foreign Affairs who had also served as the UN High Commissioner for Refugees. Steven L. Burg and Paul S. Shoup, *The War in Bosnia and Hercegovina: Ethnic Conflict and International International Intervention* (Armond, New York: M.E. Sharpe, 1999), p. 265.

## XV. THE OWEN-STOLTENBERG PLAN FOR A UNION OF THREE REPUBLICS

Stoltenberg and Owen started a new round of talks in May 1993. Owen made several attempts to explain why the international community, particularly the leading powers, had failed to stand firm behind the Vance-Owen Peace Plan. To a large extent, the United States considered Bosnia and its war to be a European problem, one for the European Union to solve. Further talks with the Bosnian delegation were convened, and Owen invited all members of the Bosnian Presidency to attend. Thus work began on another peace plan, known as the Owen-Stoltenberg Plan for a Union of Three Republics.

The main idea of the Owen-Stoltenberg Plan was to create three ethnic units within Bosnia. These three ethnic territories would form the Union of Bosnia and Herzegovina. The biggest problem, however, was drawing ethnic borders that would satisfy Bosniaks, Croats, and Serbs alike. The government delegation, on the other hand, had formulated principles from which we never departed. The position of the United States at this time was clear. Its representatives declared that they would support a peaceful solution which suited the legal government of Bosnia, or, as they put it, the Sarajevo government. The US gave top priority to the principle that Bosnia was a UN member state, a legal state with internationally recognized borders. Secondly, they insisted that the Bosnian, or rather the Bosniak territorial unit, could not be less than 32% of the territory of Bosnia. The third principle was that Bosnia must have an exit to the sea via Neum and to Brčko harbor via the city of Brčko.[74] The fourth principle was that Sarajevo must remain united and have capital city status. The Americans also

---

[74] Brčko is a town in northern Bosnia's Posavina region on the south bank of the Sava River. It was captured by BSA forces early in the war. The Bosnian

insisted upon the return of the pre-war populations to the territory from which they had been expelled by force. The cities of Brčko, Doboj, Neum and Sarajevo were the cause of the most acrimonious disputes between the delegations during the negotiations.

During these negotiations, Professor Filipović, Miro Lazović and I urged the Presidency in Sarajevo to invite Selim Bešlagić, an opposition party leader and Mayor of Tuzla, to join the Geneva delegation.[75] When the difficult discussion of Brčko's status began, there were many different ideas on the table. Karadžić, as he had done throughout the negotiations, advocated access to the Brčko harbor through separate flyovers and tunnels. In his view, Bosniaks and Serbs, or Croats and Serbs, should not even meet on the same road. Selim Bešlagić reacted furiously to the suggestion: "Not even a lunatic would accept this." Bešlagić was very soon discouraged by the way the negotiations were going and during the first break he returned to Tuzla.

Karadžić endlessly repeated his offer to trade the parts of Sarajevo under Serb control for land in Eastern Bosnia. He wanted to create at any price an ethnically pure territory running parallel to the river Drina, from Bijeljina to Foca. He offered to exchange the Sarajevo suburbs of Vogošča and Ilijas for the Eastern Bosnian towns of Srebrenica and Žepa. We talked this over once in our delegation, but rejected all possibility of trading land and populations, for by accepting such a proposal we ourselves would participate in the evil called ethnic cleansing. Goražde was always on the table to be traded for those suburbs of Sarajevo called Serb Sarajevo, while Karadžić's delegation persisted in offering its option of an ethnically divided Sarajevo. The state delegation kept,

---

Serb nationalists felt they needed to retain control of Brčko in any peace settlement to assure a land corridor between their Western Bosnian territories in the Krajina and the land they controlled in Eastern Bosnia. This left the problem of establishing passage from the government-controlled territories to the Sava River and to Croatia to the north.

[75] Tuzla was the only major city in Bosnia where a social democratic party prevailed in the 1990 elections. There, Selim Bešlagić, candidate of the Union of Bosnian Social Democrats (UBSD), was elected Mayor, a post he held throughout the 1990's. In February 1998 the UBSD merged with the SDP and became effectively the Tuzla branch of that party.

however, to its insistence on a united Sarajevo. Lazović and I frequently endorsed the idea of a temporary UN protectorate for Sarajevo to neutralize the wartime divisions, and preserve the pre-war ethnic structure of Bosnia's capital by stopping the exodus of Sarajevans. Izetbegović and Silajdžić accepted this idea in principle, but they did not press for it, as they had little confidence in the efficiency of international management. The mandate eventually given to US Ambassador Eagleton, as the first international community representative to oversee the reconstruction of Sarajevo, turned out to be something less than a protectorate. It had no power and did not last long.

There were two unresolved issues in the Owen-Stoltenberg Plan. The first was how the ethnic partitioning would be carried out, and the second was how to ensure viable central institutions for the Union of Bosnia and Herzegovina. On the first question, the state delegation insisted that the process of drawing borders between the three republics must not be allowed to lead to further ethnic cleansing. We used Sarajevo and Tuzla as examples. Tanja Ljujić-Mijatović, Miro Lazović, and I grew passionate when we talked about these cities. We pointed out the risk that the ethnic division into three republics would lead to the mass exodus of Serbs and Croats from Sarajevo. This would mean a radical change in the ethnic structure of the capital city, which even in war and in spite of so much slaughter had preserved the nucleus of its pre-war multiethnic composition. At this point Lord Owen entered the discussion. Even the cold Owen became almost emotional at this point. He confirmed our fears, and added, "I have been in Sarajevo. I saw that people of different nationalities are living together even in wartime. There is a high degree of tolerance and solidarity among them. You, as individuals and as members of the Presidency," he said, turning toward Ljujić-Mijatović, Lazović and myself, "are an example of this way of life, and of these relations between the peoples."

We believed that the preservation of a multiethnic Sarajevo would mean reasonable hope that a multiethnic population structure and interethnic trust could be revived in Bosnia. On the basis of this faith I endlessly urged that Sarajevo have a separate status in the peace plan. My view was that we should have a unified city under a temporary international administration until all essential services were restored and interethnic trust had been re-established. We succeeded in preserving a sense of the unique significance of Sarajevo throughout negotiations on the Owen-Stoltenberg plan.

The Presidency met in Zagreb in July 1993 on the occasion of our return from Geneva. Owen and Stoltenberg had issued a call for the talks to continue. But, during the Presidency's meeting at the Bosnian Embassy in Zagreb, we found ourselves divided. President Izetbegović and Ejup Ganić preferred to continue their journey on to Sarajevo rather than return to Geneva, but the rest of the Presidency members all chose to travel back to Geneva the following day, to carry on with the negotiations. There was a rumor that the aircraft we were taking might be in potential danger. But most of the Presidency members decided to take it anyway, and all of us except Izetbegović and Ganić returned to Geneva as planned.

In Geneva, the next issue discussed was that of the central organs proposed for the Union of Three Republics, and their jurisdiction. On this question, too, there was absolutely no agreement between the state delegation and Karadžić. One morning co-chairs Stoltenberg and Owen placed a paper on the table containing nine points or principles for the structure of the union. None of these contained any elements of a proper confederation or union, much less any elements that would guarantee a strong structure for the central organs of the Bosnian state. All nine points were based on the independence of the three ethnic republics, Bosniak, Croat and Serb, and provided only for the possibility of their future cooperation within the Union on questions of common interest. No issue was actually specified as being of common interest, and no central state organ was given constitutional status. Everything was left to possible future consensus.

After we had carefully analyzed the concept for division that had been offered, the atmosphere grew painful. I felt sick. Lazović noticed and asked me what was the matter. I told him, "I feel ill. This is too much for me. I neither can nor will take further part in this." Owen now suggested we should take a break and dine together in the afternoon and evening with co-chairs Stoltenberg and Owen, presidents Tuđman of Croatia and Milošević of Serbia, and all the members of the Bosnian Presidency who were then in Geneva, along with Lazović as Speaker of the Parliament and Akmadžić as Prime Minister. This was a working dinner, and Stoltenberg and Owen made the opening speeches. They repeated their assessment of the situation in Bosnia, emphasizing the danger of a humanitarian catastrophe, the need to stop the war, and the importance of obtaining an agreement. Their basic theme was that all sides must agree to end the war. Abdić, Lasić, Boras and Akmadžić entered into the subsequent discussion, which included analysis of various individual aspects of finding a solution. Momir Bulatović was also present at the dinner.[76]

Tanja Ljujić-Mijatović, after her initial presentation, stressed that she was born in Bosnia, grew up in Sarajevo, was educated there, had lived there for her entire career, and had become a professor of its University. All this she achieved in coexistence with her neighbors, Croats, Bosniaks and Jews. She then attacked the theory that a common life for all nations is impossible in Bosnia, and that this impossibility was the basic cause of war. She refuted this with concrete examples of how people lived before and during the war, with examples of the prosperity of Bosnia's people. She also emphasized that Bosnia could have a hopeful future only if the peace solution ensured the equality of the three nations and all citizens, and included punishment for war crimes. As for the political order of the state, she proposed a federal model. Miro Lazović propounded a similar theory. He added that all people, regardless of nationality, wanted to stop the war in Bosnia, stop the killing, and continue in peacetime to resolve the historic questions that emerged in the transition from a communist to a democratic society and a pluralist political system.

The ideas that I myself offered were similar, but I talked in more detail about a possible constitutional structure for Bosnia, based on the concept of a modern Federation, in which key problems would be solved by a council of citizens and the issues of developing and preserving the identity of the peoples would be resolved by a council of nations. This was a familiar idea that dated back to the program earlier adopted by the Presidency. Then I begged Presidents Tuđman and Milošević to hear me out on the issue of cooperation between Bosnia's nations and their neighbors. If Croats and Serbs live mixed in Bosnia, then it should be obvious that their relationships within this state are of positive significance for cooperation between the Croat

---

[76] Bulatović, a Milošević loyalist, was the President of Montengro, which together with Serbia made up the Federation of Yugoslavia as reconfigured in April 1992. Bulatović remained President until unseated by an oppponent of Milošević, Milo Đukanović, in 1998.

and Serb nations generally, and between Croatia and Yugoslavia specifically. I went further and asked what they felt about the various solutions successfully achieved by contemporary social democracies in Europe on both social and national questions.

After this Tuđman declared himself ready to speak, and spoke at length. He drew many comparisons between episodes in Europe's past and the history of the South Slavs. I had asked him to give, as a historian, his opinion on the possibility of cooperation between the peoples of Bosnia, given that they had lived together for centuries with other peoples and states of Europe. His initial thesis was that the fall of Communism was accompanied by a volcanic upheaval of national energy, leading ultimately to full-blown war in Croatia. He described how the Serb forces, meaning the Croatian Serb forces, with the might of the JNA at their backs, had destroyed almost every Croat house in the Croat-populated areas of the Krajina, Slavonia, and Baranje. He pointed out that nothing like this had ever happened before. He said that even the Second World War had seen less destruction. He argued that the time of national movements and ideologies had arrived, and that national issues were bound to be resolved in ways more radical than at any previous period in the region's history.

After an excellent dinner and much talking, we got up from the table. An atmosphere of goodwill had been created, and now Lazović, Tanja and I hoped to talk to privately with Milošević and Bulatović. Bulatović told us that he agreed with our comments on the war in Bosnia, and on a possible solution. But of course, he only said this when talking to us in private. He had not stood up and said so publicly during the dinner. Next we tried to talk to Milošević. Our aim was to tell him clearly that his support for the Pale leadership would not lead to any resolution of the Bosnian tragedy. But Kasim Trnka, special adviser to the delegation, immediately put some questions to Milošević about the 14th Congress of the League of Communists of Yugoslavia (SKJ).[77] Sparks started

---

[77] The Fourteenth Extraordinary Congress of the League of Communists of Yugoslavia, held in January 1990, was the last effort to resolve the severe conflicts that had developed within the party among delegates form the various Republics. After the Slovenian delegation walked out, the Congress dissolved, spelling an end to the SKJ.

flying on the question of whom to blame for the collapse of both the SKJ and Yugoslavia, and we lost the chance to introduce our own topic.

But at the working dinner itself, those of us on the Presidency had succeeded in establishing that any further negotiations must incorporate the concept of a federal structure for Bosnia. The two co-chairs of the peace conference, Stoltenberg and Owen, accepted this.

We now returned to Zagreb and asked President Izetbegović and Ejup Ganić to join us in preparing a proposal for a federal structure for Bosnia. President Izetbegović had obligations to meet in Sarajevo, so he authorized Ganić, as was his practice throughout the war, to come to Zagreb and chair the next Presidency session. (Against Presidency regulations, Izetbegović never designated anyone other than Ganić to stand in for him at such meetings.) On a very hot July day in 1993, at the Austrian Embassy in Zagreb, we spent the whole day discussing what concept for a federal Bosnia we would offer the co-chairs of the peace conference. Our advisers, Professors Kasim Trnka and Kasim Begić, provided the necessary expertise. We mostly discussed how to implement the principle of parity and achieve consensus within the central organs of the state. There was disagreement between the Croat members of the Presidency and Ganić, and to some extent among all of us, on how widely consensus should be required for decision-making by the central organs of the Bosnian federation. By the afternoon, after a prolonged discussion, we had reached agreement on these issues and on the concept of the federal structure generally.

We returned to Geneva for further negotiations with this proposal in hand, and the co-chairs arranged for a meeting in Brussels between the Presidency and the foreign ministers of the European Union member countries. The chair was Willy Claes, the Belgian minister of foreign affairs. The meeting was useful: we were all able to air our views on a federal structure for Bosnia. During the following discussion, in the round Chamber of the European Union in Brussels, Claes gave us his response. "Gentlemen, we are in Belgium, and Belgium is also a multi-national country. For thirty years we have debated how to achieve an internal structure offering the best political order, a federal order. But we haven't had a war. You, gentlemen, have a war in your country, and now the issue is primarily of stopping the war, not finding an internal structure.

One thing is certain; the internal structure of Bosnia must have at its foundations the equality of the three nations that live in this country. All else can be subordinated to achieving peace and stopping the war."

Claes's tough words were the note on which the meeting ended. We gave a joint press conference, at which there were a number of questions. The journalists who were present reported that Ljujić-Mijatović, Lazović, myself, and - according to the speech he made - Fikret Abdić, were all advocating for the preservation of a united Bosnia and the equality of its three constituent peoples, Bosniaks, Croats and Serbs. We all spoke out strongly on behalf of stopping the war. After the press conference a journalist from Belgrade's *Naša Borba*, Mirko Klarin, came up to me to ask for an additional interview. He said some encouraging words to me, and to Tanja and Lazović, about the job we were doing, and how we were representing Bosnia.

Subsequently one more round of talks followed in Geneva, based on the Owen-Stoltenberg Plan. The new variant of their plan foresaw three ethnic units with a joint capital city, Sarajevo, and with borders, borders that we found deeply unsatisfactory, between the Bosniak, Croat, and Serb ethnic units. Owen led most of these discussions.

The sessions of the Bosnian Parliament and the Bosniak Assembly convened after our return from Geneva were especially grueling.[78] I followed the session of the Bosniak Assembly closely. The Assembly, after much discussion, decided to accept the peace plan proposed by Owen and Stoltenberg, but only on condition that the formerly Bosniak-majority territories which had been taken by force must be returned to the Bosniak territorial unit, given that the Bosniak nation had been expelled by force from the whole of Eastern Bosnia. The Bosnian Parliament subsequently held two debates on the possible formation of an entity that would be called the Bosnian Republic, but would in essence be a Bosniak republic

---

[78] The Bosniak Assembly was an unofficial but highly gathering of Bosniaks that met twice in 1993. In this instance it met to consider the Union of Three Republics plan and then presented its views to the Bosnian Parliament, which effectively rubber-stamped them. It was at the first of these two meetings that the delegates voted to change the group name from "Bosnian Muslim" to "Bosniak."

on Bosniak territory. The idea included the expectation that the Bosniak entity would receive international recognition as a sovereign state. Muhamed Kupusovic, an SDA delegate and Mayor of Sarajevo, led the first debate. Hasan Muratović, then member of the government and later Prime Minister, led the second. Thereafter the Bosnian Parliament, of which a large majority of delegates were SDA members and Bosniaks, followed the lead of the Bosniak Assembly and endorsed the peace plan with the same conditions as those imposed by the Bosniak Assembly. This demand to reverse the armed seizure of territories where Bosniaks had lived for centuries was interpreted by Owen and Stoltenberg's as a rejection of their proposed peace plan.

# XVI. THE SGV: ITS FOUNDATION, PRINCIPLES, AND ACTIVITIES

In June 1992, when Sarajevo was under siege and bombardment, a group of Serbs founded the Forum of Citizens of Serb Nationality of the City of Sarajevo. This was one of the first expressions of the collective wishes of the Serbs who chose to remain in Sarajevo with their Bosniak and Croat neighbors, and who acknowledged the legal government of Bosnia. The first meeting was held in the Institute of Physical Culture and chaired by the first president, Dragutin Braco Kosovac, a pre-war Prime Minister of the Bosnian Government and a director of Energoinvest. Despite the challenge of traveling through widespread shelling, many people gathered to condemn the bombardment of Sarajevo and the ethnic cleansing that had already commenced in Eastern Bosnia. All appealed to the Pale leadership to stop shelling Sarajevo, enter into negotiations, and find a solution that would end the bloodshed, aggression and war.

The Forum undertook forceful initiatives in promoting the demands of its participants. Nenad Kecmanović and I had then just joined the Presidency, but we were present at the Forum meeting as citizens of Serb nationality. I remember the landmark speech of Dr. Trifko Guzina, who had been an SDS activist and member of that party's Advisory Board before the war. He criticized everything that his former party was doing, and condemned the use of force to solve problems, which he saw as leading to the destruction of coexistence between the nations. He denounced the destruction of Sarajevo, and the attacks on its people and their property. He pointed out that over 150 000 members of the Serb nation lived in Sarajevo when the war began.

The Forum adopted a statement that condemned the use of force and ethnic expulsion, demanded the immediate cessation of all bombardment, and called for negotiations. The statement described the killing of civilians in Sarajevo as a crime, and stated categorically that no one had the right to commit crimes in the name of the Serb nation. This was the first voice of the Serb nation in Sarajevo, the voice of civic-minded people who had made it their destiny to defend co-existence against aggression. They thus stood firmly opposed to the extreme nationalist politics of the SDS.

In early 1993, Professor Ljubomir Berberović proposed the idea of creating a Serb Consultative Council. He proposed this step during a leisurely conversation on a cold morning over a sandwich - for at that time there was nothing to eat or drink in the Presidency except sandwiches and tea. The crux of the idea was to broaden the mission of the Sarajevo Serb Forum to unite the activities of Serbs who had stayed to support a sovereign, multiethnic and united Bosnia. All had confirmed their belief in a secular and democratic state of equal citizens and peoples by voting at the referendum in early 1992 in which the majority of Bosnian citizens voluntarily supported the historic development of the sovereign Bosnian state. All had shown their dedication to this platform, both as individuals and as activists in civil and multiethnic political parties, cultural, sport, humanitarian and other associations.

Professor Berberović produced a sketch of the principles for the Serb Consultative Council. After some discussion with others who supported the idea, Berberović wrote the final version of the Council program, consisting of four points. The first point called for achieving a stable and lasting peace in Bosnia through a just agreement. The second point upheld the coexistence of equal peoples and nations in a sovereign and internationally recognized state. The third point called for parliamentary democracy, and the fourth for the recognition of human and civil rights in accordance with international standards. These became part of the founding document of the Serb Consultative Council adopted in 1993. Regional Serb Consultative Councils were formed in Sarajevo and other cities. Tuzla was among the first to form its own Council: headed by Mišo Božić, a businessman and well-known citizen of Tuzla. The Council's aim was principally to promote a solution that would bring peace. Among its other activities, the Council sent representatives to meet with the co-chairs of the Conference on the Former Yugoslavia, Lord David Owen and Thorwald Stoltenberg, to discuss the peace plan.

The idea gained momentum when other groups organized similar associations. The Bosniak Assemblies of 1993 and the formation in 1994 of the Croatian National Council gave psychological weight to the idea of forming an equivalent Serb Council. This was conceived of as a single council of the Serb nation in the territory under the control of the legal Bosnian government and the Bosnian Army. Within the Serb Consultative Council, extensive consultations took place that included activists from numerous political parties, the cultural society *Prosvjete*, the humanitarian agency *Dobrotvor*, and refugee associations from abroad. The Serb Consultative Council passed a resolution to convene an inaugural Assembly of Citizens of Serb Nationality.

The intention was that this assembly, as a civic initiative, should undertake to form the Serb Civic Council (SGV – *Srpsko građansko vijeće*). The original plan was to call this group the Serb National Council, but a day or two before the Assembly, during final preparation of the papers, Professor Berberović and I discussed this one more time, and I suggested it should be called the Serb Civic Council rather than the Serb National Council. He and I agreed, and we thus became the godparents of the SGV. During the war many people abroad, principally Bosniaks and Croats, asked me, "Why didn't you simply call it the Civic Council, so that we too could be members?" But I recommended this title for a reason. Prior to the war there were around 1.3 million Serbs in Bosnia, the majority of whom lived in cities and towns. Many of the latter - and there is an estimate that this was around half a million Serbs - did not vote for the SDS: instead they gave their political backing to the parties and people of civic orientation. They voted for citizens' rights as the foundation for a social structure, independent of party, political, religious and other associations, and for the constitutional equality of all three indigenous Bosnian nations. At the first multiparty elections in 1990, they voted for the civic parties: the Social Democrats, the Reformists, and the Liberals. Many took part in the 1992 referendum and voted for an independent and sovereign Bosnian state. This fact was for me decisive, and this was what motivated me to recommend including the word 'Serb' in the title of the council, as subsequently accepted by the Assembly.

This Assembly was held on March 27 1994. In spite of wartime conditions, 428 delegates gathered from Sarajevo, Tuzla, Zenica,

Mostar, Konjic, Gračanica, and other places within the state of Bosnia, although most were from Sarajevo and Tuzla. Among the delegates were a significant number who were serving in the Bosnian armed forces. There were also a large number of local and foreign guests, including Charles Redman, then acting as envoy of the US President in the Bosnian peace negotiations, and the Russian ambassador to Zagreb Kerestedžijanc who was serving as the envoy of Victor Churkin, the Russian Deputy Foreign Minister.

At this first assembly some notable documents were passed. The first was the Declaration of the Assembly of Citizens of Serb Nationality, which defined all-important questions concerning the war, a political solution, the internal structure of Bosnia, and the development of the state. In particular, it defined the Assembly's position on war crimes, namely that war criminals of Serb and other nationalities must be brought to justice, and that responsibility for war crimes must be borne by those individuals and forces which committed them, but not by whole nations in the name of collective guilt. As for the state structure, the Assembly declared itself in favor of a federal model for the Bosnian state.

The second document adopted by the Assembly was a summons to the citizens and nations of Bosnia to hold an assembly of interethnic trust. The idea was to organize a joint assembly of the Croat, Bosniak and Serb peoples in order to build a platform for the renewal of trust, the fight for a common life and a unified state. This idea was very well received in the media, but never came to be realized in practice, for the situation was too desperate.

The third document passed by the Assembly proposed an amendment to the draft Constitution of the Federation (to be discussed in Chapter XXII).

Finally, the Assembly formally founded the SGV and elected its 33 members. Those elected were activists in the Serb nation who had distinguished themselves locally by their activities on behalf of a multiethnic and united Bosnia. When preparing for the first Assembly of Citizens of Serb Nationality, Professor Berberović, Žarko Bulić and I had communicated to other activists our decision to nominate Žarko Bulić, Sarajevo lawyer and president of the Bosnian Bar association, as President of the SGV. Everyone accepted this proposal, and I would have said the same of Žarko himself. Two days later, however, which was all the time left before the Assembly was due to convene, Bulić asked for the choice to be reconsidered on the grounds that if he accepted this responsibility, he would no longer be able to continue his professional activities as a lawyer. He therefore appealed for an alternative to be found.

During those two days I was in Tuzla, at the holding of regional preparations for the Assembly. Late in the evening Professor Berberović called me. He reached the point immediately: would I accept the position of President? He said that I could not refuse, given all the circumstances, particularly the need for the SGV to establish international cooperation, to create an international position for itself, and to have access to international diplomatic leaders in the quest for a peaceful solution. He added that my activities and my position were such that I had to accept, and pointed out that this was wartime, and therefore everything must be done and every opportunity used to transform our ideas into reality. I personally wanted the SGV President to be somebody who was not involved in the execution of government, but I had only a short time to decide, as Professor Berberović again called me for a meeting and asked me once more to accept. Thus I was elected President of the SGV president at the First Assembly of Citizens of Serb Nationality.

The SGV was founded on the understanding that Bosnia's society and state must develop on the foundations of civil society and the ideas that have evolved during the development of contemporary democracy. Contemporary democratic achievements derive from concepts that have enabled the growth of the market economy, the evolution and protection of human rights, parliamentary democracy, and the establishment of national equality, based on democratic freedom and individual and collective human rights.

The second Assembly of Citizens of Serb Nationality was scheduled for April 1995. During the preparations for the Second Assembly, an SGV delegation traveled to Belgrade, led by Boro Bjelobrk, an SDP delegate in the Bosnian Parliament. In Sarajevo, we had spent over a month trying to organize the trip. Telephone lines and transport connections were frequently cut off, and travel was arduous. The route involved passing through the Sarajevo tunnel and along the dangerous route to and over Mount Igman. From there the road led to the Adriatic Coast at Split, from Split to

Zagreb, from Zagreb to Hungary, and through Hungary to the Federal Republic of Yugoslavia. Several organizations in Belgrade had agreed to receive our delegation: these included the Association of Bosnians and Herzegovinians, a multiethnic association led during the war by Ljubo Babić; the Civil Alliance; and several others. With these preparations completed, the delegation set off.

During every hour that followed, we anxiously awaited news that they had safely passed Igman, and arrived in Split for the journey to Zagreb. Obstacles cropped up at every stage of the journey. It was not even certain if they could enter Yugoslavia at all, for a delegation that had previously attempted to do so had been turned back at the border. But the delegation eventually entered Yugoslavia and was enthusiastically received in Belgrade. Its arrival drew the attention of the independent media and the civic opposition parties in particular. In addition to Boro Bjelobrk, the delegation included Nada Mladina from Tuzla and Boro Spasojević, an SGV activist from Sarajevo. The delegation's hosts in Belgrade included the Serb Renewal Movement, the Civil Alliance, the Circle of Independent Intellectuals, the association "Living in Sarajevo", and many other organizations.

The delegation made a public presentation, arranged by the Belgrade Circle of Independent Intellectuals. This presentation succeeded, as the members of delegation said, in reaching out to those who opposed what Karadžić's military and political machinery were doing to Bosnia. The meeting revealed the freedom-loving, democratic spirit of Belgrade: these were the individuals and associations who had stood against the war. The SGV delegation members were each greeted as a symbol, as a sign of moral victory, for these were not Serbs from Pale, but people who had emerged from the steel circle forged round Sarajevo, where death struck every day. Bjelobrk and the other members of the delegation talked about themselves, about life in war-torn Sarajevo and the other towns from which the various delegation members had come, and they spoke of what hope they could see of ending the war. They also presented the ideas of the SGV. This first appearance of the SGV in Belgrade obtained good media coverage, both in the local press, and by international media organizations.

The delegation also met with His Holiness, the Serbian Orthodox Patriarch Pavle. With him they discussed the reconstruction of religious life in the towns of the Federation, and the possibility of

Orthodox priests returning to be with their people. This did not yield any immediate results; later, however, a priest did come to Tuzla, and another to Sarajevo.

The delegation also met with various officials in Belgrade, notably with Dragan Tomić, then speaker of Serbia's parliament. The SGV delegation members saw and heard for themselves that official Belgrade viewed the Bosnian Serbs as Serbs only, without making any attempt at distinguishing them from the Serbs of Serbia and elsewhere. The delegation learned from Tomic that Belgrade had accepted the peace plan of the Contact Group, although the Pale leadership was still against it. Tomic told the delegation that it was unjustifiable for 30% of the population to demand 50% of the territory of the state. These were the first signs of spring, the thawing of relations between Belgrade and Sarajevo, and the first establishment of political relations with the free-minded people and democratic forces in Serbia and Yugoslavia.

Following the delegation's visit to Belgrade, many guests came from Belgrade to the second Assembly, which adopted the report of the delegation'a president, Bjelobrk, as one of its documents. Around 400 delegates participated in the Second Assembly held in April 1995, and several documents were passed. The first document outlined the views of the SGV on the establishment of peace in Bosnia and on the internal structure of the Republic of Bosnia and Herzegovina. The declaration stated that a solution to the Bosnian question is possible with the participation and engagement of the international community as a factor able to achieve consensus on a peaceful resolution, and to ensure implementation. The declaration affirmed the earlier SGV view that Bosnia as a state is comprised of its equal citizens and its three equal nations, and therefore the best structure for the state would be a Federation. The internal organization would best consist of cantons or regions founded on cultural, historic, economic, and geographic criteria as well as ethnic criteria. However, the declaration rejected the notion of ethnicity as a primary criterion. The declaration asserted that peace was in the best interests of the Serb, Croat, Jewish and other nations living in Bosnia, and essential for economic revival and the renewal of interethic trust. Finally, the declaration reiterates that no individual or organization, including the SDS, can claim the right to represent the entire Serb nation. It demands that the SGV participate in the peace negotiations, to express the will of that part of the Bosnian Serb nation which had never accepted the policy of ethnic cleansing and ethnic division of Bosnia.

The Second Assembly also passed a resolution on the establishment of respect for human rights in Bosnia, the first time that such a resolution was adopted. This demanded that human freedoms and human rights should be universally protected, and the development in Bosnia of institutions to ensure this protection.

The Assembly addressed a letter to the heads of state of the countries comprising the Contact Group, the body that had taken the lead in seeking an agreement to end the war. It stated, "The three year war has shown that a historic deception of the Serb nation has taken place. The homogenization of the Serbs was implemented in order to defend the concept of Yugoslavia. It has now been revealed that Yugoslavia was only a station on the road to an ethnically pure Serbia." Here, I will add that it was, of course, absurd to create an ethnically pure Serb state in Bosnia in order to join it with multinational Serbia, where 35% of the population is non-Serb.

The third Assembly was held in peacetime, on 14 July 1996, half a year after the signing of the Dayton Peace Accords. During its work, the third Assembly received immense support from many representatives of various associations, political parties from the Federation, and political parties and associations from abroad, as well as political associations and independent journalists from the RS. This was the first time that somebody from the RS was present at a gathering of Federation Serbs, including those who were living there as displaced persons. The guests were activists from Bijeljina, Doboj and Banja Luka.

The Third Assembly defined the post-war peacetime goals of the SGV, namely the foundations for the reconstruction and reintegration of the Bosnian state. The SGV undertook to promote economic revitalization, the return of refugees, and the democratization of society. Special emphasis was laid on the universal protection of human rights and the renewal of interethnic trust. The "Declaration on the interests of citizens of Serb nationality in building peace and the state of Bosnia and Herzegovina" stated in its opening paragraph, "The greatest general good for citizens of Serb nationality and all peoples of Bosnia and Herzegovina is peace and the strengthening of peace. Peace is possible only through cooperation of the Serb, Bosniak and Croat nations in all institutions of contemporary Bosnian society." This referred to the central institutions established by the Dayton Peace Agreement: the Presidency, the Bosnian Parliament, the Council of Ministers, and the Constitutional Court.

Another document laid out the SGV position on the elections scheduled for September 1996, the first held under the terms of the Dayton Peace Agreement. The document noted that the SGV particularly welcomed the "Joint List" of civic multiethnic parties, and stressed the issues which were of particular interest to the SGV: the reintegration of the state within its internationally recognized borders, the renewal of trust between peoples and nations, the return of refugees and displaced persons to their homes, and the arrest of all those indicted for war crimes.

The Third Assembly also passed a resolution concerning the integration into Sarajevo of those areas that had been controlled by Karadžić's forces during the war, where the Serb population had been a majority. The Assembly concluded that the mass departure of Serbs from the reintegrated areas of Sarajevo was a project of the Pale leadership, executed in order to complete the ethnic division of the nations and to produce total national homogenization – in other words, an ethnically pure territory - in the Republika Srpska. In my opinion, Momčilo Krajišnik played the key role in the mass exodus of Sarajevo's Serbs from the reintegrated areas of the city. The whole action was manifestly against the interests of the people themselves. After their exodus, the former Sarajevo Serbs lacked homes and property and were jobless. They became, in fact, the most dissatisfied element of the Republika Srpska's new population.

# XVII. WARTIME VISITS TO MOSCOW AND BELGRADE

After the failure of the Owen Stoltenberg Plan for a Union of Three Republics, the US became directly involved in the search for peace. In February and March 1994, American diplomats helped negotiate the Washington Agreement, the first successful phase in the search for a comprehensive peace for Bosnia. The Washington Agreement ended the armed conflict between the ABH and the HVO and led to the creation of the Federation of Bosnia and Herzegovina. Together, the US, Russia, France, England and Germany agreed to form the Contact Group to promote a broader peace agreement, that would end the war waged by Karadžić's Bosnian Serb nationalists. Thanks to their influence in the UN Security Council, Contact Group member countries were able to produce the founding principles for a peace agreement for Bosnia. One of these principles was that Bosnia must retain its international and legal continuity as a state, its integrity and unity within internationally recognized borders. The second principle was that the state should be equally governed by each of its three nations, Croat, Serb and Bosniak. The third principle was that the situation the conflict had created on the ground should be resolved by defining two Entities: the Republika Srpska, which would occupy 49% of Bosnia's territory, and the Federation of Bosnia and Herzegovina, which would cover 51%: this was the Contact Group's founding concept. Two further conditions were envisaged for the peace plan: that the leading powers should manage its implementation in association, and that a formula for internal division would be necessary. The latter now became the subject of all negotiations with those who represented the military and political forces currently operating in Bosnia.

When the Contact Group started work, the Pale leadership issued a clear rejection of their proposal. During 1994, the Contact Group went on failing to produce significant results, until the US peace initiative got under way, at the end of the year. The US took over the leading role in seeking a peace solution, using a combination of military action in Bosnia, and diplomatic pressure on the power centers of Belgrade and Zagreb - which had and still have immense influence on Bosnia's political and military forces.

In summer 1994, the SGV appointed a delegation of its members to visit Moscow: Miro Lazović, Speaker of the Bosnian Parliament, Gavrilo Grhovac and Rajko Živković as officials of the SGV, and myself. This was the first visit to Moscow ever made in wartime by a delegation from Bosnia. It was also the first visit paid by Bosnian Serbs. We had a meeting scheduled with Vitaly Churkin, deputy to Andrei Kozyrev, Russia's Foreign Minister. Kozyrev had earlier visited Sarajevo, and as chance would have it, I had hosted his visit to the Presidency and the subsequent press conference.

We used our meeting with Churkin to discuss the Contact Group Plan. It was a unique opportunity for Churkin to hear the SGV's vision for achieving a lasting peace. We stressed the idea of a peaceful, political solution, with the involvement and commitment of the international community, as a guarantee that the peace plan would be implemented. We acquainted Churkin with facts that were little known in Moscow, particularly that many Serbs still lived in cities on Federation territory. We also told him the facts about Serbs in Bosnia generally and the current distribution of the Bosnian Serb population. According to the estimates of international organizations, half a million citizens of Serb nationality had been forced by war to seek refugee status: many of these were educated people from the cities.

We told Churkin that the Serbs living in territory under Karadžić's control numbered around 800,000, and within this group was a ruling elite which managed the army, police, political activity, and local municipalities. Within this elite there flourished an extremism founded on ethic hatred, and dedication to ethnic cleansing and ethnic expulsion. We stressed the need to distinguish between this extremism and the wishes and interests of the Serb nation as a whole. We said we knew that the ordinary people living in the territory held by Karadžić's forces, above all wanted the war to end. No one wanted their sons to go to war and never come back; no one wanted their children dead, and the nation deprived of its young people. But the war machine had gained such momentum that the Pale leadership believed they could continue to defy not only the rest of Bosnia, but the whole world.

We also told Churkin that the relations of trust between the Serb, Bosniak, Croat and Jewish nations, created in the course of building a common life, had been essentially preserved, especially in Sarajevo, Tuzla, and other towns. We stressed that in Bosnia, the coexistence of the nations is subject neither to the political will of this or that regime, nor to this or that ideological concept of government and society. Instead, it is simply a matter of destiny, a natural order arising from the presence in the same territory of people of different faiths and nations. We denied the theory that coexistence is impossible and told him it was a false ideology used to justify crime, ethnic cleansing, and the creation of an ethnically defined Serb territory with the intent of joining it to Serbia, or rather the Federal Republic of Yugoslavia. Churkin's answer was clear. He had visited Pale several times, he said, and he personally believed that Karadžić and the Pale leadership were addicted to war, and that war profiteering blinded them to the suffering of their people. But the need to stop the war was our main topic, and we stressed that Russia, as one of the Contact Group members, should take part in finding a political solution that would engage the international community in implementation of the peace agreement.

We also met with a representative of the Russian Orthodox Patriarchy: the Archimandrite Feofan, foreign relations assistant to the Russian Patriarch Aleksei. On our way to this meeting, our delegation stepped into the outer circle of the Patriarchate, a huge space with candles burning on all sides, full of people, especially women. We suddenly noticed that one of our group, member, Gavrilo Grahovac, had stopped and that several women were busy kissing his hand: thanks to his beard and his dark coat, he looked exactly like a visiting priest. He drew himself up and, in the manner of a real priest, raised his hand to bless the faithful who had gathered round him.

When we entered the Patriarchate itself, the deputy of Patriarch Aleksei greeted us cordially. For him too it was a new experience to meet people from Sarajevo, not Pale, who were Serbs, but not

Karadžić's Serbs. He asked us to tell him first of all about the situation in Bosnia, and about those Bosnian Serbs who were neither in Karadžić's army nor his party, and who did not acknowledge him. We tried to say something about ourselves, about Bosnia, the situation in Sarajevo, and about Serbs in Sarajevo and in other cities. We talked to him about the religious lives of Serbs, Bosniaks, Croats and Jews, and the specifics of inter-religious tolerance in Bosnia. We did not hide the fact that during the war there had been unprecedented destruction of religious buildings, especially mosques. We said that about a thousand Muslim places of worship had been devastated by Karadžić's forces. We told him how many buildings belonging to the Catholic Church had also suffered, both monasteries and churches, and that a number of Orthodox churches had been devastated, especially in the Neretva valley.

When we told him how many mosques Karadžić's forces had destroyed, he was deeply disturbed, and asked if this was really possible, why nobody knew about it, and how could anyone commit such an act against faith and against God. He then told us that the Patriarch Aleksei intended to go to Belgrade and meet with the Serb Patriarch Pavle, and that he wanted to do something to stop the bloodshed in Bosnia and help peace. When we heard this, we proposed an alternative. We suggested that Aleksei, Patriarch of Moscow and all Russia, rather than traveling to Belgrade to meet with the religious dignitaries of Croatia and Bosnia, should meet them in Sarajevo itself. We stressed that the visit of the Russian Patriarch to the Bosnian capital would be in itself the most effective expression of his moral position towards the destruction of Sarajevo and Bosnia. Archimandrite Feofan was very much taken with our proposal, and said that he would discuss it. It was agreed that over the next few days Patriarch Aleksei, as a dedicated worker for peace and cooperation between nations, would give us his reply.

We next visited Ibrahim Đikić in the Bosnian embassy. That afternoon Đikić told us a fax had come, announcing that the Russian Patriarch Aleksei would be glad to visit Sarajevo to meet with religious representatives from Croatia, Bosnia and Serbia. We immediately informed Sarajevo, as this news seemed to us of great importance, given the influence the highest religious dignitary of Russia could have on the Russian public and Russian policy when it came to a peace solution for Bosnia.

The next day we traveled to Ljubljana and from there to Zagreb, where a press conference had been arranged. We had already spoken to the press in Ljubljana about our visit to Moscow. I phoned President Izetbegović from Slovenia, and told him of the new turn of affairs in Moscow, particularly of Patriarch Aleksei's wish that the meeting of religious dignitaries should take place in Sarajevo instead of Belgrade. President Izetbegović advised me to consult with Reis Cerić, whom I immediately telephoned. Reis Cerić accepted the idea, but felt that the meeting should take place in the city itself rather than at the airport as had been originally intended by the Russian Patriarch.[79]

I saw that there would be difficulties ahead, as there had previously been difficulties over Cerić's meeting with his Holiness the Serb Patriarch Pavle because the latter had failed to condemn publicly the crimes committed against Bosniaks, especially the destruction of their religious monuments. I suggested that the Reis should bear in mind what the meeting would achieve, and that it would also involve the Bosnian Catholic Archbishop Vinko Puljić and the Zagreb Archbishop Cardinal Kuharić. In speaking with Reis Cerić I did not place any special emphasis on the fact that the Russian Patriarch would be present, as his presence would also mean that of Patriarch Pavle. However, it turned out, as I feared, that neither the Russian nor the Serb Patriarchs were prepared to enter the city of Sarajevo proper, and Reis Cerić refused to meet them at the airport. Thus the meeting of these religious dignitaries never took place in the form envisaged. In the end, the meeting was held at Sarajevo airport and without Reis Cerić.

The Russian Patriarch's, readiness to come to Bosnia, confront the truth about the slaughter in Sarajevo, and carry this truth back to his own country, revealed much about the attitude of the Russian Orthodox Church. But for me the crowning moment came when Archimandrite Feofan said, "We, in Russia, have around 20 million residents of Muslim faith. We respect all their religious freedoms. We cannot accept the fact that people's mosques are being destroyed just because they are of a different faith."

---

[79] The Reis-ul-ulema is the supreme authority of the Islamic Religious Community in Bosnia and Herzegovina. Cerić assumed that position in 1993 after having served as imam at mosques that served the Bosnian Muslim communities in Chicago and in Zagreb.

After the press conference in Zagreb, we stayed another day at the Hotel Esplanada. Ivo Komšić was in Zagreb at the time, and over breakfast in the Esplanada he introduced me to Veljko Knežević, then the Yugoslav envoy to Croatia. (Knezević was later appointed the Yugoslav ambassador to Croatia.) The conversation that followed focused primarily on our visit to Moscow, our meetings there, the general situation in Bosnia, and the situation of Serbs in the Federation, especially in Sarajevo. We shared with Knezević the position of the SGV on a peace agreement for Bosnia, the questions facing the Serb nation in Bosnia, and the extremism of the Pale leadership. Knežević showed deep interest, and we agreed to meet again. In our second dialogue with him, we discussed these topics further and, in turn, we heard from him about the Serbs in Croatia and his government's ongoing disagreement with various policies of the leaders of the Krajina Serbs. My impression was that Veljko Knežević, a Croatian Serb who was born in and worked in Croatia, was not only well informed about relations between Serbs and Croats in Croatia, but also profoundly concerned about relations between the three peoples in Bosnia. I felt that he genuinely cared about finding a peaceful solution.

During this meeting I was inspired by the notion that a delegation of the SGV should visit Belgrade, to speak with President Milošević about the issues we had already raised in Paris, Brussels, Strasbourg, London and Vienna. Veljko Knežević was sympathetic to this idea, but it remained to be seen how our proposal would be received in Belgrade. After a while, however, the message came that our proposal had been accepted. The SGV visit would be arranged for early July 1994, and would include a meeting with President Milošević. On our side we chose to make this visit secretly, with no publicity. Just before we left, Knežević gave me a letter to deliver to his nephew who was studying in Sarajevo. This nephew had married a Bosniak from Tuzla and was spending the war in the Sarajevo suburb of Dobrinja with his family. This very human episode speaks volumes about Knezević's connections with Sarajevo and of his many friends there.

After learning that the trip to Belgrade had been agreed, we agreed at the top levels of the SGV that our delegation should consist of Žarko Bulić, Deputy President of the SGV, and myself. But when a date was decided upon, Bulic turned out to have obligations that took him out of Sarajevo. In the end I traveled with only my bodyguard, and with the assistance of the Bosnian ambassador to Zagreb. In preparation for my journey to Belgrade, in addition to consulting with Deputy Presidents of the SGV Professor Berberović and Žarko Bulić, I spoke with President Izetbegović. I told him of our intentions, and we discussed what message he wished to send to Milošević. At this time the Contact Group was making progress, and the bases of the peace agreement for Bosnia had already been defined. These specified that Bosnia should remain as an integral state within its internationally recognized borders, but was to be divided into two entities comprising 49% and 51% of Bosnia's total territory. The international leading powers were showing a strong will to back this peace agreement with significant numbers of peace-keeping troops. There was also, at that time, a great deal of discussion about precisely how the territorial division should be made.

Izetbegović told me that he was prepared to travel to Belgrade and meet with Milošević, if the Serbian President gave clear guarantees for the international and legal identity of Bosnia as an integral state. On the question of how to divide certain parts of Bosnia, President Izetbegović told me that he himself accepted the basic points of the Contact Group Plan and would be ready to accept the plan itself.

Having completed my preparatory consultations, I traveled to Zagreb and here I met again with Knežević, who told me what to expect at the border crossing from Hungary to Yugoslavia. I borrowed a car from the Bosnian Embassy, and my bodyguard and I set off through Croatia and Hungary to the border of Yugoslavia. We reached the border at the appointed time and found ourselves awaited by representatives of the Yugoslavia Ministries of Internal Affairs and Foreign Affairs. We continued our journey in the same car we had taken from Zagreb, accompanied by a second car that served as our escort. In Belgrade we were housed in a building belonging to the Serbian Ministry of Internal Affairs. That evening, my host was a Bosnian, a man called Krajišnik, who was full of questions about the events in Bosnia and about people he had known before the war.[80] The next day at breakfast I was told that

---

[80] This man is not to be confused with Momčilo Krajišnik, the SDS political leader.

President Milošević would see me at eleven in the morning, in rooms near the Museum of the 25th of May.

The interview lasted well over two hours: Milošević was very ready to talk. It was not my first encounter with him, for I had already seen him a couple of times during the Geneva negotiations, but this was our first real meeting. I finally had the opportunity to talk about the many issues I wanted to raise with him. To begin with I told him about the Serbs living in the cities of the Federation, the lives and problems of the Serbs who had remained to live together with Bosniaks and Croats in Sarajevo, Tuzla, Mostar, Zenica, and other cities. As for Serbs in the Federation, I gave him all the available statistics and facts of their situation after two years of war. I did not miss the opportunity to point out that the large number of Serbs killed in the war should be taken into account. I stressed that, of the 80,000 to 100,000 Serbs remaining in the Federation, the highest death toll was in the cities, chiefly the result of shelling by Karadžić's forces. Milošević listened carefully, although he asked no questions.

Then I reminded him how large the Serb populations had been before the war in the cities of Sarajevo, Tuzla, Zenica, Bihac, Travnik, and others. I stressed that next to Belgrade, Sarajevo had been the city with the largest Serb population within socialist Yugoslavia. I gave him data from estimates then available, that several hundred thousand Serbs had left the territory of the Federation, either because of general hardship; or their personal need to escape the war, and that of these the greatest number had initially fled as refugees to Serbia and Montenegro. They would subsequently leave Serbia and Montenegro for Western Europe and overseas, especially Canada, Australia and New Zealand. I saw by his reaction that Milošević was in the main already acquainted with this problem.

Then I told him of the foundation of the SGV, its development, its program, and its position on a peace solution, giving him all the SGV's ideas for solving the Bosnian question. I emphasized the historic position of the Serb nation in Bosnia, reminding him that this was one of the three Bosnian nations, which in the past had the position of an equal nation, and that because of certain historical experiences in the period of Tito's socialist Yugoslavia and the construction of a socialist Bosnia, members of the Serb nation held a greater share of positions in the economy, culture, education, social and state services than their percentage of the total Bosnian population. I gave him concrete examples, citing the significant number of Sarajevo Serbs who held leading posts, pointing out that they were particularly well represented in the university and in the allocation of housing. Their relations with the Bosniaks and Croats were developed to an enviably high degree of mutual trust and tolerance. When this subject came up, President Milošević invoked some of his memories from the time when he visited Sarajevo as director of a Belgrade firm doing business in Sarajevo and Bosnia. He had visited several times and knew many people, among them a large number of Bosniaks, with whom he had enjoyed good cooperation. He was, said, personally convinced of the former good relations between the Bosniak and Serb nations in Bosnia.

From this recollection of the past, he went on to ask many questions, expressing himself as astonished by events then taking place: bloodshed, murder, the expulsion of whole populations, and a return to mediaeval times. It was not unpleasant for me to listen to talk of this sort, even though there was no attempt to identify those responsible for this policy in the Republika Srpska, nor any acknowledgment that these acts had been inspired and supported by Belgrade and by Milošević personally. But it was clear that Milošević had already tried to call a halt to the Republika Srpska's activities and was in conflict with the Pale leadership over the peace initiative of the international community I told Milošević of the SGV's view that the Bosnian question could not be solved by the use of military force against any of its peoples. Long-term damage had been done to the Serb nation by taking territory by force from Bosniaks and Croats, and expelling whole populations. The Serbs could have neither peace nor stability nor happiness in Bosnia if they aspired to the property of the other nations.

Milošević listened to this carefully. Finally, I gave him the main points of Izetbegović's message. I told Milošević that Izetbegović expressed a genuine willingness to stop the war and accept the principles of the draft solution offered by the Contact Group. The second point was that President Izetbegović was ready to meet and discuss all issues surrounding the peace agreement, if President Milošević would sign a statement acknowledging Bosnia as a sovereign, independent and integral state. I also passed on Izetbegović's message that he was ready to discuss the issue of partitioning Bosnia in accordance with the percentages given by the Contact Group.

Then it was Milošević's turn to talk. It should be remembered that this was Milošević's first contact with a Sarajevan, in this case a Serb, who was a member of the state government, (although officially I was visiting in my capacity as President of the SGV). Milošević said resolutely that the war must be ended. He declared that nowhere else in the world today, especially in Europe, did peoples resolve their inter-ethnic relationships by war. He said that any normal person must feel abhorrence at such slaughter: that the world at large lives in a more civilized manner, and finds civilized solutions for its problems. He then gave his own views on the Bosnian war and made his anger with the Pale leadership very plain. He accused them, by implication, of failing to respect both the will of the international community and proposals from Belgrade, including Milošević's own ideas for a peace plan. He did not say so explicitly, but it was clear there was an ongoing conflict with the Pale leadership, and that Milošević was dissatisfied with their position on peace and their continued efforts to resolve matters by force.

I remember very well what Milošević said next: "The world wanted Bosnia and Herzegovina to be a sovereign and independent state. This is a fact which the world made clear." This suggested a new attitude toward the political and legal identity of Bosnia as a state. Both the Pale leadership and Belgrade had always questioned Bosnia's status, taking the view that the international community had forced the recognition of Bosnia while the necessary historical preconditions were not yet ripe. The war was fought, in essence, in order to annex Bosnia, in whole or in part, to rump Yugoslavia. The idea of a united and sovereign Bosnia had been wholly rejected. But with this very specific statement, Milošević showed — this was in the middle of 1994 — that he respected the international community's requirement that Bosnia should be a sovereign independent and united state within its internationally recognized borders.

Following up on the message I bore from Sarajevo, I suggested to President Milošević that he should perhaps write a few words for me to take back to President Izetbegović. When he stood up, right at the end of our meeting, he said, "Well, all right, just so long as we aren't formal about it. We shouldn't be formal – what we think, what we want, is what's important. There's no need to make any kind of conditions in advance of our meeting. It's important that we want this meeting to be of use to our countries, to our peoples." And thus he let it be known that he would send nothing in writing to President Izetbegović.

Then he asked me, "Are you sure that Izetbegović genuinely and absolutely wishes for the cessation of war?" I repeated what I had already said and added, "Yes I am." The question followed, "Do they trust you as much as you trust them?" I made no comment on this. Instead I simply said that the majority of ordinary people wanted the war to stop and to live in peace, and that my wartime cooperation as a member of the Presidency, with President Izetbegović, had convinced me there was genuine readiness on his part to stop the war, albeit with certain preconditions. One of these conditions, which I did not consider it necessary to specify again, was that all parties, including Serbia, should respect the territorial integrity and international status of Bosnia. This would also be in accord with the wishes of the international community.

I started my journey home the next day. On my return to Sarajevo, I spoke to President Izetbegović and gave him the essence of the dialogue with Milošević, specifically that part of our conversation that related to Izetbegović's message and his interest in a meeting. Izetbegović only added that he felt and believed Milošević and Karadžić were genuinely in conflict over stopping the war. Izetbegović then asked me, "How is it possible that you and Milošević disagree so much, considering that as socialists you and he are of the same political orientation?" I did not think it was necessary to comment on this statement, just as I had not commented on Milošević's question as to whether Izetbegović and the rest of the Sarajevo leadership trusted me as much as I trusted them.

It was clear that pressure from the international community was growing stronger and that a peace plan would soon follow. This was confirmed by later events, in particular the American peace initiative of 1995 that involved a combination of military, diplomatic and political maneuvers. Holbrook, as Clinton's envoy, worked the Zagreb-Sarajevo-Belgrade axis hard. When I later managed to talk to Holbrook, I begged him to pass on my visiting card and try to interest Milošević in meeting with a delegation of the SGV or with the Serbs who held posts in the Bosnian Presidency and Parliament. Some time afterwards Holbrook passed on the message that he had acquainted Milošević with this proposal, and that Milošević in principle was willing, but that at the time there was no opportunity available for such a meeting.

I did not go to Dayton. Lazović went as Speaker of the Parliament and member of the Serb nation. On his return, Lazović told me that Milošević was interested, as before, in events in Sarajevo and had sent me his greetings. My priority at the time was resolving the status of Sarajevo, and this was why I had advocated meeting with Milošević prior to Dayton. I wanted as much done as possible to preserve Sarajevo's pre-war ethnic structure. I fought for a solution for Sarajevo similar to that achieved in Dayton, but one that would also include international supervision and administration for a defined period. But, in the end, neither the international community nor the Sarajevo government acted in any way to prevent the exodus of Serbs from Sarajevo, after the Dayton Peace Agreement was signed.

## XVIII. JOINT ACTION FOR DAYTON BY THE SGV AND THE HNV

When preparations for the Dayton accords first got under way, between August and September 1995, the foreign ministers of Bosnia, Croatia, and Serbia (or rather Yugoslavia) met in Geneva. At this meeting, chaired by the international community and representatives of the US, an understanding was ratified which would later be known as the Geneva Agreement.[81] By this Bosnia was divided into two entities: the Republika Srpska (RS) and the Federation of Bosnia and Herzegovina, which was the entity of the Bosniaks and Croats established by the Washington Agreement. Under the terms of the same agreement, Bosnia was to "continue its legal existence with its present borders and continuing international recognition." But by way of central institutions, very little was specified.[82] This was not even a confederation - merely a loose union of two entities.

Discussions followed of what this solution might mean, and where it was leading. Some felt that this was the last step before the final division of Bosnia. It was asked why an entity with the title of Republika Srpska was proposed: who decided this and how?[83]

---

[81] "Agreed Basic Principles," Geneva, 8 September 1995.

[82] Article 3 of the Basic Principles provided for a Commisison for Displaced Persons, a Human RightsCommission, joint public corporations, an arbitration system, and a Commission to Preserve National Monuments.

[83] The proposed entity, of course, bore the same name ("Republika Srpska" – RS) as the break-away entity proclaimed by SDS Serbs in late 1991. The Basic Principles also specified that each entity would "continue to exist under its present constitution (amended to accommodate these basic principles)."

But the Geneva Agreement merely formalized something decided much earlier in the negotiations. The Contact Group's proposal for internal territorial division using the territorial percentages of 49% and 51% was the nucleus for the creation of the two entities. I myself was not in Sarajevo when the Presidency approved the decision on this issue, but if I had been, there was nothing we could have done to avoid such a structure, which was the principal proposal of the international community, based on the Contact Group's formula for stopping the war. The actual names given to the entities could have little influence on the agreement as a whole.

However, after the Geneva Agreement of September 1995, the issue of whether Bosnia would be left a loose union with only a few joint bodies to unite it, whose operation would be based solely on consensus, grew more urgent. The principal uncertainty was whether Bosnia would have any central institutions at all. A sense of resignation was taking over throughout Bosnia, but in the SGV we refused to give in, and debated what action to take. Our political friends in the Croat nation, within the Croat National Council (HNV), were thinking along the same lines. We now received an invitation from the London-based Alliance for Bosnia and Herzegovina. During the war this organization united all people, particularly British locals, who advocated for a multiethnic integral Bosnia of equal nations. They wanted delegations from both the SGV and the HNV to come to London to present our ideas, and to do what we could to challenge the Geneva Agreement.

In September 1995 we set off for London, with the additional intention of paying a subsequent visit to Washington. The twelve-person SGV delegation included, apart from myself, Deputy SGV President Žarko Bulić; Presidency member Tanja Ljujić-Mijatović; General Jovo Divjak, at that time assistant to the commander in chief of the Bosnian Army; and Mićo Rakić, a former Yugoslav ambassador to the US. In the HNV delegation were Ivo Komšić, Stjepan Kljuić, and the writer Ivan Lovrenović. While in London we were accommodated in a student hall of residence. Stjepan Kljuić, who was inclined to Sarajevo-style witticisms, said one morning at breakfast, "This hall is destined to be well-known. Never in its history has it accommodated so many officials of one state in such a short space of time, and most probably never will again."

What were we trying to do, and what did we accomplish? We encountered praiseworthy commitment and energy on the part of our hosts, the Alliance for the Defense of Bosnia and Herzegovina – especially from the family of Quentin Hoare and his wife Branka Magaš; from Professor Adrian Hastings and others. We held talks with officials in the Foreign Office, with leaders of the Conservative Party, and with Margaret Thatcher. We also held a public rally in the city, a presentation and a press conference. In all these meetings we raised the issue of central organs for the state of Bosnia. Nada Dugonjić, a reporter for the Sarajevo daily *Oslobođenje*, wrote stories that gave the people back in Sarajevo some hope that Bosnia would not end up in the form currently envisaged in the Geneva Agreement.

In our talks with top officials in the Foreign Office, our main argument was that Bosnia, in order to function successfully as a state, must have those institutions that comprise a state. We told them, "Find any state in Europe which functions without a government, parliament, constitutional court, and chief of state." People heard this argument with interest and expressed willingness to discuss the matter further; but said, "You are aware, this result reflects the will of those who took part in the agreement," and we felt we were up against a considerable barrier. We failed to reach our goal of persuading the officials of Great Britain that the agreement now being prepared, on the eve of Dayton, had no chance of a successful future if the state of Bosnia lacked central institutions.

To the issue of central institutions we added that of Sarajevo. The view of the SGV and the HNV was that Sarajevo should remain the capital of Bosnia and have the status of a district.[84] We felt that Sarajevo had preserved its multiethnicity through the hardest times of the siege and therefore retained the largest nucleus for reconstituting a multiethnic structure throughout Bosnia. We also stressed the need for international administration or arbitration for Sarajevo for a specific length of time to ensure the survival of its multinational structure. The press conference we gave was crowded, and there was plenty of interest, as we explained our ideas for peace in Bosnia. We talked about the proposals of the HNV and the SGV, emphasizing their support for central institutions of the state.

---

[84] "District" became the word for a territory administered directly by the international community, somewhat like the District of Columbia in the US. Sarajevo was never made a district. Only the northern Bosnian town of Brčko, as a result of international arbitration, was made a district in 1998.

Several members of our joint delegation also gave an interview to a political columnist for the London *Times*, resulting in an editorial commentary that sparked off a wider debate in the press over the question of central institutions for the Bosnian state.

During our stay in London, researchers and members of the foundation "Legal Life" paid us a visit, and we also gave them several interviews. They subsequently researched all facts about the SGV and nominated the group for the peace prize awarded annually by the foundation. Professor Hastings was particularly active in this work. (On the basis of the data gathered, the SGV was nominated for this award, and received it in 1995). Members of the SGV delegation were also able to visit other cities of Great Britain. Some went to Manchester, where they were particularly encouraged by our refugees and by others who supported Bosnia. Others went to Ireland, where they were warmly received.

A reduced party traveled to the US: Komšić, Kljuić and Lovrenović from the HNV, and six of us from the SGV. The London Alliance for the Defense of Bosnia and Herzegovina, and the Washington-based Council for Peace in the Balkans paid our travel and accommodation expenses.

Marshall, our host and the president of the Council for Peace in the Balkans, together with Sven Alkalaj, the Bosnian ambassador to Washington, met us on our arrival in the city. The joint delegation of the SGV and HNV included four members of the Presidency – Ljujić-Mijatović, Komšić, Kljuić and myself. Part of the delegation was accommodated just outside the city center, and the other part in the city center itself, in a hotel. Lovrenović, Vešović, Bulić and General Divjak stayed in a villa in the suburbs, where their hosts were a Bosnian refugee family from Prijedor. They were entertained on a daily basis by Semo Cikotić, military attache in the Bosnian embassy. On the evening of our arrival we were given a schedule showing the program and the meetings organized for us. It was already arranged that we would meet with Bob Dole, then leader of the Republican majority in the American Congress; with Anthony Lake, President Clinton's National Security Advisor; and with Democratic Senator Joseph Biden. These were to be our contacts with the holders of political power in the US. Meanwhile General Divjak was invited to an interview in the Pentagon.

We also talked with various associations and institutes engaged with the Bosnian question. The main aim of our visit to the US was to highlight the issue of central organs for the Bosnian state, in order to achieve a better solution than that of the Geneva Agreement. We succeeded in saying something of this to Bob Dole, first of all, although his other commitments cut the meeting short. We had a longer talk with his colleagues, but it was essential, even in this brief dialogue, to win his support. When Kljuić greeted him on our behalf, Bob Dole noted, "It's all going well at last. You are having success on the ground, you are having success in the diplomatic field, and you now have a chance to go further."

Of all our political interviews, during which we tried to communicate the joint mission of the two councils to American officialdom, our meeting with Clinton's adviser Anthony Lake lasted longest and was devoted solely to the issue of Bosnia's political future. We asked what kind of a future there could be if there were no central state institutions. We had agreed we would each give our thoughts on this issue, and Stjepan Kljuić was the first to do so, as soon as opportunity offered, ending with a simple, but highly important message. "We are not asking for anything which our state doesn't already have. Bosnia should be a multiethnic state, have a structure based on federal principles, and have central organs which function and provide cohesion and successful growth for the country." We used our meeting with Anthony Lake to bring this issue to the fore, and I believe we succeeded.

This was subsequently confirmed at the New York conference of the foreign ministers of Yugoslavia, Croatia, Bosnia, and the countries of the Contact Group, who were all involved in preparing for the Dayton peace conference. The New York Statement, which complemented the Geneva Agreement, ensured the principle of the existence of central organs of the Bosnian state.[85] These were specified as a three-member Presidency, a Parliament, the Council of Ministers, and a Constitutional Court.

In our meeting with Senator Biden of the Democratic Party, he showed a good understanding of, and a high level of engagement with, Balkan events. However, he started the interview by saying: "You are aware that we say in the US, if something does not work, that it's "Balkan" - it's a symbol of the Balkans." After that, all

---

[85] "Further Agreed Basic Principles (additional to those issued September 8, 1995, in Geneva)," New York, September 26, 1995.

discussion between Senator Biden and ourselves was at cross purposes. However we had a specific subject we wanted to raise with him, just as we had initiated the topic of central state organs with Anthony Lake. We told Senator Biden of the need for an international presence in Bosnia to guarantee implementation of the peace agreement. Such a presence would mean the involvement of the US as the leading power in the NATO alliance.

Senator Biden followed our arguments carefully, but said it was hard to get the US public to accept the notion of sending American youth anywhere on the globe, and that doing so would be especially difficult where the Balkans were concerned. There were two obstacles. The first was the Vietnam syndrome, with all that it signifies: the American public's memory of the slaughter of Americans in Vietnam and all the other negative consequences of that war. Why die in someone else's country for a cause that is ultimately the responsibility of the locals? The second obstacle was the US regard for human life. The loss of a single American life could motivate the public to demand that the President, government, and members of Congress should be held accountable.

The Senator both directly and indirectly reminded us that we were at war. He never used the term aggression, or civil war, but simply spoke of war, a war in which ethnic groups and neighbors had turned their guns upon one another to resolve their quarrels, even though the use of force in such a situation offers no solution. He agreed, however, that international support could be of significance in halting the war. Then he digressed, telling us, "I have received many delegations from all over the world, including from the region of Yugoslavia and Bosnia. I understood everything - I try to understand everything. But there was one thing I could never understand. You speak the same language, you have the same mentality and your physical appearance is almost identical - so how do you know whom to kill?"

Always, in these talks, we tried to raise the issue of Sarajevo's status, to ensure its inclusion in the preparations for the final peace negotiations at Dayton. We had prepared a special petition, signed by Komšić and myself on behalf of both our Councils, stating that Sarajevo should be the capital city, that its multiethnic structure should be preserved, and that it should have district status - like that of Washington, D.C. We suggested there should be international support in the form of a temporary administration or special arbitration. This proposal too was received with understanding, but less so than the others. We had a strong feeling that the need for central organs was accepted - that it would be difficult to explain the absence of these organs from the future state of Bosnia to the American public. It also seemed possible to persuade the public that the price of peace meant the presence of international forces, and thus the US should be involved. The city of Sarajevo, however, was obviously not on the same level with the other issues.

Our stay in the US drew the attention of various journalists, public officials, and institutes for democracy. Mićo Rakić, formerly Yugoslav ambassador to the US, was in our delegation, so all these contacts were well publicized. There was much interest among the American people, and our own public received regular reports. We soon agreed with TV Bosnia and Herzegovina's New York reporter, Enver Selimović, on regular coverage of the work of our joint delegation. The delegation was also greatly assisted by Nedžib Šaćirbey, the SDA representative for the US, with whom we met several times. By the time our visit was nearing its end, and we had successfully carried out our "March on the White House", had talked to Anthony Lake and met with Bob Dole, it was obvious that our two Councils, and the four members of the Presidency within them, were a united force which had won acceptance in Washington.

One morning over coffee with Ambassador Alkalaj, we were talking over the achievements of the visit when Nedžib Šaćirbey joined us and suggested that we should send a letter of support to President Izetbegović in Sarajevo. During this period he was himself struggling with the issue of obtaining a better solution for Bosnia, including central institutions, while the Bosnian public was angrily demanding rejection of the Republika Srpska as a separate entity. Our delegation felt there was no need to send messages of support to Izetbegović, as we were already providing the best possible form of support for our joint cause: the principles of the Platform on the work of the Presidency in wartime, and of a united and integral state. Our feeling was that Sacirbey had made this suggestion with the full knowledge of Sarajevo: probably the Bosnian public would have welcomed a statement of support from both our councils. We ourselves however believed that our mission to Washington, and the united action of the two councils, was in itself the best demonstration of solidarity.

The issue of Banja Luka arose during our visit to the US. It was September 1995, and Banja Luka was facing the threat of imminent attack.[86] I received a request for an interview from Slobodan Pavlović, the Washington reporter of the Belgrade paper *Nezavisna Borba*. He asked if I supported the offensive, and the approaching fall of Banja Luka, adding that the situation there was fast deteriorating as widespread fear gripped the city, and people were packing their bags. He noted that there might be a new Serb exodus, on a much larger and more serious scale than the exodus of the Serbs from the Knin Krajina in Croatia. I told *Nezavisna Borba* that the most important thing was to stop the war, find a peaceful solution, and preserve the integrity of Bosnia. If the fall of Banja Luka would lead to a mass departure of Bosnia's Serbs, the entire peace initiative and the possibility of preserving Bosnia as a united and multiethnic community would be called into question. This was not well received in certain journalistic circles, including those of Zagreb. Later, however it became clear that the overriding need to achieve peace and preserve a multiethnic and united Bosnia had also prevailed with President Izetbegović. Had the Serbs left Banja Luka and the Bosnian Krajina, they would have left Eastern Bosnia altogether and the country would perhaps have gone in a totally different direction. Moreover, the subsequent return of Serbs to Bosnia might have entailed a new and larger war, of which the bloodshed might have encompassed all the Balkans, perhaps even Europe.

Finally, near the end of our stay in Washington, there was a press conference at which Komšić, Kljuić, Ljujić-Mijatović and I presented the results of our visit. We at last had the feeling that our ideas were being accepted. I suspect that our views were previously unknown in Washington, meaning the Americans had not previously had the chance to review them. The strength of our ideas was increased by the fact that the leaders of the two Councils, the SGV and the HNV, were advocating these proposals together. For their members were people who had remained to live together in war, were determined to live a common life in a multiethnic society, and were equally determined that this should be cemented by a peace agreement.

---

[86] At this time a joint HVO-ABH offensive had driven the BSA from parts of central and western Bosnia and was moving swiftly toward Banja Luka, the largest city in the RS.

One day the history of Bosnia's war will be set down objectively, and the initiatives behind the Dayton Peace Accords will be described in full, together with all the efforts made on behalf of the democratic, multiethnic forces of Bosnia, to ensure the unity of the state through the existence of central organs. When this finally happens, the joint visit of the SGV and HNV to London and Washington will surely be considered a most significant event in creating a political climate that affected the decisions of the leading world powers. Our protest started in London and ended in Washington, but in both places we made the point that Bosnia could not survive without central state institutions. It was after our interview with Anthony Lake that the diplomatic action of the US intensified, and the New York negotiations were held.

## XIX. THE DAYTON PEACE AGREEMENT

Spring and summer 1995 were the most significant period of preparation for Bosnia's peace: during this time the decisive American initiative was gaining momentum. This initiative had several strategic points. The first aimed at stopping the war, and this was achieved by a combination of diplomatic and military pressures, resulting in roughly similar levels of defeat and victory for all military forces engaged in the Bosnian war. The second strategy was to apply diplomatic pressure to the governments in Belgrade and Zagreb, as the generators of the Bosnian war, to make them accept the formula of the Dayton peace solution. The final element of the initiative was to preserve the integrity and international legal status of Bosnia and the continuity of the state. Thus, although the peace plan could not ensure all aspects of democratic growth and reconstruction, it could at least enable social development in Bosnia to unfold in this direction. The final element was the implementation of the peace process. The commitment of the international community to any peace agreement implied the participation of US forces.

The man who worked to realize these strategies in the name of the US and its President was the American negotiator, Richard Holbrook, a man whose unusual strength, penetration and clarity exerted a strong influence on those with whom he negotiated. Holbrook succeeded in making all the necessary preparations to define the basis of a peace agreement, one that would be accepted and validated by all parties, at the American air base near Dayton in the autumn of 1995. Thus the peace agreement for Bosnia acquired its name: the Dayton Peace Accords.

What took place during this period of preparation? On several occasions I was a member of delegations that spoke with Holbrook during summer and autumn 1995. He was then diligently traveling the Zagreb-Sarajevo-Belgrade circuit, and each time he arrived he had a fresh solution to offer or new question to raise. One of these was the issue of the electoral system. In September 1995 our delegation met Holbrook and his colleagues in the cabinet of President Izetbegović. There were several of us: Krešimir Zubak, then President of the Federation; Hasan Muratović, Komšić, Izetbegović, Ganić, a Bosnian Army representative, and I. Holbrook asked us, "Gentlemen, what ideas do you have for the election system?" There was little time for discussion of this issue, however, since plenty of other items were on the agenda. Komšić and I however felt that the members of the central state institutions should be elected on a system that would enable all citizens of Bosnia to vote for the Presidency, members of the state parliament members of the Council of Ministers. The system should also include some safeguards to ensure the equality and fair representation of all three constituent nations.

This was a very short debate, and no conclusion was then reached. However, President Izetbegović commented that the Serb side was not ready to accept any kind of solution that would mean abandoning their dominance of a closed entity. As we went into the hallway, toward the room where the press conference would be held, I found myself walking with Mr. Zubak, who said to me, "The Croat nation will never again allow its representatives to be chosen by any other nation." Thus I learned what formula the Croat side would prefer in further talks with Holbrook. The Serb side insisted the most strongly, but the Croats took a virtually identical view of the question. It was hard, of course, for the Bosniaks to fight this attitude alone in further talks, and perhaps they, too, actually had a preference for this option.

At one point during September 1995, President Izetbegović and I were dealing with some business together. When we finished, he asked me who would represent the Serb nation in the state delegation to Dayton. I proposed Miro Lazović, the Bosnian Parliament Speaker. I made no other suggestions; I felt this was good enough. It was accepted. Lazović was the only Serb representative from the Federation and the joint organs of the Bosnian state to take part in the Dayton negotiations.

Once the delegation had set off for Dayton, public expectation focused on the peace talks. Information trickled in, but insufficient. Then the news arrived that the negotiations were nearing their end, but how they would finish was rendered uncertain by the problem of Brčko. Later we learned from the delegation that at one point, because of the dispute over Brčko, the entire peace package was thrown into doubt. Happily, however, it was finally agreed that the question of Brčko's status would be resolved subsequently, by international arbitration.

When President Izetbegović and the rest of delegation arrived back in Sarajevo, Kljuić, Ganić, Duraković and I waited for them in front of the Presidency Building. Outside were several hundred citizens of Sarajevo who had come crowding into the street in elation, because the peace agreement had been signed. When we entered the Presidency Building together, the President looked out into the street from the Great Salon. He saw for himself the crowds of people demonstrating their joy that the Dayton negotiations had ended the war, and that an agreement had been signed which would bring peace to Bosnia. There were high hopes that international presence would make peace a reality. It was clear that ordinary people, of all three nations, wanted nothing but peace.

What did the Dayton Accords achieve? First of all, they stopped the war. They preserved the continuity of Bosnia as a state and provided international guarantees of the sovereignty, integrity and unity of the Bosnian state within its internationally recognized borders. The sovereignty of the Bosniak, Serb and Croat nations was ensured by the sovereign state of Bosnia as a united state of all its citizens and constituent peoples. This will probably remain unique in history as an international legal contract, since the constitution of the state of Bosnia actually derives from the peace agreement.[87] Moreover, the peace agreement incorporated an international guarantee of its implementation. The Dayton Peace Agreement is buttressed by the presence of international peacekeeping forces and the international community's High Representative.[88]

---

[87] The "Constitution of Bosnia and Herzegovina" is Annex 4 of the "General Framework Agreement for Peace in Bosnia and Herzegovina," initiated in Dayton on 21 November 1995 and signed in Paris on 14 December 1995.

[88] Annex 10, "Agreement on Civilian Implementation of the Peace Settlement," provided for the designation of a High Representative to monitor the implementation of the peace settlement. In practice this person and his staff has come to be known collectively as the Office of the High Representative (OHR). The OHR has acquired added authority, including the right to impose legislation, at meetings of the international Peace Implementation Council since 1996.

The agreement contains the bases for reintegration of the Bosnian state: economic revival, the return of refugees, the democratization of society, protection of human rights, and the renewal of interethnic trust. The Dayton Peace Agreement defined the internal structure of Bosnia, based on the concept of two entities, and limited the military forces that took part in the war. These are, as I see it, the positive aspects of the Agreement. However, the constitutional structure incorporates the inherent risk that ethnic division of the state of Bosnia will continue in the direction initiated by the war. Why? Because the two entities have a strongly ethnic basis, particularly one of them – the Republika Srpska with its overwhelming ethnic majority of a single nation – while the structure of the central state organs is based on the entity structure. Moreover, the election of representatives of the central organs depends on ethnic partitioning and ethnic membership. The dominance of ethnic bases and ethnic components has been built into the entire system of the state, and this means endless possibilities for opposition and conflict and for obstruction of the processes of agreement, decision-making and integration.

The Dayton peace agreement is, figuratively speaking, a crossroads between war and peace. It made possible the journey toward peace, integration of the state, reconstruction and democratization. But it is equally possible to travel in the opposite direction, towards disintegration and division. Two important factors could prevent this. One is the long-term presence of the international community and its forces. In my opinion, a decade is needed. During this period, through its political, economic and military presence, the international community could contribute to the strengthening of peace and to building the structures of civil society in Bosnia. By this I primarily mean the transformation to an economy based on consensus and free trade, developing institutions for the protection of human rights, securing the principle of universal protection of humanity; building democratic institutions in the spirit of genuine political pluralism, and ensuring the existence of free media and non-governmental organizations.

The second factor preventing division would be the creation of a new political structure for Bosnia, based on the political organization of Bosnian citizens and parties. Such an organization should be built on the social and political foundations of social interests, and contemporary political concepts such as liberalism, social democracy, the concept of right, left, and center politics, rather than primarily on an ethnic basis. New interests and political groupings must substitute for and put an end to political organization on the basis of ethnic homogeneity.

## XX. THE SERB NATIONAL QUESTION IN BOSNIA

The SDS proclaimed that Bosnia was a practical impossibility, both as a unified state and as a common way of life. It wanted to carve out a separate state structure to be ultimately unified with Serbia and Montenegro. This conflicted, above all, with the interests of the Bosniak and Croat peoples of Bosnia. These two nations did not live merely in defined pockets of the country; they lived all over Bosnia; as did the Serbs. The consequence was conflict between the Serbs and the other two nations. So the issue of the Serb nation's future in Bosnia is an issue for more than just one nation: it involves the future of Bosnia's Croats and Bosniaks, and the interests of the international community.

The SDS elite, victorious in the elections of 1990 in coalition with the HDZ and the SDA, elected to use force to realize its vision for a separate Serb republic in Bosnia. The use of force led to aggression, militarily and materially supported by Belgrade. From its inception, this campaign involved the ethnic cleansing of all non-Serbs.

Execution of this plan was attempted on 70% of the territory of Bosnia during 1992 alone, and expanded to an all-out war lasting over four years, ending only in late 1995 with the Dayton Peace Agreement. The Dayton solution disallowed the notion of a Serb republic as an independent state wholly separated from the other two nations of Bosnia, and eligible to join Serbia and Montenegro. Thus the historic journey toward a unified and sovereign Bosnia was acknowledged by Slobodan Milošević himself, who signed the Dayton Peace Agreement in the name of both Yugoslavia and the Serb nation.

The SDS campaign thus ended in defeat, due to its conflict with the fundamental principles of international development. However, even after Dayton, the SDS elite continued to spread illusions and intensify the indoctrination of the Serbs in the Republika Srpska. Their story was that the Serbs had won their own state, which existed in total independence, had nothing to do with Bosnia, and would follow its own road of independent development. This meant continuing the conflict with the international community and forcing the Serb nation into poverty and isolation. Small nations and states, whether in Europe or elsewhere in the world, cannot travel the roads of their historic destiny alone. Instead, their future is prescribed by the chief trends in the international community, as expressed by a consensus of the major global powers.

The SGV's approach is diametrically opposed to that of the SDS. The SGV supports a sovereign, independent and united Bosnia within its internationally recognized borders. Within this state, the Serb nation has its own political and legal identity and the incontrovertible constitutional and political right for this identity to be expressed within the framework of Bosnia's sovereignty. The SGV views Bosnia as a common state in which the peoples of Bosnia - Serbs, Croats and Bosniaks - each have sovereign rule.

The second key difference between the SGV philosophy and that of the SDS lies in their respective attitudes toward coexistence as the centuries-old traditional way of living in Bosnia. The SDS wholly opposed this in proclaiming that common life is impossible. The party kept this view quiet during the electoral campaign of 1990, expounding it only after winning the elections. This was their ideological rationale for concluding that our common life had to be destroyed through ethnic cleansing, expulsion, and the creation of ethnically pure territories. At the end of the twentieth century, this led to the creation of a new apartheid. Nowhere else in Europe does there exist, thus defined, such an attitude on the part of one nation toward others with whom they live as neighbors. This ideology produced methods of warfare and crimes against civilians strongly reminiscent of fascism.

The disastrous outcome of these policies is now evident. The destruction of common life can only push the Serb nation into a closed ethnic enclave isolated from the other two nations of Bosnia and from international trends, as well as from the economic help of the international community. During the first year of implementation of the Dayton Peace Agreement, the policies of the SDS leadership deprived the RS of international aid and thrust the Serb nation deep into an economic, social and psychological crisis. The destruction of common life led the Serb nation into a trackless desert.

Ivan Stambolić, speaking at the second session of the Assembly of citizens of Serb nationality, in wartime, 1995, observed that "the first thing the Serb nation should do is free itself from the fear that it cannot live together with other nations." If common life is impossible for the Serb nation, its members may be forced flee afresh in yet another exodus, as the result of economic migration and pressure from the Bosniaks and Croats, who may seek to take back by force their territory lost in war. At stake are the Posavina, the Bosnian Krajina, Eastern Bosnia, and Eastern Herzegovina."

The SGV view is the polar opposite of that of the SDS. It sees that the common life of all three nations in Bosnia is an existential precondition for life in Bosnia, springing from its ancient way of life as a unique intermixing between the peoples throughout the country. There were once recognizable groupings based on religious membership. Subsequently, all three peoples developed as nationalities, but through demographic co-existence on common territory, so that life together became their historic destiny. Common streets, common buildings, common schools, universities, and industries developed. Mixed marriages proliferated, flourishing in an atmosphere that fostered mutual religious, cultural and national tolerance.

The SDS contends that the state of Bosnia, and the coexistence of nations within that state, is not viable. This contention ignores all dialogue developed in the past between the Serb nation and its fellow nations in the spheres of economy, culture, politics, and neighborly interpersonal relations.

The SGV, in contrast, supports the broader civilizing trends that are moving human society toward democracy and positive relations between nations. Its members believe that economic, political, and cultural cooperation with other ethnic groups in Bosnia is in the best interests of the Serb nation. Similarly, unless the RS representatives participate genuinely in the work of the central state organs such as the Parliament, Presidency, and Government, the RS itself could suffer further economic breakdown and jeopardize its future existence. One example of these dangers is the difficult position of those Sarajevo Serbs who now live in the RS, clustered on the inter-entity boundary with the Federation, in Lukavica, Kasindol, Tilava, Miljevići, Pale, Jahorina and Sokolac.[89] These Serbs stand to lose their potential

---

[89] These suburbs of Sarajevo remained in the RS under the terms of the Dayton Peace Agreement.

economic and cultural development if they cannot work, get an education, and receive medical treatment in the city of Sarajevo. Thus the SDS ideology has jeopardized the growth of the region and the developmental influence of its leading centers.

The SDS, the main party in the Serb entity, has consistently obstructed the work of the central organs of the Bosnian state. These joint bodies have been created for the common good of all citizens and nations of Bosnia, to establish the preconditions for economic and cultural growth. Each of the peoples depends for its own prosperity on the general prosperity of the state. The attitude of the SDS toward the central organs demonstrates its disregard for the prosperity of the Serb nation.

As noted in previous chapters, the SGV has always advocated for the existence of central constitutional organs, and voiced the need for the Serb nation to participate and cooperate within these bodies. Whereas the SDS demanded a model consisting solely of two entities and no central organs at all, at the time of the Geneva Agreement, the SGV and HNV vigorously urged London and Washington to include common institutions as an essential component of the peace plan for Bosnia. We likewise asked for Sarajevo to retain its status as the capital city of the state. During the war, the SDS dreamed of possessing the whole city. When this clearly could not be achieved militarily, the SDS promoted the idea of a divided Sarajevo. When the Dayton Peace Agreement provided that the city should be reunited and that some suburbs under SDS control should be transferred to the Federation, the SDS decided that the Serbs living in those areas should leave the city altogether. This led to a massive exodus of the Sarajevo Serbs, which took place in spring 1996. The Serb population from Sarajevo's suburbs was displaced throughout the cities and towns of the RS, from Brčko and Bijeljina to Trebinje. The largest group has remained in locations around Sarajevo, just across the inter-entity boundary, in suburbs that include Lukavica, Kasindol, Pale and Sokolac.

The SDS nurtured the idea of building a "Serb Sarajevo." In wartime this consisted of Ilidža, Vogošča, Ilijas, Hadžići, Trnovo, and part of Novo Sarajevo, but the Dayton Peace Agreement transferred these territories to the Federation, in order to reintegrate them into the city of Sarajevo. "Serb Sarajevo" then became a cluster of suburban and rural communities on the periphery of the city.

These outlying settlements can call themselves whatever they choose, but this is no city, for it has no nucleus. Even with the substantial economic aid needed for infrastructure, roads, factories, and various cultural components, this could only be a suburb of Sarajevo, and not the city itself. Sarajevo itself developed historically as a city of all those who lived in it: as a multiethnic city.

Sarajevo contains the largest traditional cultural component of the Bosnian Serb people. The SDS refusal to accept the city of Sarajevo as the political, cultural and economic center of all peoples has meant provincializing the Serb nation, thereby depriving it of the cultural and historic preconditions to develop as a state-building nation of Bosnia. The SGV believes the multiethnic structure of Sarajevo must be renewed, along with the rest of Bosnia, in the framework of universal refugee return. Inside this project, as envisaged by the SGV, the urban nucleus of the city must be reconstituted as a civic whole. All three constituent nations, and the Jewish and other people with them, should have constitutional and statutory solutions by which they can equally participate in the government of the city.

Another key question for the Bosnian Serbs is their relationship with Serbia itself. This is less a matter of relations with the regime in power, for every government passes, but of their relationship with the Serbian and Montenegrin Serbs in the Federal Republic of Yugoslavia. This relationship must be based on contemporary civilized norms so as not to risk the Serb nation's relationship with the other two nations of Bosnia, with whom they coexist in all aspects of life. This relationship must ensure that it remains possible for the Bosnian Serbs to live in peace with all their neighbors.

Cooperation between the Bosnian and Yugoslav Serbs is in the best interests of the Serb nation as a whole. Economic prosperity and cultural growth can only take place if these relations in no way jeopardize the legal and political position of the Serb nation in Bosnia and the international status of Bosnia. This could be modeled on the experience of the relations of Germans in Switzerland with the German people in Germany, or likewise on the relations of the French in Switzerland with the French nation in France. All these relationships enhance the cultural identity and economic prosperity of these peoples. The Serb nation in Bosnia and Herzegovina cannot have a stronger legal or political relationship with the Yugoslav

Serbs than the Bosniaks or Croats of Bosnia have with their co-nationals outside Bosnia.

Finally, the SDS and SGV have very different views on Bosnian Serb relations with the international community. In the Dayton Peace Agreement, the international community has defined Bosnia's international status, upheld its continuity, and validated the equality of all three Bosnian nations. It has also assumed responsibility for implementing the agreement by committing military forces, and economic resources to the task. The SDS, however, is highly suspicious of the international community's role and sees it as a world police-squad, an occupying force imposing its own will and its own interests. According to the SDS, the international community has nothing but malevolence for Serbs and is deliberately endangering Serb national interests.

The SDS approach has led to economic isolation and paltry levels of economic assistance. Of the total aid package granted to Bosnia by the intentional community to Bosnia in 1996, the RS received only two percent. The purposely isolationist stance of the RS is anachronistic. No nation can stand wholly apart from the international community in today's world. In contrast, the SGV has advocated full cooperation with international institutions and respect for the general trends of the new world order. The SGV believes that the establishment of peace, economic renewal, the return of refugees, the building of democratic institutions, and a civil society, are impossible without the international community's involvement. In the interests of the Serb nation, and its equality with the Bosniak and Croat nations, the SGV supports the international community's continued presence in Bosnia for at least a decade. It also favors the integration of Bosnia into European institutions, including the Council of Europe, the European Union, and the NATO alliance, through the "Partnership for Peace" program. By following this path, Bosnia should avoid the danger of ethnic division and the negation of its statehood by either Zagreb or Belgrade.

At the Sintra Summit in June 1997, the world community established a formula for Bosnia's political and economic future. According to this formula, none of the ethnic groups may attempt to resolve its relations with other groups by force. Second, no ethnic group can decide on secession nor seek to sever any part of the territory and population of Bosnia from the whole. Third, no ethnic group can seek to impose its will upon another ethnic group. Finally, the extension of the international community's presence in Bosnia offers an opportunity for political growth and prosperity of each nation and for Bosnia as a state of citizens and equal nations.

The Bosnian Serbs face three possible options for their future. The first is that of reintegration into the Bosnian state, following the premises of the Sintra Summit. The second option is to create a purely Serb state on Bosnian soil, to develop independently or eventually become a part of Serbia. The third possibility is that Serbs in Bosnia might suffer the fate of the Serbs who formerly lived in Croatia: a mass exodus would take place, while those left in Bosnia would lose their status as an equal nation and become a national minority (as they are in Croatia).

I myself am fighting for the first outcome: the reintegration of Bosnia. This is what the SGV is fighting for, as are all democratic forces in the numerous civic parties, whether or not they have Serb members. The outcome will ultimately rest on the stabilization of Southeast Europe and the future stance of the international community regarding the unity of Bosnia as a state. Much depends on the international community's involvement and the economic, political, and military resources it will deploy over the long run in Bosnia. Much also depends on the progress of democratization in Bosnia, Croatia and Serbia, and the democratization of the Serb nation, both within the RS and in the rest of Bosnia. Another important contributor to progress would be the conversion of what are now ethnic parties into civil parties. For as long as any ethnic body in Bosnia continues to be politically structured as an ethnic party, this contributes to the other nations' preference for similar structures, and feeds their extremism.

Bosnia relies on the ongoing commitment of the international community to implement the Dayton Peace Accords. It is important that those who committed war crimes, both from the Serb nation and the other two nations, are brought to justice. If the democratic forces in Bosnia help develop trust among the nations, they will contribute to separating Serbs from the SDS regime. This in turn will move the majority of Bosnia's Serbs to support the idea of a multiethnic and united Bosnia. If it happens otherwise, and the Serb nation's fear increases, the subsequent conflicts would lead to one of the two remaining options: an independent Serb state and its eventual secession, or the final disappearance of Serbs from Bosnia.

The SDS has fed the ideologies that produced hatred and promoted Serb fears of living with the Bosniak and Croat nations in Bosnia. But despite the trend toward partition, isolation, poverty, and secession, the SDS continues to harbor hopes of acceptance by the international community. Radivoje Kontić, then Prime Minister of Yugoslavia, in a meeting at Davos in Switzerland, in February 1996, which Miro Lazović and I attended, told me the following about the Pale elite: "You know that the problem is not only their vision of joining Yugoslavia - the problem is that they want more than that. They want to be an independent Serb state with all the prerogatives of international acknowledgement." But the extremism now dominant in the SDS has no chance of succeeding with the international community. Untold harm could be done to the Serb nation before this drama plays itself out. Its current course could undermine the whole concept of a multiethnic and united Bosnian state, and has the potential to destabilize Europe as a whole.

## XXI. CONSTITUTIONAL CHANGE

The Washington Agreement ended hostilities between the Bosniaks and Croats and created a new political entity, the Federation of Bosnia and Herzegovina.[90] This was a major step forward in securing a broader peace for Bosnia. Coincidentally, the agreement was in the process of being considered for approval by the Bosnian Parliament just at the time the Serbian Civic Council was created at the first Assembly of Citizens of Serb Nationality, held on March 27, 1994.

The Washington Agreement left unresolved the status of those Serbs who lived on the territory of the Federation. Many Serbs, rejecting the separatism of the SDS, had remained and fought with the Bosniaks and Croats against the military might of the Republika Srpska. During the war those Serbs helped to preserve the common life, mutual trust and tolerance that was fostered through the centuries in the regions that now make up the Federation. But they were ignored in the Constitution drafted for the proposed Federation. Various specialists had monitored the development of the draft Constitution, and they pointed out that Article One, Point One of the Constitution failed to provide that the Serb nation living in the Federation would have equal, constituent status with the other nations.[91] Other constitutional provisions followed this pattern, setting aside state offices for Bosniaks and Croats but

---

[90] "Framework Agrement for the Federation," 1 March 1994, Snežana Trifunovska (ed.), *Former Yugoslavia Through Documents From its dissolution to the peace settlement* (The Hague: Martinus Nijhoff, 1999), pp. 83-93. Hereafter cited as *Former Yugoslavia Through Documents*.

[91] In the "Proposed Constitution" of the Federation, Article 1, Point 1 stated that the "Bosniacs and Croats, as constituent peoples (along with Others) and

making no provision for Serb participation. The House of Peoples was to have two chambers, one for Croats and one for Bosniaks, but none for Serbs.

The Serb Civic Council therefore proposed an amendment to the draft Federation Constitution. The amendment stated that the Serb nation should be recognized as an equal constituent nation, on a par with the other two nations of the Federation, regardless of the unresolved status of Serbs in Bosnia overall. Of course, at that time no final solution to this question could even be guessed at, for war was raging under its own impetus between Karadžić's territory and the Federation. The proposed amendment was endorsed at the first Assembly of Citizens of Serb Nationality. It read, "In Article One of the Founding of the Federation, Point One, Item one, instead of the words Bosniaks and Croats, the words used should be Bosniaks, Croats and Serbs." Two days later, acting as the Constituent Assembly of the Federation, the Bosnian Parliament took up the amendment for discussion but neither passed it nor rejected it,[92] deciding only that it should be placed in the context of a total peace solution for Bosnia. The Parliament went on to approve unanimously the Federation Constitution at its session on March 30, 1994.

The war dragged on for another twenty months, including some of the most brutal shelling of Sarajevo and the slaughter of over 7 000 Bosniaks at Srebrenica. The peace process led step by step to the Dayton peace negotiations, and the Dayton Agreement was signed at the end of 1995. The Constitution of Bosnia and Herzegovina, Annex 4 of the Dayton Agreement, refers to "Bosniaks, Croats, and Serbs, as constituent peoples (along with Others)."

The Constitution of the Dayton Agreement, in recognizing three constituent nations, set up a direct conflict with the constitutions

---

citizens of the Republic of Bosnia and Herzegovina, in the exercise of their sovereign rights, transform the internal structure of the territories with a majority of Bosniac and Croat population in the Republic of Bosnia and Herzegovina into a Federation." Point 2 specified that "Decisions on the constitutional status of the territories of the Republic of Bosnia and Herzegovina with a majority of Serb population shall be made in the course of negotiations toward a peaceful settlement..." *Former Yugoslavia in Documents*, p. 95.

[92] The SGV document was noted and attached as "Additional Information" in the form of Enclose I to UN Document S/1994/382. *Former Yugoslavia in Documents*, pp. 119-21.

of the two entities that were defined by the Agreement. The Federation Constitution, of course, recognized only Bosniaks and Croats; the Republika Srpska Constitution mentioned only the Serb nation in its Preamble. Thus the people of the RS could only have "Serb rights," whereas anyone belonging to a different nation would have none. In the Federation, Serbs were altogether without rights as a nation. It was left to the two entities to bring their constitutions into line with that of Bosnia and Herzegovina: this they failed to do.

We in the SGV decided to organize a special declaration to urge that all three nations be designated as constituent nations on the entire territory of Bosnia. We presented this idea to the Parliament of Bosnia and the Parliaments of each entity. In the RS there was no intention of even listening to this idea, much less of dealing with its consequences. In the Federation too, there was no possibility of considering the question at this time, since the HDZ would not associate itself with any such approach.

We next turned to the Presidency of Bosnia and Herzegovina. The Dayton Constitution created a Presidency of three members: one Serb from the RS, and two members from the Federation, one a Croat and the other a Bosniak. The Presidency member from the RS at that time was Momčilo Krajišnik, the SDS activist, who would not even receive our delegation. Krešimir Zubak, the Croat member of the Presidency, was also an HDZ leader at the time: he gave us his support, saying it was just a question of time before it would be approved. However, he then referred us to Bozo Rajić, the President of the HDZ in Bosnia. We simply avoided that meeting, for we knew that nothing could come of it.

Then in 1998 we called on Alija Izetbegović, the SDA leader and, at the time, President of the Presidency. We got his support in the first interview, and in the second talk we officially requested that he, in his role as a member of the Presidency, should submit a formal legal proposal to the Constitutional Court to place this issue on its agenda.[93] He accepted, and explained that his whole rationale

---

[93] The Dayton Constitution (Annex 4) provided that the Constitutional Court have nine judges, four selected by the House of Representatives of the Federation. two selected by the Assembly of the RS, and three selected by the President of the European Court of Human Rights. In practice the latter three have been jurists from countries in Western Europe.

of political thought and social values supported this idea. He favored it not only because it was democratic, but also because it was in the interests of the Bosniak nation. Bosniaks wanted to live where they had lived before, on the entire territory of the state, equal with all members of the other nations throughout Bosnia. We were enheartened by his response, for we know that it meant that sooner or later the Constitutional Court would make that decision. There was, of course, a whole range of responses to our initiative, from good cooperation with Izetbegović to none at all with Krajišnik.

Since 1998 the fight for the equality of the three nations has dominated the activities of the SGV. In that year we were joined in our initiative by three other non-governmental organizations: the Association of Independent Intellectuals Circle 99, the HNV, and the Council of the Congress of Bosniak Intellectuals. That year we sponsored together a seminar on, "How to Establish Constituent Nations on the Entire Territory of Bosnia and Herzegovina" which included representatives from the international community. The four groups reached a common position in support of the three constituent nations concept. We presented this to the ambassadors of all the Contact Group countries, to the High Representative, to the UN Mission to Bosnia, and to the OSCE, all of which gave their support. Carlos Westendorp, then the High Representative, publicly supported the initiative as vital for the fight for human rights and the equality of all ethnic communities in Bosnia. He saw it as being very much in the spirit of the Dayton Agreement. But he also voiced the international community's confidence in the Constitutional Court's decision on this matter.

That decision was 28 months in the making, measured from the time Izetbegović submitted the request in early 1998 until the Court's ruling in July 2000. Under normal conditions it might have happened earlier, but in our country and in our circumstances, it might well not have happened at all. Much has changed in Bosnia during the five years since the Dayton Agreement. Since I had gone through all phases of the battle for this idea, I knew that there were forces that would have obstructed the decision had it been reached in the first year after Dayton, when the SGV first raised the issue. At that time the local players were largely unchanged, a fact that was reflected in the views of local judges of the Constitutional Court. The international representatives listened to the arguments we were advancing, but they were not in a position to do more. Now, six years after we first proposed to amend the Constitution of the

Federation, the international community and the Constitutional Court had altered their stance.

Even so, the fact that four local judges still voted against this decision does not bode well for us in Bosnia who want this land to have peace, with all its peoples enjoying equal human rights. Their votes against show that we are still living with the consequences of war, and that the political, spiritual, and mental structures that led to war are still with us. During the war they led to the politics of expulsion and ethnic separatism; now they translate into opposition to the Dayton Agreement, and a failure to recognize that the international community has entered a new century. Still, of greater importance is the decision itself, and its eventual implementation. Who voted for it, and who voted against, are now matters that belong to history.

The Constitutional Court international justices reached their conclusions on the basis of their own comprehension of the issues involved. The international community consistently and patiently supported this decision, not only by its statements, but also by its active support for the involvement of international court justices. They attended all the seminars, discussions, and conferences, and concluded that the solution of this issue is the key to implementing the Dayton Agreement, to the internal integration of Bosnia, and to the return of each person to his or her home.

The Court's decision makes two things clear. The first is that human rights issues are paramount for defining Bosnia's future. Equally important, the Court showed that local initiative can succeed, that Bosnians can take responsibility for their own destiny, take the lead in implementing the Dayton principles, and be responsible for the political stability of Bosnia.

When the Constitutional Court's decision was announced, some colleagues and I were returning by car to Sarajevo from Bujojno, where we had attended an organizational meeting of the SGV. We celebrated the entire way home. I embrace this decision as the victory of an idea for which we fought together, as allies and colleagues. It provides some compensation for our long struggle for a common life, for the preservation of Bosnia, and for its international affirmation.

The Court's ruling provided immediate psychological relief. Never again will there be in law second-class citizens anywhere on the territory of Bosnia. This spells an end to the systematic discrimination against over 1.3 million people, whose homes were located in an entity where their nationality was not recognized. Such discrimination led to war, to the creation of ethnically divided territories, and to the death or expulsion of whole populations. It secures principles of national equality that will pave the way for Bosnia to be integrated into European institutions. People can find solace in a kind of psychological peace, knowing that they are recognized as citizens with ethnic, cultural, and religious identities. This is what Cardinal Puljić means when he refers to the right of each person to an identity: a home, membership of a local community, property, religion, and all other forms of identity.

The remaining challenge is to implement this far-reaching ruling in the institutional structures of Bosnia. The Constitutions of both entities, in their first articles, must be amended. The Parliaments of each entity must change their constitutions and laws to reflect the state-level constitutional principles, and assure the legal equality of all nations. Many practical consequences will follow from such changes. The principles of constitutional equality among the three nations will influence electoral laws, the rights of representation, the right to vote, and the eligibility of citizens to be candidates for a wide variety of offices. It will lead to changes in the structures of both entities. In the Federation, for example, the composition of the House of Peoples will surely have to change. There must also be far-reaching changes in the RS. Two variants are possible. Issues of vital interest to each nationality can be assured through a special council, which would rule on issues of language, culture, and tradition. Also, in all state institutions, whether at the cantonal or entity level, all three nations must be represented in all bodies and in all state structures. If this is implemented, no one will ever again be forced to ask if they dare build a church or mosque.

With these changes the book will be permanently closed on those who want to divide Bosnia along ethnic lines. And the book has been opened for Bosnia as an integral and sovereign state that can, with gradual steps, enter a united Europe.

# INDEX

Abdić, Fikret, 86, 108, 110n.50, 113; and accession of Pejanović and Kecmanović to Presidency, 67; call for united Bosnia, 184; creation of Autonomous Region of Western Bosnia, 112; 1990 election results for, 38; role of in drafting Presidency Platform, 74; support of Pelivan for Prime Minister, 70
ABH. See Army of Bosnia and Herzegovina (ABH)
Academy of Arts and Sciences of the Republika Srpska, 84
Academy of Sciences and Arts of Bosnia and Herzegovina, 81
Ačić, Milan, 88, 89
Advisory Board for Defense Issues, 90, 98
Advisory Board for the Protection of Constitutional Order, 85
Ahtisaari, Mati, 161, 162
*Akademik*, 76n.36
Akmadžić, Mile, 70, 71, 110, 117, 154, 180, 181
Aleksei, Patriarch, 199, 200
Alispahic, Bakir, 98
Alkalaj, Sven, 212, 215
Alliance for the Defense of Bosnia and Herzegovina, 210, 211, 212
Alliance of Reformist Forces of Yugoslavia (SRS—*Savez reformskih snaga Jugoslavije*), 3, 4, 56
Alliance of Workers of Bosnia and Herzegovina, 21
Amendment 60, 2, 6, 7
American Institute for Democracy, 125
Anđelovic, Fra Petar, 120, 121, 123
Arbitration Commission. See Badinter Commission

Arms embargo, 170, 171
Army of Bosnia and Herzegovina (ABH): Advisory Board for Defense Issues, 90; Board of Morale, 90; conflict with HVO, 117–119, 121–122; creation and development of, 75, 85, 89; dismissal of Halilović as commander of, 94–96; display of religious symbols by, 98–99; in ending the siege of Sarajevo, 93–94; formation of, 75n.35, 85n.40; Islamization of units of, 97n.43; murder of Serbs by renegade commanders, 142–143; Serb units in, 87–88
Article One, 1974 Constitution, 2n.1
Assembly of Citizens of Serb Nationality, 189, 195, 233–234; constitutional amendment passed by, 190; Declaration of, 190; founding of SGV by, 190; interethnic trust, 190; second meeting of, 191–192; third meeting of, 194
Assembly of the Republic of Bosnia-Herzegovina, 1, 5, 6
Assembly of the Serbian People of Bosnia-Herzegovina, 6
Associated Republics of Yugoslavia, 41
Association of Independent Intellectuals Circle 99, 236
Autonomous provinces, 2, 3
Autonomous Region of Western Bosnia, 112

Babić, Ljubo, 192
Babić, Živko, 168
Backović, Zaim, 79
Badinter Commission, 7
Bajramović, Ismet, 79, 136
Bambur, Fatima, 140–141

## INDEX

Banja Luka, 36–37, 129, 216
Banović, Milenko, 91, 92
Beganović, Mustafa, 71
Begić, Kasim, 183
Belgrade Circle of Independent Intellectuals, 192
Belgrade Initiative, 6
Berberović, Ljubomir, 82, 188, 190, 191, 203
Bešlagić, Adnan, 172
Bešlagić, Selim, 178
Bičakcić, Edhem, 77, 155–156
Biden, Senator Joseph, 212, 213–214
Bijedić, Mustafa, 160
Bijelica, Krstan, 107
Bilić, Vladimir, 167
Bjelobrk, Boro, 191, 192, 193
Boban, Mate, 7, 115n.55, 117, 136n.65, 154
Bogićević, Bogic, 90, 112, 155
Boras, Franjo, 38, 70, 110, 111n.53, 113, 154, 181
Bosnia-Herzegovina, Republic of, 6
Bosniak Assembly, 184n.78, 185, 189
Bosniaks, 4; Islamic fundamentalism and, 173, 174; killing of Serbs by, 144; mass slaughter of in Goražde and Žepa, 143; name change from Bosnian Muslims, 19n.9, 184n.78; number of in Bosnia-Herzegovina before 1993, 1; as refugees, 138n.66, 139n.67, 146n.69
Bosnian Academy of Sciences, 76
Bosnian Army. *See* Army of Bosnia and Herzegovina (ABH)
Bosnian Front, 25
Bosnian League of Reformist Forces, 29
Bosnian Muslims. *See* Bosniaks
Bosnian Serb Army (BSA): early success of, 8–9; formation of, 68n.32; war crimes committed by, 73
Boutros-Ghali, Boutros, 170
Božić, Miso, 188
Brčko, 33, 36, 177–178, 221
Brigić, Ivan, 90
Brkaćin, Ante, 136n.65
Brković, Don Luka, 119

Budiša, Drazen, 111
Bugojno: persecution of Serbs in, 146; Serb population of, 129
Buha, Aleksa, 165
Bukvić, Edib, 154, 155
Bulatović, Momir, 181, 182
Bulić, Žarko, 190–191, 202, 203, 210, 212
Bush, George H.W., 171

*Caritas* charity, 120
Catholic Church, 120–122, 201; in Bosnia-Herzegovina prior to 1993, 2; role of in preserving peace, 119–122, 201; tolerance of in Bosnia, 173
Cease-fire agreement, 11
Cecur, Savo, 134
Čegar, Zoran, 105, 134–135
Central institutions, 179–180, 210, 211–212, 213
Cerić, Reis, 201
Chetniks, 24, 39, 82, 97, 148
Churkin, Vitaly, 190, 198
Cico, Muhamed, 151
Cikotić, Semo, 212
Circle of Independent Intellectuals, 192
Citizens of Serb Nationality, Declaration of, 190
Citizens of Žepa Association, 139, 140
Citizens parliament, 53–58
Civil Alliance, 192
Civil Democratic Party (GDS—*Građanska Demokratska Stranka*), 46
Civil rights, 188. *See also* Human rights
Claes, Willy, 183–184
Clinton, Bill, 171–172
"Collective guilt," theory of, 145
Committee for the Protection of the Constitutional Order, 141
Committee of the Association of Communists of Yugoslavia, 88
Common life and equality of nations, concept of, 22, 25, 48, 161
Communism: collapse of, 1; nationalism under, 2; transition to democracy from, 1, 2–5
Concentration camps, 114, 118

# INDEX

Conference of the Socialist Alliance, 14
Constituent nations: constitutional recognition of, 2, 12, 19n.8, 233n.91, 235–238
Constituent peoples: constitutional recognition of, 11; court rulings on recognition of, 12, 237; failure to recognize Serbs as, 11; rights guaranteed to, 7; secession, right of, 6, 7
Constitutional Court of Bosnia-Herzegovina, 235n.93; and formation of political parties, 16n.4; recognition of constituent nations, 12, 237
Constitution of the Republic of Bosnia and Herzegovina, 19n.8, 233–238; constituent people, recognition of, 11; government structure under, 154; provision for in Dayton Peace Accords, 221n.87, 234–235
Contact Group; influence of on UN Security Council, 197; letter from Assembly of Citizens of Serb Nationality to, 194; member countries, 172n.71, 197; peace agreement drafted by, 203, 205; proposal for internal territorial division, 210
Contact Group Plan, 127, 163, 198
Continuity, 221
Čosić, Dobrica, 24, 139, 175
Council for Peace in the Balkans, 212
Council of Europe, 230
Council of Nations, 167, 169
Council of the Congress of Bosniak Intellectuals, 236
Criminal prosecution, 92, 137
Croatia, Republic of, 2, 7; elections in, 1; resistance to League of Reformists, 31; war in, 5
Croatian Army, 40
Croatian Community of Herzeg-Bosna, proclamation of, 7
Croatian Defense Council (HVO—*Hrvatske vijeće obrane*), 75n.35, 87; conflict with ABH, 117–119, 121–122
Croatian Defense League (HOS—*Hrvatske obranbene snage*), 136

Croatian Democratic Union (HDZ—*Hrvatska demokratska zajednica*): alliance with SDA, 5; election coalition with SDA and SDS, 37–38, 39, 40; formation of, 4, 17; future, peoples' impression of, 34; hostility toward DSS, 34–35; support for sovereign Bosnia, 41, 48
Croatian National Council (HNV—*Hrvatsko narodno vigece*), 122, 189, 210, 236
Croatian Party of Right, 136n.65
Croatian Peasant Party (HSS—*Hrvatska seljacka stranka*), 111, 122
Croats: calls for equal treatment of, 20–21; number of in Bosnia-Herzegovina before 1993, 1; political party of, 4; in Sarajevo, 119–120
Cutileiro, Jose, 8
Czech Republic, 27

Day of the Army, 85n.40
Day of Uprising, celebration of, 14, 27, 29
Dayton Peace Accords, 219–223; achievements of, 221–223; civil implementation of peace settlement (Annex 10), 221n.88; Constitutional Court, 235n.93; Constitution of Bosnia-Herzegovina (Annex 4), 221n.87, 234–235; election system, 220; ethnic homogeneity, provisions for, 222–223; human rights, protection of, 222; initiative behind, 216; internal structure defined by, 222; international presence, guarantee of, 222; international support for, 231–232; provisions of, 11–12; refugees, return of, 222; resolution of Sarajevo crisis, 130, 228; Serb republic as independent state, disallowance of, 225
Decentralization, 2–3
Declaration of Sovereignty, 48
Declaration of the Assembly of Citizens of Serb Nationality, 190
Delalić, Ramiz, 141, 142n.68, 143

Delić, Rasim, 87, 96
Democracy, transition from communism to, 1, 2–5
Democratic Socialist Alliance (DSS— *Demokratski socijalisticki savez*): declaration of principles for building Bosnian society, 21–22; efforts to avoid war, 56; election coalition with SDP, 33–42; formation of, 4, 14; response to 1990 elections, 43; support for Serb-Bosniak agreement, 46–47
Demonstrations, 53, 55
Đikić, Ibrahim, 200
Dinar, fall of, 28
Diplomatic pressure, 219
Disdarević, Zlatko, 16
District, defined, 211n.84
Divjak, General Jovan, 86, 210, 212
Dodik, Milorad, 37
Doko, Jerko, 86
Dole, Bob, 212, 213, 215
Draskovic, Vuk, 36
Dretelj concentration camp, 118
Drinčić, Miroslav, 107
Drino, Mehmed, 154–155
Droca, Veljo, 134
DSS. *See* Democratic Socialist Alliance (DSS—*Demokratski socijalisticki savez*)
Dugonjić, Nada, 211
Đukanović, Milo, 181n.76
Duraković, Nijaz, 108, 155, 221; efforts to avoid war, 49; prediction of war by, 35; pre-election rallies, participation in, 33, 34–35; as president of Montenegro, 181n.76; selection of for Presidency, 110, 112; state of the army, concern for, 96, 97, 99
Đurdev, Professor Branislav, 81–82
Đurđević, Mile, 151
Đurić, Momcilo, 86

Eagleburger, Laurence, 171, 179
Economic Bank, 149
Economic reforms, introduction of, 27
Efendić, Hadžo, 154

Ekmečić, Milorad, 77–78
Elections: under communist rule, 1; corruption in, 38; under Dayton Peace Accords, 220; multiparty, 1, 2, 29; nationalist parties in, 4–5; of 1990, 3–5, 13; of 1996, 157, 195; "others" category, 19, 110n.50; party coalitions during, 33–42, 50; pre-election rallies, 33–35; of Presidency members, 19; Serb voting patterns, 130, 189; SGV position on, 195; voter confidence, 38
Ethnic cleansing, 198; efforts to curb, 179, 187; and failure to build coalitions among political parties, 26; following Geneva peace proposal, 118; justification of, 199; under Karadžić, 118, 131, 162, 178, 198; resistance to, 111; by SDS, 147, 162, 166, 225, 226
Ethnic expulsion, 198, 226, 238
Ethnic hatred, 198
Ethnic homogeneity, 222–223
Ethnic homogenization. *See* Homogenization
Ethnic partitioning, 118, 179–180, 222
Ethnic purity, 63, 130, 178, 194, 195, 226
European Community (EC): International Conference on the Former Yugoslavia (ICFY), 10, 153n.70; mediation efforts by, 6–7; recognition of independent Bosnia-Herzegovina, 8, 54n.26, 57n.29
European Community Conference on Yugoslavia (ECCY), 7, 8
European Union (EU): discussions with, 170; negotiations mediated by, 40; peace activities of, 153n.70, 173; representatives of, 127; and siege of Sarajevo, 93

Federal Socialist Republic of Yugoslavia (SFRY), 1, 2–3, 13, 41, 88, 199
Federation of Bosnia and Herzegovina, creation of, 10–11, 197, 209, 233
Feofan, Archimandrite, 199

Fetahagić, Sead, 62
Filpović, Muhamed, 178; condemnation of SDS, 58; efforts to avoid war, 56; in formation of MBO, 46n.19; initiative re: Presidency following collapse of Parliament, 57; meeting at UN, 170; as member of Geneva delegation, 159, 162, 166, 167, 169, 170, 178
Foco, Salih, 54
Foreign aid, 157, 158
Foreign currency reserves, decline of, 28
Forum of Citizens of Serb Nationality of the City of Sarajevo, 136, 187–188

Ganić, Ejup, 109, 110n.50, 113, 156, 180, 220, 221; and accession of Pejanović and Kecmanović to Presidency, 67; "collective guilt" declaration, 145; proposal for federal structure in Bosnia, 183; state of the army, concern for, 95, 97; support of Pelivan for Prime Minister, 70
GDS. *See* Civil Democratic Party (*Gradanska Demokratska Stranka*)
General Framework Agreement for Peace in Bosnia-Herzegovina. *See* Dayton Peace Accords
Geneva Agreement, 213; provisions of, 209; SGV challenge to, 210
Geneva peace talks, 159–168; delegates to, 159–160. *See also* Owen-Stoltenberg Plan for a Union of Three Republics; Vance-Owen Peace Plan
Genocide, premonitions of, 48
Germany, diplomatic relations with, 170, 172
Gogalo, Josip, 144
Gojer, Gradimir, 112, 155
Goražde: exchange of, 178; mass slaughter of Bosniaks in, 143; siege of, 139, 140
Grahovac, Gavrilo, 198, 199
Grbo, Ismet, 21, 43, 49, 50
"Greater Serbhood," 24

Greater Serbia, 48, 78, 81, 164
Grebo, Zdravko, 15, 49, 90, 103
Guzina, Dr. Trifko, 79, 135–136, 187
Guzina, Dalmatia, 135

Hadrović, Resad, 160
Halilović, Sefer, 36, 75, 79, 86, 88–89, 90, 96–97, 113, 140
Harris, Marshall, 212
Hastings, Adrian, 211, 212
Haverić, Tarik, 15
HDZ. *See* Croat Democratic Union (HDZ—*Hrvatska demokratska zajednica*)
Heliodrom concentration camp, 118
Herceg-Bosna, Republic of, 7; Catholic Church in, 119–122; conflict between ABH and HVO, 117–119, 121–122; constitutional issues concerning, 116; creation of, 115–128; Geneva proposal, response to, 117–118; goal of, 115; phases of, 116–122; significance of, 116
Herceg-Bosna Council, 127
Hierarchy of trust, 149
Historic uniqueness, concept of, 22, 25, 36, 46
HNV. *See* Croat National Council (HNV—*Hrvatsko narodno vigece*), 122, 210
Hoare, Quentin, 211
Holbrooke, Ambassador Richard, 130n.64, 207–208, 219–220
Homogenization, 24, 26, 33, 39, 42, 44, 130, 144, 93, 195. *See also* Ethnic cleansing
HOS. *See* Croatian Defense League (HOS—*Hrvatske obranbene snage*)
Hotel Zagreb, 80, 136
House of Peoples, 234
HSS. *See* Croat Peasant Party (HSS—*Hrvatska seljacka stranka*)
Huković, Seid, 83, 84
Human rights: actions to preserve, 144, 188; affirmation of by ZAVNOBiH, 16n.3; call for at Geneva peace talks, 161; first formal resolution on, 194;

Human rights (*continued*): importance of in Bosnia's future, 237; as integral to democracy, 191; Karadžić's violation of, 131; protection of in Dayton Peace Accords, 222; respect for, 137
Humanitarian aid, 120, 144, 156, 159, 173
Humanitarian catastrophe, danger of, 170, 180–181
Husić, Mehmed, 166
HVO. *See* Croatian Defense Council (HVO—*Hrvatske vijece obrane*)

Ibrišimović, Nedzad, 97
Implementation Force (IFOR), 11, 130n.64
Independence: European Council recognition of, 54n.26, 57n.29; referendum concerning, 7–8
Industrial production, decline of, 28
"Informative talks," 133
Intellectuals: imprisonment of, 79–80, 136; SDS focus on, 24
Inter-ethnic relations, 20, 35
Inter-ethnic tolerance, 36
Interethnic trust, 138, 190, 222
Intergroup relations, 1–2
Internal division, formula for, 197
Internal territorial division, 210
International community, pressure from, 207–208, 209
International Conference on the Former Yugoslavia (ICFY), 10, 153n.70
International diplomacy, role of in accelerating hostilities, 6
International intervention: need for, 171, 214; role of leading powers in, 197; and siege of Sarajevo, 93
International Peace Conference, 57
Interrogations, 92, 133
Islam: in Bosnia-Herzegovina before 1993, 1; European prejudice against, 174; Reis Cerić as representative of, 201n.70; tolerance of in Bosnia, 173
Islamic Conference, discussions with, 170
Islamic fundamentalism, 173, 174
Izetbegović, Alija, 215, 216; and accession of Pejanović and Kecmanović to Presidency, 62, 66; and accusations against Đorde Zarić, 149; advocacy for survival of Yugoslavia, 31; American Institute for Democracy award, 125; Bosnian sovereignty, support for, 48; compromise by, 141; constituent nations, support for, 235, 236; constituent peoples, recognition of, 12; Contact Group Plan, support for, 205; editing of Presidency Platform by, 74; election as President of the Presidency, 5, 67, 108, 113; extension of term, 113–114; in Geneva peace talks, 180; and growth of nationalism, 34; hopes for Bosnia's future, 44–45; inspection of Seventh Muslim Brigade, 97–99; last meeting with SDS representatives, 66–67; as leader of SDA, 4, 37, 67; meeting with Milan Panić, 106–107; meetings with Ambassador Holbrooke, 220; and organization of the army, 87, 89, 90, 94–96; pre-election promises, 39; proposal for federal structure of Bosnia, 183; refusal to block SDS referendum on sovereignty, 49; Sarajevo, future of, 179; and Silajdžić as Prime Minister, 155, 156–157; statement re: Sarajevo Serbs, 140; in televised debates, 18; and unity of political parties, 22; withdrawal of support for Belgrade Initiative, 6

JNA. *See* Yugoslav National Army (JNA—*Jugoslovenska narodna armija*)
Journalists, departure of, 151
Jovanović, Kosta, 18, 151
Jozić, Jozo, 111

Kadić, Rasim, 37
Kadrić, Hasan, 167
Kalinić, Dragan, 30, 50
Kapetanović, Amira, 161, 167
Karađorđevo agreement, 116, 123–124

Karadžić, Radovan, 234; and accession of Pejanović and Kecmanović to Presidency, 62, 65; calls for war by, 36–37; commitment to war, 171, 199; early peace attempts, response to, 9; ethnic cleansing under, 118, 131, 162, 178, 198; ethnic purity, measures to ensure, 178; in Geneva peace talks, 161–162, 163, 165, 180; headquarters, location of, 21; influence of on JNA, 5, 8; last meeting with SDS representatives, 66–67; loyalist Serbs, attitude toward, 10; mass slaughter of Sarajevo civilians, 142; and national homogenization, 24; organized opposition to, 192; paramilitary troops loyal to, 54n.26; paranoia aroused by, 145; pre-election promises, 39; pre-war talks with Milošević re: future of Yugoslavia, 41–42; rejection of political unity by, 23–24; response to 1990 election results, 43–44; as SDS president, 4, 17; and Serbs in Sarajevo, 130–131; Serbs living under,198; separatism and, 24; and status of Brčko, 178; in televised debates, 18; threats against Muslims, 6, 48; Vance-Owen Peace Plan, rejection of, 174–175; vision for future of Bosnia, 161–162

Karavdić, Zlatan, 20, 21, 29

Karić, Vehbija, 61

Kecmanović, Nataša, 102, 108

Kecmanović, Nenad, 166; accession to Presidency, 9, 59–71; assistance given to families by, 135–137; condemnation of SDS, 58; defection of, 9; efforts to save Professor Leovac, 79; and Forum of Citizens of Serb Nationality (Sarajevo), 187; influence of, 104, 106; as leader of Reformists, 29, 30, 50; pleas for peace by, 56, 63; as representative of Serb nation to Presidency, 105–106; resignation of, 103, 108; role of in drafting Presidency Platform, 74; trip to Belgrade, 101–106

Keraterm camp, 170

Kerestedžijanc, Ambassador, 190

Khuarić, Cardinal, 201

Kinkel, Klaus, 170, 172–173

Klarin, Mirko, 184

Kljuić, Stjepan, 113, 121, 155, 221; and accession of Pejanović and Kecmanović to Presidency, 67; election to Presidency, 111, 112, 113; and equal treatment of Croats, 20–21; failure to take political responsibility, 144; HNV delegate to London and U.S., 210, 212, 213, 216; hopes for Bosnia following 1990 elections, 45; ouster of, 7; pre-election promises, 39; as president of HDZ, 21n.10; resignation of, 109, 110, 154; role of in drafting Presidency Platform, 74; state of the army, concern for, 97, 99; support for Pelivan as Prime Minister, 69–70

Knez, Željko, 86

Knežević, Veljiko, 202, 203

Koljević, Nikola, 165; meeting with Kecmanović, 102; 1990 election results, 38; resignation of, 8, 9, 57n.29, 59, 108;

Komšić, Ivo, 108, 220; efforts to avoid war, 49; failure to take political responsibility, 144; formation of Croat Peasant Party, 111; HNV delegate to London and U.S., 210, 212, 214, 216; pre-election rallies, participation in, 35–36; state of the army, concern for, 90, 97, 99; in televised debates, 18

Kontić, Radivoje, 232

Kordić, Dario, 118

Koschnik, Hans, 127

Kosovac, Braco, 107, 134, 187

Kosovo province, 3

Kovać, Nikola, 70, 80

Kozyrev, Andrei, 198

Krajišnik, Momčilo, 203n.80, 235; and accession of Pejanović and Kecmanović to Presidency, 62–66; early peace attempts, response to, 9; influence of on JNA, 5; loyalist

Krajišnik, Momčilo *(continued)*: Serbs, attitude toward, 10; as president of the Assembly, 5; pressure on Pejanović to join separatist movement, 50, 163–164, 165; role of in exodus of Sarajevo Serbs, 195; as Speaker of Parliament, 108
Kreševljaković, Muhamed, 148
Kulović, Hamdija, 151
Kuposović, Muhamed, 155, 185
Kurspahić, Kemal, 16
Kusturica, Dino, 78

Lagumdžija, Zlatko, 49, 70, 75, 77
Lake, Anthony, 212, 213, 215, 217
Lasić, Miro, 20, 109n.49, 110, 144, 154, 181
Latinović, Đorde, 109
Lazović, Miro, 112, 113, 123, 155, 198, 232; and accusations against Đorde Zarić, 149; as candidate for Parliament Speaker, 110; in Dayton peace talks, 208, 220; as delegate to Geneva peace talks, 159, 162, 167, 170, 178, 180; meetings in Germany, 169; as president of SDP Club of Members, 46; resignation of, 110; support for united Bosnia, 184
Leading powers, intervention by, 197
League of Communists, 1, 3–4, 37; change of name, 4, 15n.2; criticism of, 18; future, peoples' feelings about, 34; role of Socialist Alliance in, 15; Sarajevo Committee for Ideology and Education, 79
League of Communists–Movement for Yugoslavia (SK-PZ—*Savez komunista-Pokret za Jugoslaviju*), 55
League of Communists of Yugoslavia (SKJ), 182–183; Fourteenth Extraordinary Congress of, 182n.77
League of Communists–Social Democratic Party (SK-SDP—*Savez komunista–socijalistička demokratska partija*), 4, 15, 29–30, 35
League of Reformist Forces of Yugoslavia (SRSJ–*Savez reformskih snaga Jugoslavije*), 19, 27, 29

Left Bloc, 5, 6
Legal Life Foundation, 212
Leho, Fatima, 150
Leovac, Professor, 79–81
Liberal Party, 37, 56
Living in Sarajevo (association), 192
Ljubić, Mariofil, 74, 108, 163, 167
Ljujić-Mijatović, Tatjana, 97, 113, 155; and accusations against Đorde Zarić, 149; as candidate for Presidency, 109, 110, 112; collective guilt theory, efforts to refute, 145; in Geneva peace talks, 179, 184; SGV delegate to London and U.S., 210, 212, 216; state of the army, concern for, 96, 97, 99; vision for Bosnia's future, 181
Local initiative, 237
Lokvančić, Zaim, 160
London Conference. *See* International Conference on the Former Yugoslavia (ICFY)
Lovrenović, Ivan, 210, 212
Lozo, Obren, 150
Lučarević, Kerim, 133
Lukac, Predag, 148–149

Macedonia, support for League of Reformists, 31
Macura, Milos, 49
Magaš, Branka, 211
Magazinović, Vojo, 136–137
Major, Prime Minister John, 10
Makar, Andeljko, 86
Manjača camp, 170
Marcotić, Ante, 78
Marjanović, Radoslav, 140
Market economy, 3, 15, 28, 34, 36, 191
Marković, Ante, 3, 4, 13, 27–31, 78
Matić, Dr. Bozidar, 69. 71
Mazowiecki, Tadeusz, 143
MBO. *See* Muslim Bosniak Organization (MBO—*Muslimanska bosnjacka organizacija*)
McKenzie, General Louis, 107, 108
Media, involvement of in political parties, 17

Međović, Desimir, 15
Memorandum of the Serb Academy of Arts and Sciences, 49
Mesić, Stipe, 111
Micotakis, Prime Minister (Greece), 175
Miličević, Fra Nikica, 119, 121
Milijaš, Vojo, 61
Military judiciary, establishment of, 92
Military police: formation of, 92; weapons searches by, 133
Military prosecution, 137
Milošević, Slobodan, 225; criticism of, 106n.47; and Dayton Peace Accords, 11, 225; DSS, resistance to, 35; formation of SDS, 4; in Geneva peace talks, 180, 181, 182; influence of on JNA, 5; Karađorđevo agreement, 123n.58; League of Reformists, resistance to, 31; meeting with Ambassador Holbrooke, 207–208; meeting with Pejanović, 202, 204; opposition pleas for peace to, 56; Panić's challenge to, 101n.44; and partitioning of Bosnia-Herzegovina, 2; pre-war talks with Karadžić re: future of Yugoslavia, 41–42; role of in the resignation of Marković as Prime Minister, 13n.1; rise of, 3; stand on Bosnian sovereignty, 205–206; Vance-Owen Peace Plan, rejection of, 175
Minority rights, 126
Mladić, General Ratko, 68n.32, 175
Mladina, Nada, 192
Mono-ethnicity, 64
Monopolies, 34
Montenegro, Republic of, 3, 181n.76
Moral issues, 146
Mosques, destruction of, 200, 201
Mostar: administration of following Washington Agreement, 127n.60; battle of, 119; persecution of Serbs in, 146; pre-election rallies in, 33; Serb population in, 129
Mount Kozara, symbolism of, 3, 27
Multiethnicity, 22, 111, 144, 162, 179, 213
Multiparty elections: under communist rule, 1; role of nationalism in, 2

Multiparty system: building of, 14–15; legislation mandating, 16
Municipality, concept of, 33n15
Muratović, Hasan, 156, 157, 185, 220
Muslim Bosniak Organization (MBO—*Muslimanska bosnjacka organizacija*), 18n.6, 37, 46, 56
Muslim-Croat Federation, 116

Najdanović, Milutin, 138
*Napredak* charity, 120, 126
National division, 42
National equality, 191, 238
National homogenization. *See* Homogenization
National safety, efforts to preserve, 54–55
National segregation, 26
National territory, 42
Nationalism, growth of, 3–5, 33–34
Nationalist parties, 4–5, 42; alienation of, 25–26; formation and registration of, 16n.4; in the 1990 elections, 4–5, 33–42. *See also* HDZ; SDA; SDS
NATO: bombing by, 11; Implementation Force (IFOR), 11, 130n.64; SGV support for, 230; U.S. as leading power in, 214
New York Statement, 213
Nikolić, Ranko, 71

Omersoftić, Amila, 157
Operation Lightning, 147
Operation Storm, 147
Organization for Security and Cooperation in Europe (OSCE), 83
Organizing Committee, citizens parliament, 54, 55–56
Orthodox Church, Russian, interest of in Bosnian situation, 199–201
Orthodox Church, Serbian: in Bosnia-Herzegovina before 1993, 1; condemnation of war crimes by, 201; reconstruction of religious life, 192; in territory controlled by Bosnian Army, 107; tolerance of in Bosnia, 173

OSCE. *See* Organization for Security and Cooperation in Europe
Owen, Lord David, 10, 153n.70, 161, 163, 179, 188
Owen-Stoltenberg Plan for a Union of Three Republics, 177–185; Bosnian Parliament debates on, 184–185; central institutions, preservation of, 179, 180; endorsement of by Bosniak Assembly, 184; ethnic partitioning under, 179–180; ethnic territories, concept of, 177; failure of, 197

Panić, Milan, 101n.44, 106–107
Paraga, Dobroslav, 136n.65
Parliament: collapse of, 50–51, 54; Declaration of Sovereignty, 48; divisions in, 48–49; following the 1990 elections, 40, 47–48; meetings of in wartime, 56n.28
Parliament of citizens, 54
Parliamentary democracy, 188, 191; DSS advocation of, 22, 25; in Geneva peace talks, 161; Marković's vision of, 28; public enthusiasm for, 36; structure of, 169
Parliamentary rule, 15
Parliamentary system of government, 15
Particularism, 3
Partisan legacy, 3, 4
Partisans, 24, 37, 39, 88, 89, 171
Partisan uprising, anniversary of, 27n.13
Partnership for Peace, 230
Party for Democratic Action (SDA—*Stranka demokratske akcije*): alliance with HDZ, 5; election coalition with SDS and HDZ, 37–38; failure to support Serb-Bosniak agreement, 47; following the 1990 elections, 40; formation of, 4, 17; support for sovereign Bosnia, 41, 48
Pašalić, Colonel Arif. 96
Pavle, Patriarch, 192, 200, 201
Pavlović, Slobodan, 216

Pejaković, Josip, 56
Pejanović, Mirko, 210, 212, 214, 216, 221; academics, efforts to help, 78–79, 82–84; accession to Presidency, 9, 59–71; civic option, hopes for, 5; collective guilt theory, efforts to refute, 145; constituent peoples, recognition of, 12; in creation and development of Bosnian army, 85–90; as a delegate to the Geneva peace talks, 159–168, 169, 170, 178, 179; efforts to avoid war, 53, 63; efforts to secure peace, 119, 121; election as president of Socialist Alliance, 13; election rallies, participation in, 33–36; election to presidency of SGV, 191; emergence of, 1; family assistance given by, 135–137, 141; first draft of Presidency Platform, 74, 75; and Forum of Citizens of Serb Nationality (Sarajevo), 187; founding of SGV, 11m 189, 190–191; Koševo stadium incident, response to, 134–135; as leader of DSS, 4, 21; as a mediating voice, 123, 138, 139; meeting at UN, 170; meetings with Ambassador Holbrooke, 220; meeting with Milošević, 202, 204; and political party unity, 22–26, 28, 49; Presidency structure, role of in changing, 20; prison reform, 79–80, 91–92; refusal to radicalize mass murders, 143–144; as representative of Serb nation to Presidency, 105–106; SGV delegate to London and U.S., 217; suggested defection of to separatist side, 6, 10, 50, 163–164; in televised debates, 18; vision of Bosnia's future, 181–182, 184; visit to Moscow, 198–200; weapons search, personal experience with, 133
Pejanović, Ranko, 79
Pejanović, Spomenka, 133
Pejić, Nenad, 18
Pelivan, Jure, 5, 45, 113; election as Prime Minister, 5, 69, 70, 71, 153; resignation of, 154

Perinović, Davor, 18, 21, 22, 35
Petrović, Stanimir, 86
Petrović, Zlatko, 86
Plavšić, Biljana: in the election of 1990, 38n.17; resignation of, 8, 9, 57n.29, 59, 108
Pluralism, 3, 14, 15
Pluralization, 28
Podinić, Dragan, 91
Political parties: election coalitions, 33–42, 50; formation of, 16–17, 28
Popović, Goran, 37, 50
Population demographics, prior to 1993, 1–2
Pregl, Zivko, 31
Presidency: academics, input from, 76–78; accession of Pejanović and Kecmanović to, 59–71; after collapse of Parliament, 56–57; creation of, 235; election of members, 19; Izetbegović's election as President of, 5, 67, 108, 113; legislation regarding membership and election to, 19–20; and management of army, 94, 98; president of during wartime, 113; resignation of Kecmanović, 103, 108; resignation of Koljević and Plavšić, 9
Presidency Platform: armed forces, creation of, 75, 85; Bosnian Academy of Sciences, input from, 76; drafters of, 74; as foundation for Geneva peace talks, 159, 161; fundamental principles of, 75, 161; and internal structure of Bosnia, 74; purpose of, 73
Prime Minister: Akmadžić as, 71; Pelivan, election as, 5, 69–70; financial authority of, 157–158; Marković as, 3, 13; Matić, refusal to serve as, 69, 71; Silajdžić, election as, 71
Primorac, Zarko, 70
Prlić, Jadranko, 122–123
Prisons: conditions in, 79–80, 137, 142; Hotel Zagreb, 80, 136; interrogations in, 92, 133; wild jails, 91–92;
Private enterprise, 15
Privatization, 28

Prlić, Jadranko, 123, 125
Propaganda, 37, 102, 144, 225–226
Provinces, suggested organization of, 169
Pržulj, Marko, 141
Puljić, Cardinal Vinko, 120, 121, 201, 238
Pušina, Jusuf, 70, 81, 94, 95, 134, 153

Radio Sarajevo, 56, 167
Rajić, Bozo, 235
Rakić, Mico, 210, 215
Redman, Charles, 190
Referendum of the Serbian People, 6
Reformists, 3, 4, 56
Refugees, 138.n66, 139n.67, 146n.69, 212, 222
Regional Anti-fascist Council for the National Liberation of Bosnia and Herzegovina (ZAVNOBiH)— *Zemaljsko antifasističko vijeće narodnog oslobodenja Bosne i Hercegovine*). *See* ZAVNOBiH
Reintegration, 231
Religious identity, 1–2, 120
Religious tolerance, 173–174
Republican particularism, 3
Republika Srpska (RS), 238; Army, 40; constitution of, 235; Contact Group Plan for, 197; creation of, 116, 195; in the Dayton Peace Accords, 11–12, 222; under Geneva Agreement, 209; military might in, 233; Parliament of, 37; responsibility for policies in, 205; SDS support for, 41; as a separatist entity, 48; Serbs in, 147; in third Assembly of Citizens of Serb Nationality, 194; Vance-Owen Peace Plan, rejection of, 174–175
Right to free association, 16n.4, 24
RS. *See* Republika Srpska
Rule of law, 137
Russian Orthodox Church. *See* Orthodox Church, Russian

Saćirbegović, Muhamed, 172n.72
Saćirbegović, Nedzib, 172

# INDEX

Šaćirbey, Nedzib, 215
Šahovnica, 38n.16
Šarac, General Dzemal, 88, 89, 96
Sarajevo: as the academic and cultural center of Bosnia, 84; Bosnian Academy of Sciences, relocation from, 76; Croats in, 119–120; and Dayton Peace Accords, 130, 228; district status for, 211n.84, 214–215; distrust of Serbs in, 131, 137; ethnic division of, 166; exodus of citizens from, 144–145, 179; governing of, 211n.84; international administration of, 208, 211, 215; Koševo Stadium, detention of Serbs in, 105, 134–135; mass slaughter of civilians in, 142; multiethnic defense of, 166; multiethnicity of, 162, 179–180, 211, 229; pre-election rallies in, 33; refugees in, 138n.66; Serb deaths in, 142; Serb population in, 129, 131–132, 165, 166; Serb suburbs, 178–179, 227; shelling of, 56, 57–58, 62, 132–133; siege of, 8–9, 93–94, 117, 159, 172; solidarity and tolerance in, 179; UN protectorate for, 179; U.S. position on, 177–178; weapons checks in, 132–133
Sarajevo Committee for Ideology and Education, 79
Sarajevo Serb Forum. *See* Forum of Citizens of Serb Nationality of the City of Sarajevo
Scowcroft, General Brent, 170, 171
SDA. *See* Party for Democratic Action (SDA—*Stranka demokratske akcije*)
SDP. *See* Social Democratic Party (SDP—*Socijalisticka demokratska stranka*)
SDS. *See* Serb Democratic Party (SDS—*Srpska demokratska stranka*)
Sečerović, Senad, 62
Secession: influence of SDS against, 5–6; peoples' right to, 6
Security checks, 92, 132–133
Security Council, UN, 170, 197
Security system, need for, 137
Self-government, concept of, 161
Selimović, Enver, 215

Selmanagić, Rizo, 130
Separatist movement: in DSS, 233; Karadžić and, 24; Milošević and, 3; Referendum of the Serbian People, 6
Separatist Serb Republic, 24
Serb-Bosniak agreement, 46–47
Serb Consultative Council, 188, 189
Serb Council of Defense, 86–87
Serbia, Republic of, 2, 3; national homogenization, origins of, 33; resistance to League of Reformists, 31
Serbian Autonomous Regions, 7
Serbian Civic Council (SGV—*Srpsko gradansko vijeće*), 86, 127, 140; challenge to Geneva Agreement, 210–212; elections, position on, 195; founding of, 11, 149, 189, 190–191, 233; peace prize awarded to, 212; peacetime goals of, 194–195; reintegration of Bosnia, 231; and SDS compared, 226–230; support for sovereign Bosnia, 226; visit to Belgrade, 192–193; visit to Moscow, 198–200
Serbian Democratic Party (SDS—*Srpska demokratska stranka*): boycott of independence referendum, 7–8; calls for war, 54; common life concept, opposition to, 164; Contact Group Plan, rejection of, 198; ethnic cleansing by, 147, 162, 166, 225, 226; ethnic division, support of, 64, 165–166; exclusion from Parliament, 58n.30; extremism in, 232; formation of, 4, 17; as global representative of the Serb nation, 60–61; influence of on JNA, 5; intellectuals, focus on, 24; opposition to Serbs in Sarajevo, 165–166, 229; pre-war arms distribution by, 132; propaganda by, 37, 102, 144, 225–226; separatism in, 233; sovereign Bosnia, opposition to, 41–42, 63, 164–165, 225–229; treatment of prisoners by, 80; and unity with other parties, 23–24, 37–38, 39, 40
Serbian Orthodoxy. *See* Orthodox Church, Serbian

Serbian population, by cities, 129
Serb municipalities, 23, 64
Serb National Council, 189
Serbo-Croatian language, 1
Serb Renewal Movement (SPO—*Srpski pokret obnove*), 36, 192
Serbs, 4; in the cities, 145–151; "collective guilt" of, 145; conscription of, 164; deaths of in Sarajevo, 142; detention of in Koševo stadium, 105, 134–135; distribution of, 129–130; distrust of, 131, 137; exodus of, 130, 146–147, 179, 195, 216; fears of living with Bosniaks and Croats, 232; future of, 231; and international community, 230; in leading positions, treatment of, 149–150; murder of by renegade army commanders, 142–143; number of in Bosnia-Herzegovina, 1, 147; persecution of in Mostar, 146; political party of, 4; in Republika Srpska, 147; and Serbia, 229–230; suffering of in Sarajevo, 9, 131–132, 137, 142, 167; threats against, 148–149; in Tuzla, 129; and transformation of Socialist Alliance into political party, 35; Vance-Owen Peace Plan, rejection of, 10; voting patterns, 130, 189
Serb Sarajevo, 178, 228–229
Seventh Muslim Brigade, Izetbegović's visit to, 97
SFOR. *See* Stabilization Force (SFOR)
SGV. *See* Serb Civic Council (*Srpska gradjanske vojece—SGV*)
Šiber, Stjepan, 86
Silajdžić, Haris: election of as Prime Minister, 71, 155–156; as Foreign Minister, 153, 169, 172; future of Sarajevo, 179; as head of Geneva delegation, 159, 163, 166, 170; resignation of, 157–158
Simović, Miodrag, 70, 139
Sintra Summit, 230–231
SK-PZ. *See* League of Communists-Movement for Yugoslavia (SK-PZ—*Savez komunista-Pokret za Jugoslaviju*)

SK-SDP. *See* League of Communists-Social Democratic Party (SK-SDP—*Savez komunista–socijalistička demokratska partija*)
Slovenia: elections in, 1; support for League of Reformists, 31
Snipers, 54
Social Democratic Party (SDP—*Socijalistička demokratska stranka*), 15n.2; efforts to avoid war, 56; election coalition with DSS, 33–42; intentions and strategy of, 50; 1991 declaration of Parliament, 46
Socialist Alliance: of Bosnia-Herzegovina, 1, 13; celebrations organized by, 27; name change, 4, 14; Pejanović as leader of, 1, 4, 13–14; of Sarajevo, 164; transformation of into DSS, 14–15, 28, 35. *See also* Democratic Socialist Alliance (DSS—*Demokratski socijalistički savez*)
Socialist Federated Republic of Yugoslavia. See Federal Socialist Republic of Yugoslavia (SFRY)
Social reform, 36
Sokolović, Dzemal, 29, 30
Sovereignty: Assembly support of, 6; and Dayton Peace Accords, 221; Declaration of, 48; DSS support for, 22, 25; in individual republics, 31; Milošević's stand on, 205–206; parliamentary debates about, 46–48; promotion of among political parties, 46; SDA support for, 41, 48; SDS opposition to, 164–165
Spahić, Ibrahim, 46
Spasojević, Boro, 192
SPO. *See* Serb Renewal Movement (SPO—*Srpski pokret obnove*)
Srebrenica: mass slaughter of Bosniaks in, 143, 234; proposal to exchange for Sarajevo suburbs, 178
Stabilization Force (SFOR), 11
Stambolić, Ivan, 227
Standard of living, 27
State Security Service, 111
Stojanov, Dragoljub, 159

Stojanović, Nikola, 109
Stoltenberg, Thorvald, 175, 188
Sučeska, Avdo, 77
Suša, Gordana, 106

Tanović, Arif, 77
Tenth Hill Brigade, 142
Territorial Defense Forces (TO— *Teritorijalna odbrana*), 85n.40; ethnic makeup of, 86; weapons searches by, 132–133
Thatcher, Margaret, 211
Tintor, Jovan, 102
Tito, Josip Broz, 3, 34
Tokić, Sejfudin, 56
Tolerance, 36, 163, 173–174, 179
Tomić, Dragan, 193
Topalović, Mušan (Caco), 141–142, 143
Trnka, Kasim, 159, 161, 182, 183
Tudjman (Tuđman), Franjo, 123n.58, 180, 181, 182; actions by, 21n.10; attitude toward Bosnia, 173; founding of HDZ, 4; partitioning of Bosnia-Herzegovina, support for, 4, 7; Serb challenges to, 5
Turajlić, Hakija, 70
Tuzla, 178n.75; hardships endured in, 123; pre-election rallies in, 36; Serb population in, 129
Tuzla Second Corps, 87–88
TV Bosnia-Herzegovina, 151
TV Sarajevo, 17–19, 58

Union of Bosnian Social Democrats (UBSD), 178n.75
United Bosnia, 161
United Nations: discussions at, 169–170; humanitarian aid and, 159; peace attempts by, 10, 153n.70; Security Council, 170, 197
United Nations Protection Force (UNPROFOR), 8, 78, 102, 107, 159
United States: intervention by, 10–11, 169, 170, 171–172, 197, 212–215; position on future of Bosnia, 177–178; regard for human life in, 214; Vietnam syndrome, 171, 214; view of Bosnian war as European problem, 177
UNPROFOR. *See* United Nations Protection Force
Ustasha regime, 37, 38n.16, 97, 137
Uzelac, Uglješa, 70

Vakuf, Gornji, 122
Vance, Cyrus, 10, 153n.70
Vance-Owen Peace Plan for Bosnia and Herzegovina, 10, 162–163, 169–175; failure of, 177; international reception of, 174; Republika Srpska rejection of, 174–175; state organization under, 169
Vasić, Milan, 82, 83–84
Vasić, Professor Lejla, 82, 83
Vešović, 212
Vietnam syndrome, 171, 214
Vikić, Dragan, 95
Vlajčić, Sulejman, 58
Vojvodina province, 3
Vranić, Mirko, 88, 89
Vukobrat, Budo, 151
Vukovic, Zlatko, 135

War: calls for end to, 107; citizen protests against, 55–58; clashes between political parties and, 40; efforts to avert, 46, 47, 49, 53, 54, 56, 63; Karadžić's commitment to, 171, 199; responsibility for, 35; SDS calls for, 54
War crimes, 73, 143, 145, 147, 181, 190, 231. *See also* Ethnic cleansing
Washington Agreement, 11, 116, 120, 122, 154, 163, 197, 209, 233
Weapons checks, 132–133
Weekend brigades, 150
Westendorp, Carlos, 236
World view of Bosnian crisis, 40

Yugoslav National Army (JNA— *Jugoslovenska narodna armija*), 3, 5, 8, 31, 40, 54, 55, 68n.32, 85n.40, 171. *See also* Bosnian Serb Army (BSA)
Zarić, Đorđe, 149–150

ZAVNOBiH, 15–16, 16n.3, 165
Zenica, Serb population of, 129
Žepa: exodus of Serbs from, 146–147; mass slaughter of Bosniaks in, 143; proposal to exchange for Sarajevo suburbs, 178; siege of, 139–140

Živanović, Miodrag, 84
Živković, Rajko, 198
Zubak, Krešimir, 127–128, 220, 235
Zulfikarpašić, Adil, 6, 18, 22, 37, 46, 169

www.ingramcontent.com/pod-product-compliance
Lightning Source LLC
Chambersburg PA
CBHW022110150426
43195CB00008B/339